CRIME PREVENTION

THROUGH ENVIRONMENTAL DESIGN

# Crime Prevention
# Through Environmental Design.

C. RAY JEFFERY

*Professor of Criminology*
*The Florida State University*

 SAGE PUBLICATIONS, *Beverly Hills, London*

*To my Wife Ina*
*and my Daughter Lauren*

Copyright © 1971 by Sage Publications, Inc.

*Printed in the United States of America*

For information address:

 SAGE PUBLICATIONS, INC.
275 South Beverly Drive
Beverly Hills, California 90212

International Standard Book Number 0-8039-0086-4

Library of Congress Catalog Card No. 74-127988

SECOND PRINTING

Reform the environment—not man ...

Don't attempt to reform man. An adequately organized environment will permit humanity's original innate capabilities to become successful. Politics and conventionalized education have sought erroneously to mold or reform humanity, i.e., the collective individual.

My philosophy and strategy confine the design initiative to reforming only the environment in contradistinction to the almost universal attempts of humans to reform and restrain other humans by political actions, laws, and codes.

R. Buckminster Fuller
*Utopia or Oblivion*, 1969

## ABOUT THE AUTHOR

Professor C. Ray Jeffery was trained in sociology (Ph.D., Indiana University, 1954) and has since specialized in criminology and the administration of criminal justice. He is currently working on the application of behaviorism and environmentalism to the control of criminal behavior. Behavior is regarded by Professor Jeffery as a response to environmental opportunities rather than as a characteristic of the individual offender.

Professor Jeffery has taught at Southern Illinois University, Arizona State University, and New York University, and is presently a professor of criminology at Florida State University. He was a Senior Social Science Fellow at the University of Chicago Law School and a Social Science Research Council Fellow in the administration of criminal justice at the University of Wisconsin. Under a grant from the U.S. Office of Education he directed a research project in Washington, D.C. to rehabilitate delinquents through operant procedures.

He served as book review editor for the *Journal of Criminal Law, Criminology, and Police Science,* and is currently editor of *Criminology,* the official journal of the American Society of Criminology. In addition to having published numerous articles in professional journals and books, Professor Jeffery co-authored *Society and the Law* and authored *Criminal Responsibility and Mental Disease.*

# CONTENTS

        Organized Crime                                    226

        Introduction                              226
        Crime and Morality                        227
        Organized Crime                           229
        White Collar Crime                        232
        Summary                                   234

            Notes                                 235

PART V.   POLICY FOR CRIME CONTROL

16.    Systems Analysis, Decision Theory,
        and Crime Control                                  239

        Systems Analysis                          239
        Decision Theory                           240
        Systems Analysis and Criminal Justice     242
        Decision Theory and Crime Control         248
        Summary                                   252

            Notes                                 253

17.    Training in Criminology, Criminal
        Justice, and Corrections                           254

        Who is the Criminologist?                 254
        Training in Criminology                   255
        Sociology and Criminology                 256
        Law Schools and Criminology               257
        Social Work and Criminology               259
        Medicine and Criminology                  259
        Education and Criminology                 260
        Training in Police Science                260
        Criminology and the Future                261
        Summary                                   262

            Notes                                 263

18.    The Politics and Economics of Crime Control    265

            THE POLITICS OF CRIME                 265
        Present Governmental Policy               265
        Governmental Policy and Research          266
        Science, Humanistic Service, and Social Action  268
        Science and Values                        270

Part I

**INTRODUCTION**

Chapter 1

# Issues In Crime Control

*Criminology and Crime Control*

The timeliness of crime prevention and control is such that no prolonged discussion is needed as to why a book such as this has been written. Crime in the streets is a major political and social issue of the times. However, the orientation and theme of this work are a departure from that found in the current literature, and though many ideas presented elsewhere are reviewed here, no book specifically devoted to crime control and prevention currently exists. Sutherland and Cressey devote sixteen pages to the problem of prevention, in which they discuss such topics as community organization, recreation, case work, group work, coordinating councils, and institutional reorganization.[1] The President's Crime Commission relates crime control to resources, public involvement, and a willingness to change.[2] No major effort in teaching or research has been made in the area of crime control and prevention, though we have devoted thousands of pages and man-hours to analyzing criminals and the institutions designed for them after they commit crimes.

The attempt is made here to trace the historic origins of our crime control system, to evaluate the effectiveness of crime control measures, and to argue that a new and radically different approach to crime is called for.

The materials used are interdisciplinary: they are drawn from such traditional fields as criminal law, administration of justice, criminology, penology, sociology, psychology, and education, as well as from new fields such as systems analysis, decision theory, environmentalism, and behaviorism. The subject is designed as a textbook for a seminar or course following the criminology-penology sequence usually found in sociology departments, or a seminar in law schools or police science schools devoted to crime control. It is also designed for the lawyer, politician, policeman, behavioral scientist, probation officer, or layman who is interested in or professionally involved with the problems of crime and justice. It is not a traditional textbook in criminology or penology, but it takes up issues left over and unresolved by these courses.

*Rehabilitation or Deterrence*

The classical school of criminology in the eighteenth century put deterrence foremost in its scheme as the goal of the criminal justice system. The positive school in the nineteenth and twentieth centuries rejected the principle of deterrence while placing rehabilitation of individual offenders as the overall rationale of penological measures. The development of criminology and penology has been such as to follow the positivistic model while downgrading the classical model.

The deterrence model is still found, though as a distinct minority position, in criminal law, the courts, the police system, and the prison system. Punishment is now out of fashion, replaced by individualized treatment of a sick personality.

The rehabilitation (positive school) model is found today in studies of the individual offender, therapy, group processes, probation, parole, and community action or poverty programs. So deeply ingrained is the rehabilitation ideal that few writers have found reason to be concerned with its basic foundation or assumptions.

Positive criminology is based on certain assumptions which form a theoretical structure for criminological thinking.[3]

(1) Criminology studies the character of the individual offender, not the character of the environment in which crimes are committed.

(2) Rehabilitation of the individual offender is the major goal of American correctional practices.

(3) Individual offenders can be rehabilitated through the application of psychiatric, psychological, and sociological concepts.

(4) Punishment is not a successful means to change human behavior, and deterrence as a goal of criminal justice must be rejected.

(5) The causes of crime lie in the *past* experiences and heredity of criminals.

(6) Criminal behavior can be controlled through the manipulation of noncriminal behavior via therapy, reeducation, and job training.

(7) Criminology is concerned with treatment *after* the criminal act, rather than with prevention and control *before* the criminal act is committed.

(8) Services to individuals with problems are more valuable than basic scientific research when it comes to controlling criminal behavior.

In contrast to the above assumptions, the writer will argue that:

(1) Crime cannot be controlled through measures designed for the individual offender, but can be controlled only through the manipulation of the environment where crimes occur.

(2) Prevention and not rehabilitation must be the major concern of criminologists.

(3) Given our present state of scientific knowledge about human behavior, we do not know how to rehabilitate offenders.

(4) Punishment is a powerful means for controlling human behavior.

(5) The causes of crime are to be found in responses of individuals to *present* environmental conditions and *future* consequences of such behavior.

(6) Criminal behavior must be controlled directly through measures which influence the criminal behavior itself.

(7) Crime control programs must focus on crime *before* it occurs, not after it has occurred.

(8) Criminology must shift from a *service* orientation to a scientifically based *research* orientation.

### Models of Crime Control

Crime control can focus either on the *environment* or on the *criminal*. When we deal with the *environment*, we consider the object stolen or the person assaulted or murdered. This approach involves one in an analysis of the environment in which criminal acts are committed, e.g., the stolen property or victim. When we deal with *criminals,* we deal with the individual who commits the crime, e.g., the robber or rapist or murderer. On the one hand, we have human behavior (the criminal); on the other hand, we have environmental conditions.

.We can also deal with crime *before* it occurs, or *after* it occurs. If we deal with crime before it occurs, we are structuring the environment so as to prevent crimes; if we deal with crime after it occurs, we are treating or rehabilitating criminals.

In addition to the environment-criminal dimension and the before-after dimension, crime control techniques may be viewed in terms of direct or indirect controls over human behavior. A direct control would itself deal with the response and not operate through an intervening variable; i.e., a guard rail at a railroad crossing or a safety device on a cutting machine are examples of direct controls over behavior. Indirect controls do not control behavior except through intervening variables which attempt to influence the behavior. Training a person to keep his hands out of a cutting machine is an example of indirect control—and from experience we know that indirect controls are not adequate to ensure the safety of the individual. It is much simpler to prevent an industrial accident by building machines with safety guards than by training workers not to place their hands into dangerous equipment.

Direct controls of crime include only those which reduce environmental opportunities for crimes. Indirect controls include all other measures, such as job training, remedial education, police surveillance, police apprehension, court action, imprisonment, probation, and parole. Placing a man on probation or giving him remedial education will not prevent him from breaking the window and stealing jewelry; placing a steel bar over a window will prevent the theft of jewelry from that window.

Our current method of controlling crime is predominantly through indirect measures after the offense has been committed. The failure to control crime is in no small measure due to the strategies we select to deal with crime. It is obvious that we do not control crime if we allow it to occur before taking action. We may attempt to treat offenders or rehabilitate them *after* they have become criminals, but we should not confuse the *treatment* of criminals with the *prevention* of crime. The polio vaccine prevents polio; polio victims are treated via physical therapy after they have contracted polio.

Current emphasis is placed on *indirect* controls on the *individual criminal after* the offense has occurred. The model to be developed and supported in this book is one of *direct* controls over environmental conditions before the offense has occurred. It is economically less expensive to design an environment in which crimes are not possible than to rehabilitate all who have the opportunity to commit crimes.

The models of crime control available are illustrated by Figure 1. The model used currently in the United States is the "criminal after the crime through indirect control," as seen in the following diagram from the President's Crime Commission report, a model also adopted by the New York State Identification and Intelligence System.[4]

Crime → Police → Prosecution → Courts → Corrections

The model for crime control proposed here is as follows:

| | ENVIRONMENT | | CRIMINAL | |
|---|---|---|---|---|
| | DIRECT — — — CONTROLS — — — INDIRECT | | DIRECT — — — CONTROLS — — — INDIRECT | |
| **Before** | Reduce opportunities for crime through science and technology<br>Reduce opportunities for crime through urban planning-design | NONE | NONE | Increase legal opportunities—<br>Job training<br>Employment<br>Remedial education<br>Community action<br>Social casework |
| **After** | NONE | NONE | NONE | Administration of Justice<br>Police investigation<br>Arrest<br>Prosecution<br>Conviction<br>Sentencing<br><br>Rehabilitation and/or Treatment of Offender and Protection of Society<br>Imprisonment<br>Fines<br>Probation<br>Parole<br>Group Therapy |

Figure 1

| Environmental | Fewer | Fewer | Fewer | Fewer Cases for |
|---|---|---|---|---|
| Engineering[a] | → Crimes → | Arrests → | Court → | Correctional |
| | | | Cases | Facilities |

[a]Abandoned buildings, homes, apartments, parks, streets, victims, behavioral control techniques.

This model operates on crime before it occurs via direct controls.

Our treatment of crime can be analogized to a community that is drinking contaminated water because someone upstream is polluting the stream. We can never control water pollution until we clear up the source of the pollution. Yellow fever was checked by controlling the swamps that produced the mosquitoes which carried the infecting organism. We treat criminals, but we do not understand or study those environmental factors producing crimes; each year, consequently, the crime problem is greater than it was the previous year. Our present policies will never control crime, because they deal with the *symptoms* and not with the *causes*. We must first determine whether the causes of crime lie in the individual criminal (as current theory assumes) or in the environment. If these causes are to be found in the environment, then we must resort to environmental engineering in order to prevent and control crime.

### Plan of Presentation

Part I discusses the issues in crime control, possible crime control models, and the historical background of the deterrence versus rehabilitation arguments.

Part II examines in greater detail the deterrence model, with emphasis on criminal law, punishment, experimental psychology, the police, the courts, and prisons. The failure of the deterrence model is discussed in this connection.

Part III examines the rehabilitation model, with its emphasis on the individual offender, therapy, group processes, probation, parole, and poverty. Again, the failure of rehabilitation is discussed.

Part IV examines crime control through environmental engineering: science and technology, and urban planning and design.

Part V examines crime control policy, and the role of systems analysis, decision theory, training, and research in crime control. The emphasis in Parts IV and V is on the newer behavioral sciences: behaviorism, environmentalism, and decision theory.

The criminal justice system has been justified either in terms of a theory of deterrence or of a theory of rehabilitation. Both deterrence and rehabilitation have failed, and the criminal law at this point in history is without a sound theoretical foundation. It neither protects the rights of accused defendants, reforms or deters the criminal, nor protects the general public from crimes. Our failure to control crime is a direct product of the model we use to control crime. A new and radically different approach might be of distinct use at this time.

## NOTES

[1.] Edwin H. Sutherland and Donald R. Cressey, *Principles of Criminology* (Philadelphia: Lippincott and Co., 1966), pp. 682 ff.

[2.] President's Commission on Law Enforcement and Administration of Justice, *The Challenge of Crime in a Free Society* (Washington, D.C.: U.S. Government Printing Office, 1967), pp. 12-15.

[3.] Clarence R. Jeffery, "The Structure of American Criminological Thinking," *Journal of Criminal Law, Criminology, and Police Science,* Vol. 45, No. 5 (January, 1956), pp. 658-72; C. Ray Jeffery, "Crime Prevention and Control Through Environmental Engineering," *Criminologica,* Vol. 7, No. 3 (November, 1969), pp. 35-58.

[4.] President's Commission on Law Enforcement and Administration of Justice, op. cit., pp. 8-9.

# Chapter 2

# Theoretical Structure
# of Crime Control

## Classical versus Positive Criminology

Due to the harsh, cruel, and arbitrary nature of criminal law, a movement to eliminate the death penalty and reduce the uncertainty of "justice" emerged in the eighteenth century. Led by Beccaria (Italy) and Bentham (England), this classical school of criminology advocated limiting the power of the state by making laws specific, well known, and nonretroactive. Punishment was to be used to deter future criminals and to prevent future crimes. Beccaria taught that it was better to *prevent* crimes than to punish criminals, and he advocated *rewarding virtue* as a way of deterring criminal acts. Crimes were to be defined in legal terms so as to limit the admission of evidence without cross-examination, to eliminate secret accusations and torture, and to control the severity of punishment which could be imposed on a criminal. The classical school believed in the rule of law over the rule of men.

Bentham was a social utilitarian who believed in the greatest happiness for the greatest number. He put forth a free-will psychology of hedonism; man responded to pain and pleasure and acted so as to avoid pain and gain pleasure. Bentham devised a system of social engineering whereby there could be a calculus of pain and pleasure. The criminal law should attach enough pain to the commission of a criminal act so as to cancel out the pleasure gained from the act, thus preventing or deterring people from committing crimes. Bentham taught that *behavior is governed by its consequences*, and he viewed social control in terms of reward and punishment.

Both Beccaria and Bentham emphasized preventing a crime before it was committed, although Beccaria did not believe in using the police as a deterrent since he did not trust the arbitrary discretionary power given to police officers. On the other hand, Bentham believed in using the police to deter criminals, thereby increasing for the criminal the certainty of punishment. He also advocated the use of insurance and reward systems for informers in order to detect and capture criminals.[1]

The Italian, or positive, school of criminology was a nineteenth-century movement associated with the names of Lombroso, Garofalo, and Ferri. Unlike the classical school, the positivists emphasized protection of the state or society rather than protection of the individual. The purpose of criminal law was to *protect society* and to reform the criminal. The positivists did not believe in definite sentences or strict legal definitions of crimes; rather, they advocated indefinite criminal codes which allowed for a maximum of individual discretion and individualized justice based on the circumstances of the case. Garofalo talked about natural crimes, crimes against the sentiments of pity, and probity. The positivists wished to focus on the *offender*, not on the *offense*. Dangerous persons were to be treated for their social pathologies, though the positivists did not tell us how to decide who was to receive treatment and under what circumstances we could keep in an institution called a hospital or treatment center a man whose dangerousness was being treated. The positivists believed in the rule of men, not the rule of law.

The positivists had no faith in law as a means of social control or as a means of protecting the rights of individuals against the state. They were concerned with the personality of the offender and the procedures needed to treat criminality via the individual offender. The positivist was interested in those events occurring *after* the offense was committed.

The positivist was a scientific determinist; he believed in applying the scientific method to the study of crimes and criminals. Whereas the classical school made criminology a part of moral philosophy, the positive school made criminology a part of biology, psychology, psychiatry, and sociology. Ferri followed a deterministic concept of responsibility—that is, man does not have free will, but he is responsible for his actions by virtue of his membership in society. The measure of social responsibility is the potential danger of an action to the welfare of society.

According to Radzinowicz, whereas the classical school exhorts men to study justice, the positive school exhorts justice to study men.[2]

### Retribution and Criminal Law

The theory of retribution holds that the justification for punishment is "an eye for an eye," or, in the moral framework of Immanuel Kant, a theory of justice demands the punishment of a transgressor because our sense of justice demands it. The theory of retribution has as its basic tenets the following:

(1) the criminal act must be a voluntary and morally wrong act;

(2) punishment must fit the offense; and

(3) punishment must represent a return of suffering to the wrong-doer for his morally wrong act.[3]


Sir James F. Stephen wrote that the purpose of law is not deterrence or reform, but the moral indignation and hatred of the public against the criminal.[4] Jerome Hall, in the United States, represents today the view that moral culpability is the basis for criminal law, and punishment must be administered for the intentional or reckless doing of a morally wrong act.[5]

According to the retributive theory of justice, there is no place in criminal law for negligence, strict liability, or other doctrines by which responsibility is separated from the mental state of the offender. *Mens rea,* or the mental condition of the criminal at the time of the crime, is crucial to this philosophy, and any excusing condition such as infancy, accident, mistake, or insanity served to negate criminal responsibility. Since the retributive theory looks backward to the mental state of the defendant, not forward to his future behavior, there is no place for a discussion of retribution in a theory of crime control. As G.O.W. Mueller has observed, vindication and retribution are nonutilitarian ingredients in the correctional system, and, if our correctional system services only these aims, then it deserves to be scrapped.[6]

We still retain, however, in the criminal law, the notion of justice, as when we treat attempted murder as provoking a lesser punishment than does murder although the same human behavior (and mens rea, if you wish) are involved in both cases, the only distinction being the accuracy of the murderer's aim. Or, for example, we would not feel justified in freeing a convicted murderer after one day in prison even if we believe he was rehabilitated and would not benefit from further imprisonment.


### Deterrence and Criminal Law

The utilitarian position was forward-looking in that it sought to make future deterrence of criminal behavior the major process of punishment. This position is found today among lawyers who view criminal law as a means of social control.

The deterrence school has been based on a free will/hedonistic model of behavior, and it has retained emphasis on the moral blameworthiness and the voluntary nature of the criminal act. Bentham himself recognized that certain conditions excused the accused from moral responsibility if, under such conditions, punishment would not act as a deterrent. Conditions such as infancy, duress, and mental illness made punishment ineffective and therefore nonutilitarian. The British criminal-law expert Granville Williams views mental illness as a defense to criminal responsibility because, he argues, punishment does not deter the mentally ill.[7]

Both Professors Hart and Packer, in recent writings, have argued that the concept of deterrence must include within it the appreciation of legal responsibility; that is, the defendant's state of mind (mens rea) at the time of the crime would be a necessary condition of liability for a criminal act. The use of punishment is limited by elements of intentionality and volition, as well as by the effectiveness of punishment in deterring future criminal behavior.

Deterrence is both general and specific; general as it applies to the deterrence of future acts by the general public, and specific as it applies to the offender punished. General deterrence is incapable of being measured, since we do not know how many people would commit crimes if the threat of punishment were removed. Specific deterrence has failed if the rate of recidivism is used as a criterion, or if the failure of capital punishment to control behavior is used. Though the theory of deterrence has fallen into disrepute in recent years, legal scholars still regard it as a critical aspect of criminal law. Norval Morris and his colleagues at the University of Chicago Law School have undertaken a detailed study of deterrence and the criminal justice system. "Our dedication to corrections must not lead us to repudiate deterrence," he writes. "Our criminal law system has deterrence as its primary and essential postulate."[8]

*Positivism*

## REHABILITATION AND CRIMINAL LAW

The positive school advocates rehabilitation and treatment of offenders as the goal of criminal justice. "Treat the criminal, not the crime"; "Punishment is obsolete," and "Criminals are sick" are some of the slogans of this approach.[9] Individualized treatment replaced strict legal definitions of crimes and punishment. The "one day to life" sentence is the ideal sentence according to the rehabilitation school of criminology.

This position is based on science and determinism; determinism replaces free will. Moral culpability and responsibility are denied, replaced with a concept of strict liability or public welfare offenses.[10] The state of the criminal's mind is an issue after a determination of guilt, not before, in order to guide the judge and correctional workers in making a decision as to the proper treatment needed by the individual offender.

The rehabilitation ideal has dominated American corrections for the past hundred years. Gerhard O.W. Mueller states, "I know of no American criminologist or lawyer who does not subscribe to resocialization or rehabilitation as a foremost aim of our correctional approach."[11]

Peter Lejins distinguishes three types of crime prevention programs: punitive, corrective, and mechanical. He writes,

> when a person with a social science orientation speaks about prevention of crime today, he is usually thinking in terms of corrective prevention [which] is clearly on the ascendency and dominates interest and practical innovation, especially in the United States. . . .The emphasis is on conceptualizing theory–building and structuring in the field of corrective prevention.[12]

Francis Allen has noted that the rehabilitative ideal has so dominated American criminology that other theories have been slighted or ignored.[13]

The President's Crime Commission quotes a statement made by the American Correctional Society a hundred years ago to the effect that "Reformation, not vindictive suffering, should be the purpose of penal treatment."[14]

Lady Wootton, a British jurist, accepts scientific determinism and argues that, if the aim of law is to prevent crimes, then the conventional doctrine of mens rea is no longer applicable. According to Lady Wootton, we should look only at measures which, if taken, will prevent the recurrence of the act; that is, rehabilitate the offender and protect society.[15] Lady Wootton thus would completely eliminate the moral doctrine of responsibility and substitute a *scientific* determinism by which punishment becomes treatment through which individual offenders are reformed. The position stated by Lady Wootton is, of course, the culmination of the positive school of criminology as stated by Garofalo, Ferri, and Lombroso.

The treatment-rehabilitation ideal has come in for some heavy criticism in recent years. C.S. Lewis, in a published article, heavily condemns the humanitarian theory of punishment, by which he means both the theory of deterrence and the theory of rehabilitation. Lewis maintains that theories of rehabilitation and deterrence remove justice or just desserts from punishment and thus allow experts who are assigned the task of rehabilitation to detain a man for life under the guise of treatment. The criminal is classified "sick" and is detained until cured. The deterrence theory of punishment is likewise criticized by Lewis for allowing us to punish one man in order to deter another man; according to Lewis's theory of ethics, man should never be used as a means to an end, even though the end in itself is desirable. [16]

Francis Allen has noted that criminal law has been weakened by making it an instrument of social reform and social welfare. He mentions particularly those laws dealing with paternity, vagrancy, drunkenness, and disorderly conduct. He notes that by overloading the criminal system with new laws designed to care for the poor, unwed mothers, dependent and neglected children, vagrants, alcoholics, and sex perverts, we not only are failing to render effective social service, but we are corrupting the system of criminal justice so that it is unable to perform successfully its legitimate functions of social control. [17] Allen agrees with Lewis that the rehabilitative ideal has led to increased penal measures against delinquents, addicts, alcoholics, and homosexuals, while at the same time it has ignored or relegated to a minor position the protection of individual liberties which was of prime importance to the classical school.

## DEFINITION OF CRIMES

The influence of positivism has been strong in the United States. This is seen in (1) the definitions of crimes, (2) the study of criminals rather than of crime, and (3) rehabilitation through treatment of criminals.

Garofalo's definition of crimes as natural—i.e., against the sentiments of the community—is echoed in the anthropologist's and sociologist's definition of law as custom. Any violation of a social code is regarded as a crime, regardless of the social organization supporting the norm. The definition of crime given by Sellin reflects the positivistic influence; crime is a violation of *conduct* norms, not *legal* norms. Social rather than legal definitions of crime have been used by Reckless, Cressey, and other American sociologists. Sutherland's concept of white-collar crime involves the issue of the definition of crime to be used in sociological research. This use of socially injurious conduct rather than antilegal conduct as a measure of crime has been criticized by Paul Tappan, Jerome Hall, and others. [18] Llewellyn has stated that "Sociologists say smuggishly, 'I take the sociological and not the legal approach to crime'; and I suspect an inquiring reporter could still hear much of the same (perhaps with psychiatric substituted for sociological) though it is surely somewhat obvious that when you take the 'legal' out you also take out 'crime.' " [19] Francis Allen has stated, "It may be doubted that so complete an elimination of the legal content of the concept has well served the development of criminological·theory." [20]

The classic legal definition of crime is summarized in the *principle of legality* or rule of law—that is, specific definitions of crimes with specific punishment stated in a formal legal code. The principle of legality is in opposition to ambiguity, vagueness, retroactivity, and arbitrariness in the penal code. The doctrine of legality involves both the doctrines of *nullem crimen sine lege* and *nulla poena sine lege*—"no crime without a law" and "no punishment without a law."[21]

The major threats to the principle of legality have come in the form of statutes for special offenders—drug addicts, delinquents, alcoholics, sexual psychopaths, and the mentally ill. The offenses with which these people are charged are often very vague. Delinquency has been defined as anything from "beyond control" or "subject to immoral influences" to major felonies such as murder or rape. Sex psychopath laws or habitual offender laws often provide for long periods of incarceration without conviction for a specific offense. Alcoholism accounts for thirty percent of all arrests, and yet most cases of drunkenness are not handled within the system of due process. In some jurisdictions a man can be sentenced to jail for "habitual drunkenness." New legal decisions bar the prosecution of alcoholics as criminals and recognize alcoholism as a disease, not as a crime.[22] Under such laws, alcoholics can be committed by civil procedures for compulsory treatment (although successful treatment does not exist). Drug addicts are also now regarded as ill people, not criminals, and in many jurisdictions they can be committed for treatment even though treatment does not exist. Individuals found not guilty by reason of insanity or found incompetent to stand trial because of mental illness can be committed to an institution for life without a determination of guilt as to the commission of a criminal act. Szasz and others have criticized the lack of legality and procedural safeguards in such hearings.[23] Tappan has noted that, by following positivism, we have turned criminals into sick people and, by doing so, we justify long terms in institutions under the guise of treatment.[24]

## THE STUDY OF THE OFFENDER

Positivism was based on the tenets of science and determinism. Lombroso wanted to understand the causes of crime as they resided in the individual criminal, and following Darwin, he found these causes in the physical makeup of mankind, a product of the individual constitution. Psychologists have found the causes in the intelligence or personality makeup of the offender. Freud's theory of behavior served as a theoretical basis for a psychological explanation of the offender. Sociologists and social workers looked to the work of Quetelet and Guerry, two social statisticians who found statistical regularities as to age, sex, race, urbanization, economic conditions, and crime. From Marx, the social scientist added poverty and economic determinism. Determinism was a part of criminology by 1900, whether in the form of physical, psychological, or sociological determinism. [25]

American criminology has been dominated by positivism, especially with regard to its emphasis on studying the individual offender. "All contemporary scientific criminology is positivistic in method and in basic formulations," according to George Vold. [26] Matza has written that

the most celebrated and thus the most explicit assumption of positive criminology is the primacy of the criminal actor rather than the criminal law as the major point of departure in the construction of etiological theories. The explanation of crime, according to the positive school, may be found in the motivational and behavioral systems of criminals. [27]

Manuel Lopez-Rey has written that "the repeated assertion is made that it is not the crime committed but only the personality of the author that matters in the treatment of offenders. Such persistence has led to what we could call a criminological cult of the personality." [28] Again, "The serious problem facing contemporary criminology is not that of treatment of offenders, but that of prevention of crime and delinquency." [29]

The influence of social science on criminology has been especially prominent in the United States, and, in a later chapter, the several theories of behavior will be discussed in more detail.

### The Social Defence School

In recent years, Europeans have developed a modified version of positivism which has been labeled "social defence." The objectives of this school of criminology are the prevention of crime and the treatment of offenders; the United Nations has named its section on crime prevention and control the Social Defence Section. [30]

Social defence thus leads to the promotion of a penal policy which naturally favors the individual rather than the collective approach to the prevention of crime, and endeavors to insure the prevention of crime and the treatment of offenders. Consequently, this rational penal policy aims at the systematic resocialization of the offender

. . . .The process will be based as firmly as possible on scientific understanding of the phenomenon of crime and the offender's personality.[31]

The differences between the three schools can be seen in the following table comparing the major assumptions of each.

### Dilemmas in Modern Criminology

The issues raised by the classical and positive schools have not yet been resolved. If we follow the classical school, we place emphasis upon procedural due process and upon deterring men from committing crimes. So far we have failed to devise a system whereby criminals are deterred by the threat of punishment. If we follow the positive school, we place emphasis upon scientific determinism, the rehabilitation of the criminal and the protection of society. We have not found a way to *rehabilitate* the criminal *after* the offense has occurred, and the rehabilitative ideal has meant sacrificing individual rights as well as reducing the effectiveness of criminal law. As a result, due process for the accused has been greatly minimized in some instances, and criminal law has been asked to perform many social welfare and moral functions which it cannot adequately handle. We thus arrive at a situation wherein the law does not protect the rights of individuals accused of crimes, nor does it protect individuals from others who may commit crimes. No one benefits from the present state of affairs: the accused defendant may be convicted without certain procedural safeguards; the convicted criminal is not treated or rehabilitated; and the potential crime victim is not protected from harm or loss. Law enforcement has moved from a punitive/deterrence position to a treatment/rehabilitation position without protecting the rights of either the accused defendant or the victim of the crime. Although criminal law is seen in terms of rehabilitation, deterrence, and the protection of society, none of these goals is today justified in terms of the results.

Some writers on the subject have concluded that, rather than serving one purpose, the law serves multiple purposes—e.g., retribution, deterrence, reform, and the protection of society. Such a position allows one to preserve all possible arguments without being forced to select among them. This is not very helpful if none of the goals is achieved in fact, and if the goals are in conflict with one another.

One of the major arguments to be presented here is that the law enforcement system has been seriously weakened by the move from deterrence to treatment, for now we no longer attempt to prevent *crimes;*

**Table 1**

| *Classical* | *Positivist* | *Social Defence* |
|---|---|---|
| Moral blameworthiness and free will | Determinism, no moral guilt | Individual responsibility and free will |
| Legal protection of civil liberties | No legal protection of civil liberties | Protection of civil liberties |
| Legal definitions of crimes | Social definition of crimes | Legal plus social definitions of crimes |
| Values from ethics | Scientific studies | Science plus values |
| Criminal law retained | Criminal law ignored | Criminal law revised with sociological concepts |
| Punishment and deterrence | Protect society and reform the criminal | Treatment of individual offender |

rather, we attempt to treat or cure *criminals*. It will be argued that we cannot have both deterrence and treatment, as is so commonly assumed, since the very operations by which treatment is carried out in and of themselves are antideterrent measures. The basic behavioral assumptions of the positivists have created a situation whereby we have weakened the deterrent qualities of legal control while at the same time we have not strengthened the rehabilitative forces of the criminal justice system.

The theory of deterrence was based upon the use of pleasure and punishment to control behavior. The theory of rehabilitation denied the effectiveness of punishment as a means of behavioral control, and removed the negative consequences from criminal behavior. In a later chapter we shall review the scientific principles of behavior and relate these behavioral principles to the problems of law enforcement. A law must be enforced before it can be effective. When we fail to apply positive and negative sanctions, we fail at law enforcement.

### Summary

The classical theory of deterrence has been largely replaced by the positive theory of rehabilitation. As a result, little faith is placed in criminal law as a means of social control, while the prevention of crime *before* it occurs has been ignored to a great extent. Studies focus on the individual offender and his treatment *after* the crime has been committed. A strict legal definition of crime has been replaced by a social definition which allows serious violations of due process and legality.

The failure of deterrence has led to a further weakening of criminal law resulting from efforts to rehabilitate the individual offender. At the same time no measures equal to the challenge of crime in a free society have been devised. At this point of history deterrence has failed, rehabilitation has failed, and retribution has failed—and retribution is not about to be reinstated as a theoretical justification of criminal law. A new basis for criminal justice and crime control must be forthcoming if we are to cope meaningfully with the crime problem.

# NOTES

[1.] Leon Radzinowicz, *Ideology and Crime.* New York: Columbia University Press, 1966; Leon Radzinowicz, *A History of English Criminal Law.* London: Stevens and Sons, 1948, Vol. III, p. 426 ff.; Hermann Mannheim, *Pioneers in Criminology.* London: Stevens and Sons, 1960; George Godwin, *Criminal Man.* New York: George Braziller Inc., 1957.

[2.] Radzinowicz, *Ideology and Crime,* op. cit., p. 56.

[3.] H.L.A. Hart, *Punishment and Responsibility.* New York: Oxford University Press, 1968, pp. 231-232; Herbert L. Packer, *The Limits of the Criminal Sanction.* Stanford: Stanford University Press, 1968; Gerhard O.W. Mueller, "Punishment, Corrections, and the Law," *Nebraska Law Review,* Vol. 45, No. 11, January, 1966, pp. 58-98; Henry M. Hart, Jr., "The Aims of the Criminal Law," *Law and Contemporary Problems,* Vol. 23, No. 3 (Summer, 1958), pp. 401-439.

[4.] Hart, *Punishment and Responsibility,* op. cit., p. 168.

[5.] Jerome Hall, *General Principles of Criminal Law,* 2nd ed., Indianapolis: Bobbs-Merrill Co., 1960; Hart, *Punishment and Responsibility,* op. cit., p. 138.

[6.] Mueller, op. cit., pp. 65-72.

[7.] Hart, *Punishment and Responsibility.* op. cit., pp. 40-41.

[8.] Norval Morris and Frank Zimring, "Deterrence and Corrections," *Annals,* January, 1969, p. 138.

[9.] Packer, op. cit., p. 12.

[10.] Ibid., pp. 11-13.

[11.] Mueller, op. cit., p. 80.

[12.] William E. Amos and Charles F. Wellford, ed., *Delinquency Prevention.* Englewood Cliffs: Prentice-Hall, 1967, pp. 4-7.

[13.] Francis A. Allen, "Criminal Justice, Legal Values and the Rehabilitative Ideal," *Journal of Criminal Law, Criminology, and Police Science* (September-October, 1959), pp. 226-232.

[14.] President's Commission on Law Enforcement and Administration of Justice, *Corrections.* Washington, D.C.: U.S. Government Printing Office, 1967, p. 3.

[15.] Hart, *Punishment and Responsibility,* op. cit., pp. 193-195.

[16.] C.S. Lewis, "The Humanitarian Theory of Punishment," *Res Judicatae.* Vol. 6, 1953, pp. 224 ff.

[17.] Francis A. Allen, *The Borderland of Criminal Justice.* Chicago: University of Chicago Press, 1964.

[18.] C.R. Jeffery, "The Structure of American Criminological Thinking," *Journal of Criminal Law, Criminology, and Police Science,* Vol. 46, No. 5 (February, 1956), pp. 658-672; C.R. Jeffery, "The Historical Development of Criminology," *Pioneers in Criminology,* op. cit., p. 364 ff.

[19.] Karl Llewellyn, "Law and the Social Sciences, Especially Sociology," *Harvard Law Review,* Vol. 62 (1949), p. 1287.

[20.] Francis A. Allen, "Rafaella Garofalo," in *Pioneers in Criminology,* op. cit., p. 259.

[21.] Hall, op. cit., p. 27 ff.; Helen Silving, "Rule of Law in Criminal Justice," in *Essays in Criminal Science,* ed. by Gerhard O.W. Mueller, South Hackensack: Fred B. Rothman, 1961.

[22.] Gerald Stern, "Public Drunkenness: Crime or Health Problem," *Annals,* November, 1967, p. 147 ff.

[23.] Thomas Szasz, *Law, Liberty, and Psychiatry.* New York: Macmillan Co., 1963; Thomas Szasz, *Psychiatric Justice,* New York: Macmillan Co., 1965; C.R. Jeffery, *Criminal Responsibility and Mental Disease,* Springfield: Charles Thomas, 1967.

[24.] Paul W. Tappan, *Contemporary Correction.* New York: McGraw-Hill Book Co., 1951, pp. 10-11.

[25.] Walter C. Reckless, *The Crime Problem,* 4th ed., New York: Appleton-Century-Croft, 1961; Radzinowicz, *Ideology and Crime,* op. cit., p. 29 ff; Herbert A. Bloch and Gilbert Geis, *Man, Crime, and Society,* New York: Random House, 1962; Edwin H. Sutherland and Donald R. Cressey, *Principles of Criminology,* 7th ed., Philadelphia: J.P. Lippincott, 1966.

[26.] George B. Vold, *Theoretical Criminology,* New York: Oxford University Press, 1958, p. 39.

[27.] David Matza, *Delinquency and Drift.* New York: John Wiley and Sons, 1964, p. 3; Hall, op. cit., p. 600 ff. Jerome Hall, "Criminology," in *Twentieth Century Scoiology,* ed. by Georges Gurvitch and Wilbert E. Moore, New York: Philosophical Press, 1945, p. 342 ff.; C.R. Jeffery, "The Structure of American Criminological Thinking," op. cit.

[28.] Manuel Lopez-Rey, "Some Misconceptions in Contemporary Criminology," in *Essays in Criminal Science,* ed. by G.O.W. Mueller, South Hackensack: Fred B. Rothman and Co., 1961, p. 13.

[29.] Ibid., p. 29.

[30.] Marc Ancel, *Social Defence,* New York: Schocken Books, 1966, p. 17.

[31.] Ibid., p. 25.

Part II

THE DETERRENT MODEL

# Chapter 3

# Criminal Law, Punishment,
# and Behavioral Control

## *Introduction*

In Chapter 2 we discussed the criminal law as a deterrent to criminal behavior and the rejection of deterrence and punishment by the positivists as an effective means of controlling human behavior. Several issues will be discussed in this chapter:

(1)  the growth and development of criminal law as a means of social control;

(2)  the role of punishment in the control of human behavior;

(3)  the extension of law into the areas of private morality and public order; and

(4)  the effectiveness of law in an urban, industrial society.

## *Social Control and Social Sanctions*

Social control is based upon a system of *rewards* and *punishments.* These sanctions can be categorized as:

(1) Physical, the use of material rewards such as money, sex, or food, or the use of physical punishment such as execution, imprisonment, or fines.

(2) Social, the use of social rewards such as honors, love, praise, or recognition, or the use of social punishments such as ridicule, gossip, or group disapproval.

(3) Religious, the use of beliefs in a hereafter and rewards after death, or the use of beliefs in punishment and condemnation after

death. Conscience is involved in social control through religious and ethical beliefs.

These sanctions, physical, social, and religious, develop and are maintained as interdependent systems. Any specific social situation might involve a combination of rewards and punishments of all three types.[1] In order to be effective, a normative rule must have an effective sanction. In the case of law, the sanction used is primarily one of punishment through physical means and the use of force. The legal order is backed by social and religious sanctions—i.e., moral codes, family codes, primary group norms, and so forth—however, the ultimate sanction in our society is the legal sanction. If the informal norms of the family, the church, the neighborhood, and the educational system fail, then the more formal controls of the state system come into existence. The history of law is the history of social change from kinship law to state law.

### Tribal Law to State Law

Early primitive law was tribal law, enforced by the kinship group. The blood feud was carried out to avenge offenses between rival tribes. Offenses were considered to be against the tribe, not against an individual, and the concept of collective responsibility existed.

Primitive law has been regarded as custom, since the social norms of the tribe consisted of a class of binding rules which governed social obligations. There was at this point in human history no or little differentiation among law, custom, and tradition. "The great reality of primitive society is not civil law or criminal law, but custom."[2]

Primitive law is private law; there is no system of state law or public law. Private law consists of custom enforced by the tribe through a system of self-help or through the blood feud. The feud was checked by the use of compensation or payments, which came, in most instances, to be compulsory. A system of tariffs or compensation can be found among primitive tribes such as the Ashanti, Ifuago, and Comanche Indians, and it is also found historically among Anglo-Saxon tribes, Hebrew tribes, and Greek and Roman tribes. The earliest form of the concept of law is contained in this notion that some social agency must be developed as a means of controlling the use of physical force in human affairs. If a man were allowed to seek revenge for an offense, the result would be perpetual intertribal warfare. Law developed as a means of limiting private use of force and of channeling the use of force through a public institution.

The tribal system disintegrated in Europe, to be replaced by a state system. Law changed from tribal law to state law—law enforced on the basis of territoriality, rather than on that of kinship. Offenses were offenses against the king, not against the family, and the king had the duty of enforcing the laws of the state.

> Responsibility for carrying out retribution seems to follow a definite trend when one compares various social systems. Where cultures are relatively simple the matter of inflicting punishment on offenders is likely to be left to the kinfolk of the injured, but in societies of greater development and complexity the administration of justice is left more and more to impersonal agencies and non-relatives.[3]

The decline of kinship organization and the growth of a multi-institutional social system has been characteristic of modern social organization.[4] MacIver and Page summarize this historic change as one where the primitive fusion of institutional functions in the kinship group gave way to separate political, economic, religious, family, and ecological units. The transition from primitive society to state society is the transition from custom to law.[5]

Throughout the history of social thought, the dichotomy between rural and urban or primitive and political societies has been prominent. The following list of writers and concepts illustrates the point:

| | |
|---|---|
| Spencer | Homogeneous-Heterogeneous |
| Durkheim | Mechanical-Organic |
| Maine | Status-Contract |
| Redfield | Folk-Urban |
| Tönnies | Gemeinschaft-Gesellschaft |
| Weber | Traditional-Charismatic-Legal Rational |
| Cooley | Primary-Secondary |
| Becker | Sacred-Secular |
| Sorokin | Ideational-Idealistic-Sensate |
| Comte | Theological-Metaphysical-Positive |

Roscoe Pound has stated that "in the modern world, law has become the paramount agency of social control. Our main reliance in the society of today is upon the force of politically organized society."[6] "The broader usage [of law as custom] is common with sociologists. But certainly for jurists, and I suspect also for sociologists, it is expedient to avoid adding to the burden of the term and to use *law* for social control through the systematic application of the force of politically organized society."[7]

*History of Criminal Law*

The common law of England developed from the time of Henry II (1154-1189). Early English law was a mixture of church, state, and feudal law, but by the seventeenth century the law was clearly state law. The administration of justice and social control via law was in the hands of the king. The feud or compensation had been replaced by the punishment of the offender by the king. The state replaced the tribe as the unit of political organization.

Since the collective responsibility of the tribe no longer existed, the individual offender, not the tribe, was punished, and restitution as such disappeared for a large class of offenses. Those offenses for which no compensation was paid were called crimes, to be differentiated from tort actions, for which compensation was available.

The usual punishment for crimes during the Middle Ages was death or physical mutilation. By the eighteenth century, there were over 200 capital offenses, over 70,000 people were executed a year, and the use of capital punishment extended to very minor property offenses.

The history of criminal law during this period was that of extending the use of capital punishment on the one hand, while limiting the use of capital punishment on the other. The law was used at this time to meet the social problems related to industrialization and urbanization: drunkenness, pilfering, begging, petty thievery, prostitution, and vagrancy. The Gin Act of 1736 and the Vagrant Act of 1744 illustrate the use of criminal law to meet the problems of poverty. The early workhouses were a combination poorhouse-detention center for the poor. The Elizabethan Poor Laws of 1598, followed by several other statutes, provided that the poor were to be put to gainful employment under the penalty of imprisonment. Workhouses were used for those who were vagrants or were unemployed. The differentiation between crime and poverty was unclear at this point in history, an important fact which still has influence today.[8]

Many techniques were used to reduce the use of capital punishment. Defendants could resort to benefit of clergy—whereby a man who could read the scriptures was not subject to prosecution—charges were reduced or dismissed, prosecutors refused to press charges, and judges and juries refused to convict. Transportation to penal colonies came into prominence as a means of avoiding the use of the death sentence.[9]

The history of criminal law during the period from 1200 to 1900 A.D. was one in which penalties were increased, while at the same time techniques were devised for the avoidance of such penalties. Gradually, capital punishment was replaced by transportation, fines, or imprisonment, and imprisonment came to be the major way by which felons were punished in our society for breaking the criminal law.

*Punishment and Criminal Law*

The criminal sanction is based on the use of punishment as a means of controlling criminal behavior. The failure of punishment to deter criminals has been documented in legal history, especially in the case of capital punishment. The usual arguments run from the fact that pickpockets were engaged in picking pockets at public executions when other pickpockets were being executed to the fact that states without capital punishment do not have a higher murder rate than those that do.[10] One criminologist has noted that "American criminologists have frequently discussed the deterrent principle as unjustifiable. Indeed, some penal reformers appear to regard deterrence and all forms of punishment as stigmatic of barbarism."[11] The most recent attack on punishment is by Karl Menninger, who regards punishment as the punisher's secret need for crime and his need to displace his own guilt feelings by punishing criminals.[12]

The manner in which punishment is to be used in the criminal justice system has been debated for a long time. In the eighteenth century, a debate occurred between William Paley and Sir Samuel Romilly as to the proper place of the death sentence in the system of criminal justice. Paley argued that capital punishment should be retained for many offenses, but used in a few instances only as examples to the public. Thus there would be great discretionary power in the use of the death penalty, depending upon individual circumstances. Romilly argued that capital punishment should be reserved for a few cases, but should be applied in every case for which it was prescribed. He also argued for the certainty of punishment: "So evident is the truth of that maxim, that if it were possible that punishment could be reduced to absolute certainty a very slight penalty would be sufficient to prevent almost every species of crime."[13]

The dilemma is still with us. Historically, we followed Paley's argument in the sense that we still have the great uncertainty associated with punishment. The number of capital offenses has been reduced to a few, and today in the United States the number of executions is around one to three per year. Yet the certainty of punishment is no greater. Edwin Chadwick argued in 1829 that the cause of crime was not poverty, but the impunity with which criminals commit crimes. In many instances, there is no punishment for a criminal act. Chadwick argued for a better police force, street lighting, and better education of people in crime prevention techniques.[14] Pike has written about the ease with which criminals escape punishment.[15] Tarde noted in his work on crime that urbanization made criminal activities more rewarding and easier. In cities, there are more opportunities for crime because of the penal code.[16] Radzinowicz has commented that "in trying to account for crime in an affluent society, we cannot ignore criminal opportunities in another sense—the sheer frequency with which situations present themselves which make crime both tempting and easy."[17] Hart has argued that the legal sanction adds to the decision-making process of an individual the element of fear of punishment in an effort to make the cost of crime higher than the reward.[18] He notes that fear of death is not a strong deterrent, because it is uncertain and in the distant future.[19] He cites, for example, statistics which indicate that in England the ratio of execution to murder is 1: 12 whereas in the United States the ratio is 1: 100 or better.[20]

These writers are saying that, to be effective, punishment must be swift and certain. The failure of punishment as a means of deterring criminal behavior is better understood if we review the literature from experimental psychology, where punishment and its effect on behavior have been studied in the laboratory under controlled conditions.

Azrin has been one of the foremost psychologists working on the effects punishment has on behavior. He defines punishment as a procedure that reduces the future probability of the punished response. He notes that the more intense the punishment, the more effective the punishment. The punished response will reappear if the punishing contingency is removed from the environment. To be effective, punishment should be delivered immediately or as soon after the response as possible. The punishing stimulus must be unavoidable if it is to be effective.[21]

Punishment is usually concurrent with reinforcement—that is, the behavior which is punished is also rewarded. For example, a thief steals money (reward), for which, if caught, he is placed in prison (punishment). If the strength of the rewarding stimulus is greater than that of the punishing stimulus, the person will continue to behave in a given way even if punished. In a situation in which a desired reward can be gained by both a punished and nonpunished response, the person will select the nonpunished response to gain the reward. For example, if a person can gain food by stealing it or by asking for it, he will use the second response, since such a response results in food without punishment or the threat of punishment.

Very often a person will seek punishment (a so-called masochistic personality) because punishment is paired with reinforcement. A rat that is shocked and then fed will administer a shock to itself in order to obtain food. This is not to be interpreted to mean that the rat "likes" punishment; it is to be interpreted to mean that where the environmental contingencies for a reward include punishment, the person will accept the punishment to gain the reward providing the "value" of the reward is more than the "cost" of the punishment. It is important to remember that, in most situations, a response is paired with both *punishment* and *reinforcement,* so the relative weight of each must be considered as determinants of a response. The person responds so as to receive the reinforcement and to avoid the punishment.

Azrin concludes that punishment is the most effective means of eliminating or suppressing behavior. However, punishment has some undesirable side effects. Punishment will create and maintain avoidance and escape behavior; that is, the person will escape from a punishing situation or will avoid it whenever possible. This is negative reinforcement, the avoidance of an aversive stimulus. A criminal will escape from prison or avoid being captured. A child will refuse to go to school if school is a punitive situation, as it often is. Most of the behavior we call neurotic or psychotic is produced by punishment. Punishment creates a withdrawal response or a hostile, aggressive response on the part of the punished person; attack or retreat are the alternatives open to such a person. Aggression is one way of destroying a punishing stimulus or a tormentor. Azrin has produced "reflexive fighting" in the laboratory, wherein, if an organism is shocked, it will attack any object or person in the environment, even though the object or person is not responsible for the punishment. The psychoanalyst calls this "displacement." Punishment can lead to withdrawal from a situation, which is socially disruptive since it will terminate a social relationship. A child may withdraw from its mother, a husband and wife may secure a divorce, or a child may withdraw from school and thereby become a dropout. The policeman becomes the object of hatred and scorn because he represents the punishing agency of the community through its legal system.

If punishment is so effective in controlling and shaping behavior, why is it so ineffective as used by the criminal law? Several reasons can be cited at this time, and perhaps more given later as new experimental evidence comes into existence.

*(1) Few criminal acts are ever punished.* The arrest rate is low for offenses against property, and this does not include the many offenses unknown to the police. The impunity with which people commit crimes is a major factor in crimes. Punishment does not work if it is not used. The old saying "it is the certainty and not the severity of punishment that is important" holds as true today as it did in Sir Romilly's time.

*(2) The time gap between the criminal act and the punishment is too great.* To be effective, punishment must be an immediate consequence of the behavior. This is obviously not so in the case of the criminal act unless the criminal is caught in the act and is killed or injured in some manner. If he escapes, to be picked up days later, then is placed on trial months after that, and sent to prison years after that, the time between the act and the punishment is too great for the punishment to relate to the criminal act.

*(3) The legal system creates an avoidance and escape response system.* To be effective, punishment should be structured to as to be unavoidable. The administration of justice is such that it creates avoidance behavior: avoid detection by the police, post bail, hire a lawyer, behave so as to get an acquittal in court, tell the probation officer the right kind of story, and so forth. The defendant can resort to all types of avoidance behavior through the legal system in order to avoid or escape the consequences of his criminal act.

*(4) The criminal act pairs a reinforced consequence with a punished consequence.* The criminal gains the money or car or sex gratification prior to the punishment. The stimulus most immediate to the response controls the behavior. The fact that money is available from theft now is more crucial than the prospect of punishment in the distant future.

Eating behavior is so difficult to control because the immediate gratification of food is greater than the more distant consequence of overweight, ill health, poor physical appearance, social ridicule, and so forth. Smoking a cigarette has immediately gratifying consequences, whereas a person will not die from cancer for years. The reward for crime is immediate; the punishment is in the future, is uncertain, and may not take place, and if it does, it can often be minimized.

*(5) The punishment for a criminal act is often ineffective.* We usually use incarceration in an institution as our means of punishing criminals; such incarceration may not be very punitive to one who has grown up in the filth and deprivation of an urban ghetto. The food and shelter of the prison is often better than the person had on the streets. A warden of a Florida prison observed that the hard-core inmates regarded solitary confinement as a reward since it tested their manliness and gave them prestige in the eyes of the other inmates. When the warden fed the worst offenders baby food, however, they behaved as he wanted them to, because eating baby food was regarded as disgracing and unmanly. The punishment used must be effective for the population to which it is applied. Psychopaths are a creation of punitive situations, and punishing them further with the same brutality and physical force will not alter their behavior. New types of punishment must be structured which are less physical and more social or economic.

*(6) Punishment as we use it is positive in type*—the application of an aversive consequence, such as a shock, execution, or imprisonment. Much more effective as punishment is negative punishment, removing or taking away an object desired by the person. A child can be controlled much

more easily by taking away something he wants if he misbehaves—e.g., an ice cream cone or a movie—than by spanking him. Physical punishment is the worst type, since it brutalizes both the punisher and the person punished. Telling a child to go to his room or to remain home for the evening is more effective than the use of physical force.

As was suggested in (5) above, new types of punishment must be found which are negative in nature, removing from the criminal something he values. We use deprivation of liberty, which is very effective on some people, but not on those already living a deprived life.

### Crime, Law, and Morality

The positivists viewed crime as a social offense or any act repugnant to a social sense of morality, subject to the benevolent treatment of the therapist. From this position one can conclude that the sweep of criminal law should be broad, including within its borders many acts not usually regarded as criminal, such as alcoholism, drug addiction, prostitution, homosexuality, and pornography.

The distinction between public order and private morality is often at issue in arguments concerning the scope of the criminal sanction. Some writers, like Lord Devlin, have stated that the law must be used to enforce morality; other writers, such as Professor Hart, have opposed the use of law to enforce morality. According to Hart, private morality and sin should be separated from the public domain of criminal law.[22]

The use of criminal law to enforce morality has resulted in a corruption and overburdening of the system for the administration of justice. Such offenses as prostitution, homosexuality, gambling, alcoholism, drug addiction, abortion, and birth control occupied and to some extent still occupy an important position in the system of criminal law and absorb the resources and facilities of the criminal law, yet such laws are either unenforceable or enforceable at a minimal level and at great cost in bribery and corruption. Such offenses have been labeled by Edwin Schur as "crimes without victims."[23] The recent Wolfenden report on homosexuality in England recommended that private consensual acts between adults be removed from the province of criminal law.[24] Recently, Kadish has written in the same vein when he notes that the function of statutes dealing with vagrancy and disorderly conduct is to delegate to the police broad discretionary functions to be used in keeping the peace. Such offenses are not legal offenses, but are social offenses in the broad sense that the positivists used the term. "The use of the criminal law to enforce morals, to provide social services, and to avoid legal restraints on law enforcement ... has tended both to be inefficient and to produce grave handicaps for enforcement of the criminal law against genuinely threatening conduct."[25]

The President's Commission on Law Enforcement wrote about the ineffectiveness of broad definitions of crime dealing with drunkenness, gambling, narcotics, nonsupport, vagrancy, and some sexual behavior, and it recommended reevaluating the limitations of the criminal law as a means of social control.[26]

The argument against broad criminal sanctions has been reinforced in recent years by the writings of some sociologists who have emphasized the role of the "labeling process" in deviant behavior. These writers argue that a deviant is one who is so labeled by the society, and such labeling may further remove the deviant from the society and thus create a unified subcultural group based on values contrary to those of the society. Labeling a person a delinquent may be critical in the development of a criminal career.[27] Because of the harmful effects of many of our procedures for handling deviants, the President's Task Force concluded "in the absence of evidence on the beneficial effects of official contacts, every effort should be made to avoid the use of a formal sanctioning system and the official pronouncement of delinquency."[28] The task force report notes that "it is not at all clear that doing something is better than doing nothing."[29]

Today there exists a school of thought which advocates that we legalize many behaviors now regarded as criminal. This movement is reinforced by the youth or "hippie" movement, which not only advocates, but practices, social deviance and rebellion. Added to the burden of the criminal law is the fact that student unrest, racial tension, and antiwar protests also fall within the province of law enforcement and criminal sanctions. Much of the current antagonism against law enforcement springs out of social unrest and protest.

One member of the "labeling or social deviance" school, Professor Richard Quinney, has summarized the logic of this school when he writes that

> a great deal of the traditionally defined criminal behavior has been a response of individuals and groups to situations regarded as inadequate for the attainment of specific aspirations. Calculated violation of the law may be a rational solution to socially structured and perceived problems. Protest and resistance against unjust conditions and policies may be most appropriately pursued through activities that violate criminal laws.[30]

"When the state's use of power to control others does not rest on consent and legal guarantees, the authority of the state is illegitimate and need not be obeyed. In fact, obeying illegitimate authority would be an unprincipled act."[31]

The decriminalization, or labeling, school presents several serious problems. First, the removal of the criminal label from behavior can be considered at best only for crimes without victims. No one can seriously believe that the criminal sanction can be removed from murder, rape, arson, burglary, robbery, or assault.

Second, the removal of the label removes the criminal sanction without changing the behavior. As Edwin H. Sutherland noted, "It is true that if the law against stealing were repealed, stealing would not in a legal sense be a crime, but it would be stealing, and the public would react to it by lynch law and public disgrace."[32] The reason for having a legal system is to avoid vigilante committees undertaking the preservation of the peace. The recent attacks on student protesters by construction workers in New York City is illustrative of the danger involved.[33] By encouraging social revolt against unjust laws we are only encouraging lawlessness and further oppressive measures by the police against protesters.

Third, the position as stated by Quinney assumes there are just laws and unjust laws, but who is to judge whether a law is just or unjust? Under this system of anarchy, each man is the judge of whether or not he wants to obey the law, and only total lawlessness can result from such a political philosophy. A black is told he need not obey an unfair housing law or education law, and a student is told he should oppose the illegal war in Vietnam. Why then should not a taxpayer decide he does not have to pay taxes, or a robber that he need not respect the life or property of another individual? If we state that illegitimate laws need not be obeyed, what is left of legitimacy? If the judgment of each man replaces the will of the majority as expressed through democratic processes, what is left of the legal system? We are reduced to the old blood-feud and self-revenge notion which the law has tried to replace for the past two thousand years. Such a system leaves each citizen, including those who are protesting against unjust laws, unprotected and exposed to the violence of those who have a different notion of just and unjust.

Decriminalization of a part of the criminal justice system is an absolute necessity, but not in the way some of its proponents advocate.


## Conclusions

The criminal law developed out of a rural agrarian tradition and is now the important means by which order is maintained in an industrial urban society. The informal social controls based on custom and tradition associated with the family, religion, and neighborhoods have been weakened, thus placing new burdens on the formal controls of the state.

The law is concerned with social welfare, private morality, public order, and law enforcement. The effectiveness of the law depends to a large extent on the deterrent effect of punishment, which is lacking when enforcement is sporadic, uncertain, and far-removed from the criminal act. The law also depends in part on voluntary compliance and support from the public, which is often lacking in an urban society. Many contemporary social values run counter to the law, and the law is often viewed as a tool of oppression or as supporting a style of life not acceptable in today's world.

The philosophy of deterrence is still basic to criminal law, though the ability of the law to deter criminal behavior is of limited success at best.


## NOTES

[1.] Richard Arens and Harold D. Lasswell, *In Defense of Public Order*, New York: Columbia University Press, 1961; Paul H. Landis, *Social Control*, Philadelphia: J.B. Lippincott Co., 1956; Jerome Hall, "Legal Sanctions," *National Law Forum*, Volume 6 (1961) pp. 119-126.

[2.] William Seagle, *Quest for Law*, New York: Alfred A. Knopf, 1941, p. 33; see also E. Adamson Hoebel, *The Law of Primitive Man*, Cambridge: Harvard University Press, 1954; Bronislaw Malinowski, *Crime and Custom in Savage Society*, London: Kegan, Paul, Trench, Trubner, and Co., 1926; A.R. Radcliffe-Brown, "Law, Primitive," *Encyclopedia of the Social Sciences*, Volume 9; Karl Llewellyn and E.A. Hoebel, *The Cheyenne Way*, Norman: University of Oklahoma Press, 1941; Ray Barton, *The Kalingos*, Chicago: University of Chicago Press, 1949: Roy Barton, *Ifuago Law*, Berkeley: University of California Publications in American Archaeology and Ethnology, 1919.

[3.] Mischa Tituv, *The Science of Man*, New York: Henry Holt and Co., 1954, p. 391; see also Hoebel, op. cit., p. 288 ff; Albert Kocaurek and John H. Wigmore, *Primitive and Ancient Legal Institutions*, Boston: Little, Brown, and Co., 1915; Sidney P. Simpson and Julius Stone, *Law and Society*, St. Paul: West Publishing Co., 1948; George M. Calhoun, *The Growth of Criminal Law in Ancient Greece*, Berkeley: The University of California Press, 1927; Robert J. Bonner and Gertrude Smith, *The Administration of Justice from Homer to Aristotle*, Chicago: The University of Chicago Press, 1930; Carl Ludwig von Bar, *A History of Continental Criminal Law*, Boston: Little, Brown and Co., 1906; Sir Henry Maine, *Ancient Law*, 10th ed., London: John Murray Co., 1906.

[4.] Leonard Broom and Philip Selznick, *Sociology*, 2nd ed., Evanston: Row, Peterson, and Co., 1958, p. 35.

[5.]  Robert M. MacIver and Charles H. Page, *Society*, New York: Holt, Rinehart and Co., pp. 588-600.

[6.]  Roscoe Pound, *Social Control Through Law*, New Haven: Yale University Press, 1943, p. 20.

[7.]  Roscoe Pound, "Sociology of Law," in *Twentieth Century Sociology*, ed. by Georges Gurvitch and Wilbert Moore, New York: Philosophical Library, 1945, p. 300.

[8.]  Leon Radzinowicz, *A History of English Criminal Law*, 3 vol., London: Stevens and Sons, 1948; Frederick Pollock and Frederick Maitland, *The History of English Law*, Cambridge: University Press, 1899; Luke O. Pike, *A History of Crime in England*, 2 vol., London: Smith, Elder, and Co., 1873; Sir James F. Stephen, *A History of the Criminal Law of England*, 3 vol., London: Macmillan and Co., 1883; W.S. Holdsworth, *A History of English Law*, 7 vol., Boston: Little, Brown and Co., 1923.

[9.]  Jerome Hall, *Theft, Law, and Society*, Indianapolis: Bobbs-Merrill Co., 2nd ed., 1952; Radzinowicz, op. cit.; Stephen, op. cit.

[10.]  Harry Elmer Barnes and Negley K. Teeters, *New Horizons in Criminology*, 3rd ed., Englewood Cliffs: Prentice-Hall, 1959, pp. 314-321; Edwin H. Sutherland and Donald R. Cressey, *Principles of Criminology*, 7th ed., Philadelphia: J.B. Lippincott Co., 1966, pp. 346-352.

[11.]  John C. Ball, "The Deterrence Concept in Criminology and Law," *Journal of Criminal Law, Criminology, and Police Science*, Vol. 44, no. 3, p. 347.

[12.]  Karl Menninger, *The Crime of Punishment*, New York: Viking Press, 1968.

[13.]  Jerome Michael and Herbert Wechsler, *Criminal Law and Its Administration*, Chicago: Foundation Press, 1940, pp. 250-255; Radzinowicz, op. cit., Vol. I, p. 313 ff.

[14.]  Radzinowicz, op. cit., Vol. 3, p. 450 ff.

[15.]  Pike, op. cit., Vol. I, p. 284.

[16.]  Leon Radzinowicz, *Ideology and Crime*, New York: Columbia University Press, 1966, pp. 83-84.

[17.]  Ibid., p. 98.

[18.]  H.L.A. Hart, *Punishment and Responsibility*, New York: Oxford University Press, 1968, pp. 43-44.

[19.]  Ibid., p. 86.

[20.]  Ibid., p. 68-70.

[21.]  N.H. Azrin and W.C. Holz, "Punishment," in *Operant Behavior*, Werner K. Honig, ed., New York: Appleton-Century-Crofts, 1966, pp. 380-447.

[22.]  H.L.A. Hart, *Law, Liberty, and Morality*, Stanford: Stanford University Press, 1963.

[23.]  Edwin Schur, *Crimes Without Victims*, Englewood Cliffs: Prentice-Hall, 1965.

[24.]  Report of the Committee on Homosexual Offenses and Prostitution, *The Wolfenden Report*, New York: Stein and Day, 1963: See also Norman St. John-Stevas, *Life, Death, and the Law*, Bloomington: Indiana University Press, 1961.

[25.]  Sanford H. Kadish, "The Crisis of Overcriminalization," *Annals*, November, 1967, p. 157.

[26.]  The President's Commission on Law Enforcement and Administration of Justice, *The Courts*, Washington, D.C.: U.S. Government Printing Office, 1967, pp. 97-107.

[27.] Stanton Wheeler, ed., *Controlling Delinquents,* New York: John Wiley and Sons, 1966, pp. 57-58; The President's Commission on Law Enforcement and Administration of Justice, *Juvenile Delinquency and Youth Crime,* Washington, D.C.: U.S. Government Printing Office, 1967, p. 155 ff., pp. 417-419.

[28.] *Juvenile Delinquency and Youth Crime,* op. cit., p. 418.

[29.] Ibid., p. 418.

[30.] Richard Quinney, *The Social Reality of Crime,* Boston: Little, Brown and Company, 1970, p. 236.

[31.] Ibid., p. 313.

[32.] Edwin H. Sutherland, *Principles of Criminology,* 4th ed., Philadelphia: J.B. Lippincott Co., 1939, p. 18.

[33.] New York Times, May 9 and May 12, 1970.

# Chapter 4

# The Police

## *The Police and Deterrence*

The one criminal-justice agency most closely allied with the deterrence theory is the police department. The police justify their existence on the premise that, if criminals are detected, arrested, and punished, the crime rate will decrease. The idea of rehabilitating criminals therefore is not basic to the policeman's philosophy, and often he regards those among judges and correctional officers who do advocate rehabilitation as encouraging criminals to return to the streets to commit crimes. The police are concerned when a convicted man is released on probation or is turned free by the court on a legal technicality, and they have supported the retention of capital punishment when efforts have been made to eliminate it.

If deterrence is to be effective, the police must be effective, for swift and certain apprehension and punishment are basic elements here. The courts and correctional system cannot punish unless the criminal is first apprehended by the police. Official legal action concerning a suspected criminal commences with a complaint to the police department or knowledge of a crime by the police.

## *Police Efficiency in Crime Detection*

If we ask how efficient the operation of the police department is, we see that only twenty-two percent of all property offenses are cleared by an arrest.[1] In New York City, fourteen percent of all burglaries are cleared by arrest. It is therefore obvious that the police neither prevent nor control crime. If we compare reported crimes (a figure less than the total crime figure) to subsequent legal action, we find the following funnel effect[2]:

| | |
|---|---|
| 2,780,000 | reported crimes |
| 727,000 | arrests |
| 177,000 | complaints |
| 160,000 | sentenced |
| 63,000 | prison |

We can add to this discussion the fact that 3.5 times as many rapes and .5 times as many robberies occurred as were reported. The reported rates underestimate the actual rate of crime.[3] If we ask why this lack of effectiveness, we are told by the President's Commission on Law Enforcement that the police *lack the knowledge needed* to prevent or control crime.

The President's Commission on Law Enforcement noted that the police *do not change the conditions which cause crime.* [4] Obviously the President's Commission was referring to the so-called root causes of crime such as poverty, undereducation, and discrimination. Though police activity may not cure poverty, unemployment, or urban unrest, a high arrest rate may act as a deterrent influence. It may be that a crucial factor in the rate of crime is the lack of punishment associated with a great deal of criminal activity. Those who argue that since the cause of crime is poverty, the police cannot prevent crimes, are following the positivist tradition of rejecting the deterrence theory in favor of a rehabilitation theory. If poverty causes crime, then we should fire our police departments and give the money to the poor. If the cause of crime is the resulting consequences of criminal behavior (reward minus punishment), then the detection of offenders is an important element in our law enforcement system. In a mental hospital setting, nurses can act as behavioral engineers; i.e., shape the behavior of the patients in desirable directions.[5] The police also can act as behavioral engineers in the community to the extent that they respond to the behavior of the community in such a way as to shape law-abiding behavior.

We want our police to be more efficient, but we disagree as to the means to achieve this. We are bitterly divided today between those who want to unleash and remove the handcuffs from the police and those who cry police brutality and want more legal and political restrictions placed on police activities. The cry for "law and order" is matched by the cry for "law, order, and justice."

### Police Functions and Responsibilities

Packer has characterized two models for law enforcement: (1) the crime control model, based on administrative efficiency, where emphasis is placed on the detection and prevention of crime; and (2) the due process model, based on a judicial adversary system, where the rights of individuals accused of crime are emphasized and protected.[6]

The crime control model is based upon efficiency of operation, high rate of apprehension and conviction, rapid determination of guilt or innocence, and administrative fact-finding. According to this model, the police should have wide investigatory powers, and arrests should be made for investigatory reasons. Confessions and illegally gained evidence should be allowed into court as evidence, and the police should be trained to act in a professional manner so that the criminal could not be freed on a legal technicality.

The due process model holds that arrest must be on probable cause, confessions must not be introduced if delay in arraignment is involved, and illegally gained evidence must not be admitted into court. Police activities must be carefully controlled by the courts, not by professional police organizations. The investigatory powers of the police must be limited, and counsel must be provided for the defendant during the investigatory period.

The crime control model holds that, after arrest, the prosecutor should decide the charge; high bail and preventive detention should be used to protect the public; and guilty pleas should be expedited by the courts.

The due process model, on the other hand, holds that preliminary hearings, the setting of minimum bail, review of guilty pleas by the court, and a general review of errors by an appellate court are essential ingredients in the guilt-finding process.

Based on a study of a California police department, Skolnick characterized the dichotomy as law *versus* order; legal procedures and due process versus professional bureaucratic police activity.[7] The police view their job as one of technical proficiency in the apprehension of criminals. The courts see the protection of basic concepts of due process as fundamental to the work of both the police and the courts. One issue then is law versus order.

Another issue is *law enforcement* versus the *maintenance of order*. James Wilson draws a distinction between enforcing the criminal law (rape, murder, robbery, assault) and maintaining peace (drunkenness, family quarrels, personal assaults, public disorders).[8]

Herman Goldstein views the dichotomy as between *law enforcement* and *services* (emergency ambulance service, traffic control, social welfare services, getting cats out of trees, returning lost children).[9]

We have no well-defined role for the policeman—he is a jack of all trades. Over sixty percent of his time is spent in noncriminal matters.[10] According to Wilson, only ten percent of the calls to the police involve law enforcement.[11] We use our police to handle matters ranging from riot control and administration of the criminal law to social services. The New York City Police Department recently received a Ford Foundation grant to provide services to local citizens at the precinct level. Those who advocate greater involvement by the police in community affairs (as mentioned in the Wilson and Goldstein articles above) do so in the belief that the police must have an understanding of and cooperation from the community residents. Law enforcement is difficult in a community hostile to the police. At the same time, it is difficult to envision how social services provided by the police are going to reduce the crime rate unless one also assumes that social services prevent crime, for which proposition no evidence exists.

The question must be raised whether we are weakening our law enforcement system by using the police to maintain order, to provide social services, and to enforce the criminal law. Professor Allen has noted the weakness of the juvenile court system due to the shift from law enforcement to social services.[12] The police are under the same pressure as is the court system—namely, to rehabilitate criminals rather than to deter them through strict law enforcement. Do we have a weakening of the deterrence model because of our emphasis on the rehabilitative model? Is it possible that effective police work in apprehending and arresting criminals might reduce the crime rate? Does the apprehension and punishment of criminals reduce the crime rate? If criminals are caught, they cannot immediately commit more crimes, and upon release will commit crimes *only* in those situations where the chances of detection are slight. Punishment does deter; however, most criminals are not punished by the legal process for their criminal acts, as is seen in the twenty-two percent arrest rate for reported offenses.

A serious look must be taken at police organization, and a decision made as to whether or not law enforcement is important enough to assign the police to do it, or whether we want the police to also be quasi-social workers and community organizers. *Without detection of crime, the control and prevention of crime will never occur.*

### The Police and Public Order

In two areas (1) unenforceable laws (sex, narcotics, gambling, alcoholism) and (2) student protests, peace marches, and racial unrest, the police have been given additional burdens without compensating means for maintaining public order. In Chapter 3 we discussed the problem of unenforceable laws. When the police attempt to enforce a law for which there is little public support, and great opposition, they resort to questionable enforcement tactics such as illegal search and seizure, entrapment, use of informers, and electronic surveillance. Corruption and bribery are most often associated with the enforcement of such laws.

Problems associated with race riots, protests, and related issues occupy a major part of the concern of many urban police departments. The involvement of police in political and social issues is another example of the weakening of the law enforcement process. Not only does such intervention by the police in protest activities alienate the community from the police, but it diverts effort and resources from law enforcement to public order.

New legislation could be passed (or existing legislation enforced) governing the nature and degree of violence occurring between citizens and police. We should spell out how far a citizen can go in provoking a police officer—e.g., profanity, throwing bags filled with urine or feces, throwing rocks, and so forth. A great deal of difficulty could be avoided if we made clear to all the rules of the game before a riot or protest started. A law which made any verbal or physical assault on a police officer a felonious assault and grounds for arrest would do a great deal toward the improvement of police-citizen relations. Existing laws which permit resisting unlawful arrests should be abolished, and the legality of the arrest should be decided in court, not on the street.

Today we witness attacks by police and citizens upon one another with no legal action being taken. No protester should be struck or physically abused by the police *unless* he has *first* been placed under arrest, and then only to the extent needed to effect the arrest and to restore order. Although many rioters and protesters are physically attacked by the police, few are ever arrested or charged with crimes, and this gives the community a feeling of police brutality. *Every* person who assaults a police officer *should* be arrested and severe penalties meted out. Every person arrested should understand *disciplined force* will be used if he resists arrest, and an additional charge of resisting arrest made, for which further penalties are attached. An assault by a policeman on a citizen without a prior arrest having been made, or the use of force where it was not needed to carry out the arrest should constitute grounds for immediate dismissal of an officer from the force. As things now stand, we allow assaults by both groups on each other without legal consequences for either, and we wonder why the police of Chicago are brutal or why students in New York City roam the streets destroying property.

Effective law enforcement depends upon certain and rapid application of sanctions on violators, be they policemen or protesters. The division between policy-making and law-enforcing activities must be kept distinct, and the police should not be responsible for decisions involving the use of the streets or parks for protest purposes. Under present political conditions, we allow protesters to break the law because they feel the law is unjust. The places to test the advisability of a law are not in the streets, but in a courtroom, in a legislature, or through a referendum. The lines between lawful and unlawful protest must be carefully drawn, and all possible legal means used to enforce them so as to protect both citizens and the police.

Judge George Edwards has noted that six major social trends have changed the nature of modern law enforcement:

(1)  increase in urban crime;

(2)  effects of urbanization;

(3)  population migrations;

(4)  U.S. Supreme Court decisions;

(5)  civil rights movement;

(6)  race riots and violence.

It is within this context that the police are responsible for the dilemma of the urban environment. Edwards recommends police professionalization, disciplined use of force, more effective law enforcement, effective riot control, and organized citizen support.[14] Though Edwards lumps law enforcement, order, and services together, it is obvious from his discussion that he is talking primarily about law enforcement—the "disciplined and controlled" use of force to prevent urban crime and violence. The problems of the ghetto—education, health, housing, employment, family stability—are not going to be solved by police action, but it is also true that social improvement of the urban environment will not occur until there is law and order in the urban ghetto. Schools, business, and family life cannot function while crime and violence are occurring. The most critical function the police can perform is to provide a peaceful setting within which education, business, and living can occur.

### Discretionary Power of Police

As Goldstein, Kadish, and LaFave have written, the discretionary power of the police as to those situations which call for a decision to arrest is great.[15] The police do not arrest every time an offense is committed, even when they have knowledge of that offense. The above writers have all advocated heightened visibility of police discretion and some control of such power by the judiciary. As Skolnick points out, a number of factors influence the decision to arrest, such as type of offense, social standing of suspect, and so forth.[16] Full enforcement of the law is not realistic in light of the consequences of such a policy. The courts are now overcrowded, and any substantial increase in the arrest rate would necessitate a major increase in postarrest resources.

LaFave notes that police discretion is related to a number of variables, such as the legislature not desiring enforcement, limited enforcement resources, the victim being unwilling to prosecute, arrests being ineffective or inappropriate, arrests harming the victim, or the prosecutor feeling that a case cannot be made on available evidence. [17]

LaFave also notes that arrests are often made where there is no intention to prosecute. An intoxicated person may be arrested for his own safety. Prostitutes, addicts, drunkards, and gamblers are often arrested for harassment purposes, wherein the police attempt to control the behavior "unofficially" by making it difficult for the defendant to operate; at the same time, however, no charge is ever brought by the prosecutor's office. Often the evidence needed is lacking or the prosecutor is too busy to prosecute every case where an arrest has been made. Also, the police feel it is their duty to punish or control the gamblers and addicts since the courts will not. [18]

The importance of police discretionary power insofar as the control of crime is concerned is that there is a lack of control every time the police fail to arrest, or where arrest is a harassment tactic and no serious consequences result. In order to control human behavior, we must be systematic in the application of the consequences. Discretion and harassment are situations in which the consequences are not applied or are applied badly. For instance, the prostitute or gambler who posts bail of $25 and returns to the street within the hour is not deterred by the arrest; most family arguments involving assault do not result in charges and prosecution. [19] Do we encourage family assaults by dropping charges?

### Legal Restrictions on Police

In recent years, the Supreme Court has increasingly regulated the criminal procedures at the state level. These legal decisions have been aimed at protecting due process for those accused of crime.

In the area of search and seizure, the courts have expanded on the doctrine of U.S. v. Weeks[20] so as to apply the Weeks' doctrine (which excluded illegally seized evidence from federal courts) to states. In Mapp v. Ohio [21] the court held that Weeks applied to states; that is, the exclusionary rule applied to state as well as to federal courts. The court held in Rochin v. California [22], before the Mapp case, that the removal of narcotics from a suspect's stomach by means of a stomach pump was a violation of the due process clause of the Fifth Amendment.

The federal rule for interrogations and confessions has been that the accused must be promptly taken before a commissioner for arraignment, and any confession gained after lengthy interrogations was inadmissible (McNabb v. U.S.[23] and Mallorey v. U.S.[24]). In Massiah v. U.S.[25], the court held that evidence gained from a defendant after he was indicted and in the absence of retained counsel was inadmissible. The logic of these federal cases was extended to the states in the famous cases of Escobedo v. Illinois[26] and Miranda v. Arizona.[27] In these cases, the court moved the lawyer into the stationhouse; that is, the defendant must be advised of his rights at the time of arrest and he must be provided with counsel at this police custody stage in the legal process—before interrogation. These cases extended the right to counsel to the moment of arrest.

Similarly, the courts have limited police action in the areas of wiretapping, eavesdropping, and entrapment.

The crucial issue raised by these Supreme Court decisions is whether or not the court is handcuffing and interfering with the police in the performance of their duties. The charge is often made that such decisions protect the criminal and not the public. The cry for law and order is often the cry for less interference on the part of the court with police activities. The fact that the presidential campaign of 1968 was based on a law and order theme, as well as the fact that Justice Abe Fortas was denied confirmation by the Senate as Chief Justice, illustrates the current mood of the country. Is the court too concerned with the rights of criminals and not concerned enough with the rights of victims?

There is no doubt that the liberal Warren Court moved farther than some people would like in the direction of protecting criminals from the police. This has been done under the philosophy that the conduct of police must be policed, and that the Supreme Court must do the policing. There is an assumption here that the police will behave differently as a result of a Supreme Court decision. How effective are such controls over police behavior?

A Yale Law School study of confessions and police practices in New Haven revealed that the Escobedo/Miranda requirements were not interfering with the police or reducing the number of confessions.[28] The authors concluded that the Escobedo and Miranda decisions have not altered in any measurable way police practices, and therefore, that these decisions have not interfered with the police. The further conclusion seems to be that the criticism that the Supreme Court handcuffed the police is unwarranted.

What the New Haven study found was that Supreme Court decisions do not control police behavior. Rather than using such evidence to conclude that the police can be effective within legal regulations, as the authors of the Yale study concluded, I would conclude that the court cannot through legal decisions control police behavior.

There is no evidence that fewer violations of civil liberties are occurring today as a result of Supreme Court decisions. The reason is obvious: Supreme Court decisions do not control the environment in which the police operate. The control over behavior must be immediate and direct, and legal decisions are far-removed and remote. The policeman is controlled by his environment: the people he must control, his paycheck, his supervisors, promotions, and so forth.

Supreme Court decisions should be viewed as moral guidelines, not as *behavioral imperatives.* Moral guidelines must be implemented before they become behavioral imperatives. Violations of Miranda and Escobedo now result in rewards to the defendants and punishment of the general public (the defendant goes free and the public is faced with the fear and threat of crime). We do not control the behavior of policemen by turning criminals loose; we do control the behavior of policemen by rewarding them for good behavior and punishing them for bad behavior. A system must be devised wherein civil liberties violations by the police result in a reprimand, salary or promotion loss, transfer of duties, or some other such consequence. As we have already noted, police have great discretionary powers, and their behavior is not monitored. In fact, under present conditions, we have no way of monitoring police behavior. The first prerequisite of behavioral control is a monitoring system. Supervision of the police must be located in the environment in which they behave, not in the Supreme Court.

As a result of the Supreme Court decisions, the emphasis in some or even many criminal cases has shifted from the guilt of the offender to the behavior of the police. A defendant can go free if the police misbehave. We, therefore, control neither the police nor the criminal by legal procedures. It is absolutely essential that we separate (1) the control of criminal behavior from (2) the control of police behavior. Turning criminals loose will encourage criminal behavior but it will not deter illegal police behavior. Effective means of controlling the police must be discovered. We must use a reward/punishment system with the police as well as with the criminals if we want to shape behavior.

A related point is the well-known fact that in any bureaucratic organization the behavior of the personnel is governed as much or more by the informal rules as it is by the formal rules.[29] The informal structure of the police department would include the personal, intimate social interaction of the policeman with his fellow policemen, his superiors, and the citizens in the community. As Skolnick notes, the police are governed to a large extent by the informal control system rather than by the formal rules of the bureaucracy.[30] If, by the tone of his voice, a police supervisor lets the men under him know that he does not expect formal court orders to be followed, then the court will be ignored by the men on the beats. The reason is obvious: the policeman must deal with a supervisor who is in a position to reward or punish him today; he does not deal with the Supreme Court, nor is he rewarded by the court for obeying court decisions.

### Law Enforcement and Technology

There is a vast movement today to tie the police to a technological system. This would mean better police cars, computer-assisted operations, chemical Mace, and so forth. The details of science and technology as they apply to the police will be discussed in a later chapter on science and technology. However, it should be pointed out here that one of the major difficulties confronting the law enforcement process is the *lack of evidence that the defendant is guilty.* Unlawful arrests, illegal interrogations and confessions, illegally gained evidence, wiretapping, eavesdropping, and the use of informers are all a product of the same thing: a lack of evidence that the defendant committed a crime. The Yale study quoted above found that interrogations were used in those cases where other evidence was lacking. It is imperative that evidence of a crime be gained by scientific methods, so as to erase any questions as to guilt or innocence. We still try to determine guilt by either battle or trial by ordeal. Two lawyers battle each other in the belief that in the end we will know what happened at the scene of a crime, and we leave it to a jury of twelve men to then say that the accused is guilty or not guilty. Often the crime occurred two to five years past, and evidence is used by lawyers so as to gain a desired verdict and not so as to establish the facts of the case.

We must shift from a *trial by adversaries and jurors* to a *trial by technology.* If a man committed a crime, the fact should be known the moment the crime was committed, and the evidence should be overwhelmingly conclusive. For example, a confession by a man that he committed a bank robbery is inconclusive verbal behavior. Verbal behavior need not bear any relationship to other behaviors. A movie taken by a camera of the bank robbery is conclusive only to the point where identification can be established by film. The capture of the criminal in the act by an alarm system that holds him in place and notifies the police is conclusive evidence he was in the bank with a gun.

If we had the technological means to detect and capture criminals, we would not need a large police force or a large court system to arrest, prosecute, and convict criminals. We need to develop a system so that, as soon as a man commits a crime, he is apprehended, convicted, and sentenced by the scientific evidence. However, as Congressman James H. Scheuer has pointed out in his book on crime, scientific evidence is used in less than five percent of the criminal cases.[31]

### The Prevention of Crime

Professor James Wilson has stated, "In crime prevention, not too much should be expected of the police."[32] As is seen in the twenty-two percent arrest rate, the police act on the basis of a theory of deterrence through punishment, but the effectiveness of punishment depends entirely upon its certain and swift application. The police as now constituted do not engage in an effective fight against crime.

If we ask why this is so, we are immediately aware of several crucial factors:

*(1) Police action is initiated after the crime has been committed.* A call must be made to the police or the police must witness a crime being committed. Once the crime is committed, the police act. The typical department is organized into a peacekeeping unit which patrols the street, and there are specialized details—burglary, auto robbery, homicide, vice—to investigate serious crimes. Such an organization is marshaled after the crime is committed to investigate that crime.

A survey of police administration textbooks reveals either an absence of discussions about crime prevention, or else crime prevention is discussed in terms of youth welfare boards or educational programs. Many departments carry on police athletic leagues or summer camp programs, but such welfare programs are better carried on by welfare agencies. Prevention *before* the crime is committed is more crucial than detection *after* the crime has been committed.

*(2) The police operation is geared to the individual offender,* not to the environment in which crimes are committed. The police deal, as do judges, lawyers, and correctional officers, with offenders, not with environmental conditions.

*(3) The effectiveness of punishment is dependent upon certainty of punishment,* and the police cannot, given anything less than a police state, apprehend more than a small fraction of lawbreakers. The statistics indicate the low arrest rate for many crimes, which fact will not easily be changed. Even if the police arrested more offenders, this would only add to the burden of the courts and correctional system.

### Conclusion

The deterrence model of crime control depends primarily on the effectiveness of police work in detecting and arresting criminals. Punishment must be certain to be effective, however, and the apprehension rate is too low to make the threat of punishment a viable solution to the crime problem.

The police operate within the traditional model of crime control: the individual offender after the crime has been committed. Prevention and environmental conditions are left untouched by such an approach. Police efficiency is further reduced by legal safeguards and due process considerations, as well as by the use of the police to enforce nonenforceable laws and to maintain public safety and order. Public order and service duties weaken the law enforcement phase of police work, and the modern concept of a policeman is more that of a man who is an amateur sociologist than an agent of crime control. Urban unrest and urban politics have contributed to the use of police as social service agents operating within the theory of rehabilitation rather than that of deterrence.

Punishment as used by the criminal law and applied by the police is a weak behavioral control, and the deterrence model is an ineffective one insofar as implementation by the police is concerned.

# NOTES

[1.] President's Commission on Law Enforcement and Administration of Justice, *Police,* Washington, D.C.: U.S. Government Printing Office, 1967, p. 1.

[2.] President's Commission on Law Enforcement and Administration of Justice, *Science and Technology,* Washington, D.C.: U.S. Government Printing Office, 1967, p. 61.

[3.] President's Commission on Law Enforcement and Administration of Justice, *Crime and Its Impact—An Assessment,* Washington, D.C.: U.S. Government Printing Office, 1967, p. 17.

[4.] President's Commission on Law Enforcement and Administration of Justice, *Police,* op. cit., pp. 2-3.

[5.] See Chapter 11.

[6.] Herbert L. Packer, *The Limits of the Criminal Sanction,* Stanford: Stanford University Press, 1968, pp. 149-248.

[7.] Jerome Skolnick, *Justice Without Trial,* New York: John Wiley and Co., 1966.

[8.] James Q. Wilson, "Dilemmas of Police Administration," *Public Administration Review,* September-October, 1968, pp. 407-416.

[9.] Herman Goldstein, "Police Response to Urban Crisis," *Public Administration Review,* September-October, 1968, pp. 418-424.

[10.] President's Commission on Law Enforcement and Administration of Justice, *Police,* op. cit., p. 120.

[11.] James Q. Wilson, *Varieties of Police Behavior,* Cambridge: Harvard University Press, 1968, p. 18.

[12.] See Chapter 2.

[13.] George Edwards, *The Police on the Urban Frontier,* New York: Institute of Human Relations Press, 1968, p. 6.

[14.] Ibid., p. 38.

[15.] Joseph Goldstein, "Police Discretion Not to Invoke the Criminal Process," *Yale Law Journal,* Volume 69, 1960, pp. 543-594; Sanford Kadish, "Legal Norms and Discretion in the Police and Sentencing Process, *Harvard Law Review,* Volume 75, 1962, pp. 904-931; Wayne LaFave, *Arrest,* Boston: Little, Brown and Co., 1967.

[16.] Skolnick, op. cit., p. 71 ff.

[17.] LaFave, op. cit., p. 63 ff.

[18.] President's Commission on Law Enforcement and Administration of Justice, *Police,* p. 22; LaFave, op. cit., p. 437 ff., Skolnick, op. cit.

[19.] President's Commission on Law Enforcement and Administration of Justice, *Police,* op. cit., p. 22.

[20.] 232 U.S. 383 (1914).

[21.] 367 U.S. 643 (1961).

[22.] 342 U.S. 165 (1952).

[23.] 318 U.S. 332 (1943).

[24.] 354 U.S. 449 (1957).

[25.]   377 U.S. 201 (1964).

[26.]   378 U.S. 478 (1964).

[27.]   384 U.S. 436 (1966).

[28.]   "Interrogation in New Haven: The Impact of Miranda," *Yale Law Journal,* Volume 76, No. 8, 1967, pp. 1521-1638.

[29.]   Amitai Etzioni, *Modern Organizations,* Englewood Cliffs: Prentice-Hall, Inc., 1964, p. 40 ff.

[30.]   Skolnick, op. cit., p. 180.

[31.]   James H. Scheuer, *To Walk the Streets Safely,* New York: Doubleday and Co., 1969, p. 46.

[32.]   Wilson, "Dilemmas of Police Administration," op. cit., p. 415.

*Chapter 5*

# The Courts

*Courts, Deterrence, and Rehabilitation*

The judicial structure was based historically upon a deterrence concept of criminal law, and this position is still widely maintained among criminal law scholars, as was discussed in Chapter 3. However, during this century, the rehabilitative ideal has had an impact on the court system and has played an important role in changes that have occurred therein. Judges and lawyers are torn between deterrence and rehabilitation, with rehabilitation now widely advocated as an essential function of the judicial process. At a recent meeting of the American Bar Association, Chief Justice Warren E. Burger urged the legal profession to turn its attention toward penal reform based on ideas from correctional specialists. Attention should be paid, according to Burger, to the convicted offender and to work-release programs, early incentive releases, and other similar reform measures.[1] Burger summarized the feelings of many correctional people as well as of the Task Force of the President's Commission when he identified the problem as one of rehabilitating the individual offender.

Though we are placing the court system within the framework of deterrence, we do so with the recognition of the fact that the deterrence philosophy has been modified and supplemented by the rehabilitation philosophy.

*Role of the Court System in Deterrence*

The "funneling effect" of justice from arrest to sentencing has been commented on in Chapter 4. In the United States as a whole, twenty percent of those arrested for index crimes (FBI Uniform Crime Report) are sentenced, and thirty percent of those sentenced are in prison.[2] After arrest, the decision to dismiss is made by the police, prosecutor, or judge in up to fifty percent of the cases, and, of those charged, as many as ninety percent are disposed of by guilty pleas.[3]   .

From these figures, we know that a vast majority of criminals are not in court. Whatever effect the court system has on criminal behavior, it only touches a very small percentage of the criminal population. If we analyze the reasons for such a failure, we can list some of the factors involved.

*(1) The normative legal code must be enforced to be effective.* The courts receive only those cases for which an arrest has been made, and arrests are made only in approximately twenty-two percent of the cases, and only twenty percent of those are sentenced. The failure of legal control is directly related to the effectiveness of the police in arresting and the courts in prosecuting offenders.

*(2) The court system operates as an autonomous system* rather than as a part of an overall system of justice. Feedback of result is often not made a part of the operation of our courts. By feedback we mean knowledge of the results or consequences of decisions and communication of such results throughout the system. The courts often do not know what the police are doing, nor do lawyers and judges consider the consequences as far as the behavior of the police is concerned with respect to dismissing cases, reducing charges, or acquitting the defendant due to a lack of evidence. The police frequently behave in terms of the way they expect the courts to behave. If the courts throw out prostitution cases, then the police will harass prostitutes, but not make arrests. Likewise, the court can place convicted criminals on probation or in penal institutions without any awareness of the effectiveness of such procedures. Judges and prosecutors must be aware of the consequences of legal procedures above and beyond what goes on in the courtroom itself.

This problem is related to the often-observed fact that complex organizations often confuse ends with means. The legal system places a high priority on the rules and procedures, the means by which justice is administered, while ignoring the fact that the end results may be disastrous. The ends or goals (reforming the criminal, protecting society) are lost to sight in the process of administering the law. This is a most common defect in organizational systems, since the effectiveness of the system depends on knowledge of the results of organizational action.

*(3) The court lacks the behavioral means to implement its policy.* If the judge wishes to reform an alcoholic or a delinquent, he cannot do so within the confines of the court system; he must depend on the police, probation, parole, and correctional systems. The court is no stronger than

the components of the system. A weak probation system or prison system can destroy the effectiveness of the court system.

Another way of making the same observation is to note that reforming criminals is a matter of behavioral science, not legal procedures. The most detailed and exhaustive legal procedure is of little value if the defendant is sent to an ineffective prison system or is released to repeat his antisocial behavior. More will be said about this problem as we discuss the court system.

*(4) The court operation occurs after the crime has been committed,* and it deals with the offender, not with the crime. The court cannot prevent crime if it is involved in the criminal process after the crime has been committed. The court must wait until the offense is committed, and then it must work with the offender. Such an approach assumes that the offender can be rehabilitated by means of treatment, or deterred by means of punishment. If punishment and treatment do not work, the court process is then a failure. Again, one of the major problems is that the court does not alter the environment in which crime occurs; it tries to change criminals rather than environmental conditions.

### Functions of the Court

The court functions (1) to review the activities of the police and to determine if there is evidence to hold the accused for trial, (2) to determine the innocence or guilt of the accused, and (3) to sentence those found guilty. In addition, the appellate court reviews the action of lower courts.

A great deal of what the court is concerned with is internal administration of the system—that is, seeing to it that the court functions every day. Most of the activities concern routine matters such as arraignment, posting of bail, and entering of pleas. Such formal procedural matters become all-important to the legal process, whereas their value as agents for behavioral change becomes obscure and is lost in the process.

The two crucial functions of the court in crime control are to determine guilt and to pass sentence. Guilt-finding is a most difficult task, due to the nature of crime. As was mentioned in Chapter 4, a major problem facing the police is the lack of information concerning the commission of a crime and the guilt of an offender. Without scientific knowledge of these facts, we must resort to the present system of trial by battle, where two lawyers in the adversary system attempt to gain a conviction or acquittal. Since the purpose of the criminal trial is to convict or to acquit, and not to find out what happened, the system operates to the advantage of those criminals who can afford a good lawyer. The criminal justice system operates to the disadvantage of the poor, even if we provide free legal counsel to the indigent defendant.

A great deal of time, effort, and money are spent to determine the guilt of the accused, though such procedures do not prevent or control crime. We must first determine that a man is guilty before we can punish or rehabilitate him, but we must be aware of the fact that the longer it takes to identify the criminal, the less likely we are to deter criminals or to reform them. The present system of determining guilt must be replaced by a more efficient model based on scientific rather than legal proof of guilt. Millions of dollars a year are wasted because we do not know if the people we arrest are in fact guilty of the crimes of which they are accused, and, in addition, we do not even know the real extent to which those found guilty are guilty, or those found not guilty are not guilty. When a man is diagnosed as having a brain tumor or cancer, we can check our diagnosis with reality; in the case of finding that a man has committed a crime, we have no means of checking the results. Legal guilt and factual guilt are not the same thing.

The usual result of such a situation is an administrative procedure for determining guilt called the guilty plea, the negotiated plea, or plea bargaining. Since the prosecution lacks substantial evidence of guilt, or because it would be too expensive to hold a trial to determine guilt, the prosecutor exchanges a guilty plea for leniency in disposition. The issue becomes not one of guilt and treatment, but one of expediency and bureaucratic efficiency. The guilty plea in up to ninety percent of the criminal cases which are adjudicated places emphasis on the formal bureaucratic label of "guilty" rather than on factual truth.

One of the real anomalies of the lawyers' concept of justice is that lawyers are brought into the criminal process at the investigatory stage because of Miranda and Escobedo, and yet the same lawyers who rush in to protect their clients' rights plead their clients guilty because going to trial is an expensive and difficult task.

The prosecutor may decide not to prosecute because he lacks the evidence to gain a conviction, the evidence is inadmissible, the victim does not wish to prosecute, restitution or mediation occurs, or the political and social situation makes prosecution undesirable. The prosecutor can select any number of offenses with which to charge the defendant, depending upon the situation. Usually the prosecutor will upgrade the offense in order to be in a better position to bargain for a guilty plea from the defendant. Thus, armed robbery can be reduced to simple robbery or to larceny, or even to a less serious type of misdemeanor. Assault with intent to kill can become disturbing the peace or illegal possession of a weapon.[4]

The uncertainty of whether a charge is brought, the uncertainty of the offense with which the defendant is charged, and the uncertainty of conviction all add up to something other than swift and certain punishment. If punishment must be swift and certain to be effective, then the court system defeats the whole purpose of the administration of criminal justice. The discretionary power in the hand of the prosecutor is great, and it must be added to the discretionary power of the police as a force mitigating against the effective enforcement of the criminal law.

The other task the court performs is to pass sentence on the convicted offender. The sentencing function is carried on within the formal limitations of statutory law and the informal limitations imposed by the police, prosecutor, and probation department. There are two basic philosophies of sentencing in the United States. The Model Penal Code of the American Law Institute is based on a deterrence model, providing that there be a statutory minimum of one year and a statutory maximum as imposed by the law. The judge may increase the minimum sentence beyond one year, but the deterrent effect of the law is maintained by the one-year minimum and the maximum which the judge cannot change. Sentences can be increased by the judge if the past record of the offender requires it. The Model Penal Code is essentially concerned with categories of *crimes*, since it divides felonies into first-, second-, and third-degree categories, and it allows for judicial discretion based on the character of the offender only within statutory limitations.[5]

The Model Sentencing Act was proposed by correctional officers of the National Council on Crime and Delinquency, and its basic philosophy is rehabilitation. The act states that an offender shall be dealt with in accordance with his individual characteristics and potential as revealed by social work case studies. Preference is given to probation and suspended sentences. The act proposed a short statutory maximum with no statutory minimum; the judge has complete discretion in setting a minimum. The judge is not bound by a one-year minimum, so he has great freedom in imposing probation or short sentences. The Model Sentencing Act provides for parole for any offender at any time. Since the act is based on a rehabilitation model, it is only logical the offender must be released as soon as he is rehabilitated.[6] If this philosophy were pursued to its logical conclusion, a murderer could be released as cured one day after conviction, whereas an exhibitionist could be institutionalized until cured, even if this meant for life in a mental institution.

The Model Penal Code is based on the belief a sentence should be long enough to deter the criminal or others, as well as allowing for longer sentences for recidivists. The Model Sentencing Act is based on rehabilitation of offenders and denies the effectiveness of law as a deterrent. The Model Penal Code is the product of lawyers; the Model Sentencing Act, of probation and parole officers. Thus, each reflects a difference in emphasis as to the purpose of sentencing.

The issue of deterrence versus rehabilitation (the classical versus the positive school) is reflected sharply in the sentencing procedure. Do we sentence to deter or to rehabilitate? Do we focus on the *crime,* as the Model Penal Code does, or on the *offender,* as the Model Sentencing Act does? If we focus on the crime, we set a higher sentence for a more serious offense (murder) than for a less serious offense (robbery). If we focus on the criminal, we use an indeterminate sentence, ignore the severity of the offense, and keep the offender in custody until he is rehabilitated. The favorite slogan of the rehabilitation school is: "We don't sentence cancer patients to three years in a hospital, so why sentence rapists or robbers to a definite term in a prison?"

The whole issue boils down to the effectiveness of punishment versus the effectiveness of treatment. If punishment deters crime, then the logical use of sentencing is to deter; if treatment rehabilitates criminals, then the logical use of sentencing is to place criminals in treatment centers. Since neither is operating efficiently at the present time, we neither deter nor rehabilitate. Sentencing procedures are no better than the behavioral sciences which first must develop the means to change behavior. If we want to change human behavior, we must possess effective behavioral techniques.

Sentencing procedures also suffer from the fact that sentencing is based upon factors in existence *before* the crime was committed, and factors related to the *individual offender,* rather than upon factors to which the offender is subjected *after* sentence is passed or factors in existence in the *environment* to which the offender responds.

Besides the limitations imposed on sentencing by punishment and rehabilitation, sentencing is limited by the justice system itself. The prosecutor, police, and parole board all act as to influence the nature of the sentencing process. The police may put pressure on the judge for a lengthy sentence, the prosecutor may accept a plea of guilty to a lesser offense, and the judge may set the sentence higher or lower than otherwise because of parole regulations or because of his confidence in the parole board. If the judge has faith in the board, he will set a low minimum sentence and allow the board to determine the actual date of release; if, on the other hand, he lacks confidence in parole, he will set a high sentence and remove the discretionary power from the board.

In many instances, the sentencing procedure is an administrative compromise between police, judge, prosecutor, defendant, and parole board. The process may have no bearing on the needs of the individual, and the decisions are often based on the needs of the judicial bureaucracy. Often in a bureaucracy the means become the ends. In a welfare agency, rules and regulations, which are designed as means, become the ends of the social worker's activities, to the detriment of the welfare client. In the same way, the legal regulations become the focal point for lawyers and judges, and the end of criminal law, be it deterrence or rehabilitation, is ignored or neglected. The administration of any agency can assume a major part of the budget or effort of the agency, thus limiting its overall effectiveness.

### Rehabilitation versus Deterrence

The courts have been caught between rehabilitation and deterrence as a philosophy of criminal law. The rehabilitative ideal is seen in the juvenile court movement, probation and parole, the indeterminate sentence, the insanity defense to crime, and in correctional programs designed to make delinquent youths employable.

The courts have in recent years rendered decisions which support the rehabilitative ideal. The Durham decision[7] held that a man is not criminally liable for his behavior if he suffers from a mental disease or defect. If a man is found to be mentally ill, he is treated in a mental hospital, not punished in a prison. The court drew a distinction in the Durham case between defendants with free will and those without. This philosophical argument assumes that people with certain behavioral problems have no free will, whereas people with other behavioral problems have free will. Such a position assumes behavior labeled "mentally ill" is caused or determined, whereas behavior labeled "criminal" is not caused or determined by biological or environmental forces. This distinction is scientifically untenable, since if a man commits theft because of poverty, lack of education, or family background, his behavior is determined. There is no doubt that behavior is determined, regardless of whether we label it "mental illness" or "crime."

Several serious issues have been raised by the insanity defense.

(1) There is no definition of mental illness, and, since the Durham decision, the concept of mental illness includes neuroses, alcoholism, addiction, and psychopathic behavior.

(2) There is no treatment for mental illness. By classifying people as ill rather than as criminals we do not automatically cure them. As will be discussed later in Chapter 8, therapy has not cured our behavioral problems.

(3) We assume that those called mentally ill do not respond to punishment. There is no scientific proof that a person who behaves in a bizarre manner is not under the control of his environment—e.g., under the control of the contingencies of his behavior. A psychotic patient will behave normally when reinforced for normal behavior and will behave psychotically when reinforced for psychotic behavior (see Chapter 11).

(4) We assume that punishment cannot cure, whereas treatment can. As has been noted elsewhere, punishment is a very powerful means of controlling behavior. Also, we assume that mental institutions are not punitive, and prisons are not therapeutic. The differences between prisons and hospitals are not as great as this argument purports, and it has been observed that defendants often prefer a prison sentence to an indeterminate stay in a mental hospital. Punishment can rehabilitate, rehabilitation can be punitive, and prisons have treatment programs similar to those of mental hospitals.

(5) By classifying behavioral disorders as mental illness, we create an analogy between physical illness and mental illness, and we further assume that the physician is the proper person to treat mental illness. Thus, crime becomes a medical and psychiatric problem, rather than a social and behavioral problem. It might be more profitable to regard crime as social rather than medical. Physicians are not trained to deal with behavioral disturbances, especially those deeply rooted in environmental conditions.

A related factor is that psychiatrists are called upon to give testimony in court as to why people commit crimes, whereas sociologists, criminologists, and behavioral psychologists are not. The psychiatrist is a most powerful figure in the administration of justice, though research does not support the claims of a mental illness approach to criminal behavior, as will be discussed in a later chapter.

The mental illness concept in law is based on the theory of rehabilitation, not that of deterrence. It allows the judge to place a defendant in a mental hospital rather than in a prison. This position is expressed very well by Lady Wootton when she states that the purpose of law is rehabilitation, and the issue of mental illness becomes an issue after the determination of guilt as a guide to rehabilitation measures taken.[8] Wootton wishes to cast criminal law in the model of rehabilitation, with treatment given criminals after adjudication.

As Packer notes, the mental illness defense differs from other defenses in that it places the person in custody upon a determination of not guilty.[9] The mental illness concept is based on the assumption that we have the behavioral knowhow to rehabilitate criminals, an assumption to be discussed in Part III of this book. Such an assumption has led to grave due process questions concerning the rights of the mentally ill.

In other decisions, the court has followed the rehabilitation philosophy. In California v. Robinson[10], the court compared narcotics additions to a disease, specifically a common cold. The court decided the case on the basis of the cruel and unusual punishment provision of the Constitution as applied to "status offenses," but the major thrust of the reasoning was that addicts must be rehabilitated, not punished.

In Driver v. Hinnant[11], the court, citing the rationale of the Robinson case, said:

> The upshot of our decision is that the State cannot stamp a chronic alcoholic as a criminal if his drunken public display is involuntary as a result of disease. However, nothing we have said precludes appropriate detention of him for treatment and rehabilitation so long as he is not marked as a criminal.

In Easter v. District of Columbia[12], the court stated that it was authorized to take notice of the fact that a chronic alcoholic is a sick person in need of rehabilitation.

In Budd v. California[13], Justice Fortas stated:

> The Court has already held that a state may not punish for narcotics addiction, that to do so would violate the Constitutional provision of cruel and unusual treatment. . . .Mr. Justice Stewart's opinion for the Court in Robinson makes it clear that a state may not constitutionally inflict punishment for an illness whether the illness be narcotics addiction or the common cold.

In State v. Bess[14], the court said "We think that the demands of our penal policy which aims [sic] at the prevention of crime and the rehabilitation of the defendant will best be served if his sentence is modified to no more than five or less than two years." In Williams v. New York[15], the court noted that "retribution is no longer the dominant objective of criminal law. Reformation and rehabilitation of offenders have become important goals in criminal jurisprudence." The court went on to say that the sentence must fit the offender, not the crime.

In recent years, the failure of the rehabilitative ideal has led the court to reevaluate some of the measures taken to carry out this ideal. One of the major rehabilitative efforts was in the area of juvenile delinquency and the juvenile court. From 1890 on, the court has said that the purpose of juvenile proceedings is rehabilitation and treatment, not punishment, and, therefore, the juvenile is not protected by Constitutional protections afforded adults in criminal court.[16] The juvenile court philosophy has been seriously challenged in two recent Supreme Court decisions.

In Kent v. United States[17], the court, in a case involving a juvenile, said "there may be grounds for concern that the child receives the worst of both worlds: that he gets neither the protections accorded to adults nor the solicitous care and regenerative treatment postulated for children."

In re Gault[18], Justice Fortas reviewed the juvenile court philosophy based on the idea of *parens patriae* wherein the state stands as a parent to furnish treatment to the juvenile delinquent, not to brand him as a criminal. In Gault, the court held that constitutional guarantees, such as notice of charges, right to counsel, the right to cross-examination, the privilege against self-incrimination, the right to a transcript, and the right to appellate review must be afforded the juvenile defendant.

Justice Fortas noted that, according to the President's Commission on Crime in the District of Columbia, sixty to sixty-six percent of the juveniles referred to the court had been in court previously. "Certainly these figures and the high crime rates among juveniles could not lead to the conclusion that. . .the juvenile system functioning free of constitutional inhibitions as it has so largely done is effective to reduce crime or rehabilitate offenders."

In the case of juvenile delinquents, as seen in the Kent and Gault cases, the court has held that treatment has failed and, therefore, the juvenile must be protected by Constitutional rights; in the case of alcoholics and addicts, the court has held that they must be treated and not punished as criminals. Thus, the court is in a most embarrassing dilemma of supporting treatment for one class of offenders, but denying its effectiveness for another. Justice Stewart went to the crux of the issue in his dissent in Gault:

> And to impose the Court's long catalog of requirements upon juvenile proceedings in every area of the country is to invite a long step backwards into the nineteenth century. In that era there were no juvenile proceedings, and a child was tried in a conventional criminal trial. So it was that a 12 year old boy named James Guild

was tried in New Jersey for killing Catherine Beakes. A jury found him guilty of murder and he was sentenced to death by hanging. The sentence was executed. It was all very constitutional.

Albert Cohen, a sociology professor, has written concerning Gault:

The failure of juvenile courts goes back to the fact that despite the progress of our knowledge about juvenile delinquency, we simply do not know enough to diagnose, predict, and prescribe for a very large proportion of offenders. If all our courts were staffed by Ph.D.'s. . .we would still not know in many cases—and some would say in most cases—whether the needs of treatment would be better served by letting the offender go free or by incarcerating him for two or three years.[19]

In Powell v. Texas[20], the Supreme Court of the United States held that conviction for public drunkenness could stand where evidence did not appear that the accused lacked some control over his drinking behavior, or where evidence was lacking as to the impact of punishment on alcoholics.

Yet the medical profession cannot, and does not, tell us with any assurance that, even if the buildings, equipment, and trained personnel were made available, it could provide anything more than slightly higher class jails for our indigent habitual inebriates. Thus we run the grave risk that nothing will be accomplished beyond the hanging of a new sign—reading hospital—over the wing of the jailhouse. The Court has never held that anything in the Constitution requires the penal sanctions be designed solely to achieve therapeutic or rehabilitative effects, and it can be hardly said with assurance that incarceration serves such purpose any better for the general run of criminals than it does for public drunks. Ignorance likewise impedes our assessment of the deterrent effects of criminal sanctions for public drunkenness.

Thus in the Powell case, the court reversed the trend started by Driver and Easter and stated that deterrence was a concern of criminal law.

The climax of the dilemma came recently in the case of Rouse v. Cameron[21], in the District of Columbia, where the court held that a patient committed to a mental hospital on being found not guilty by reason of insanity under the Durham decision had a right to treatment, and, if treatment was not available or was unsatisfactory, the patient was to be released from custody. Thus a man can commit a crime, be found to be mentally sick, committed to a hospital, and then ordered released because treatment was not available. In other decisions in the District of

Columbia, the court has similarly held that a sociopath is mentally ill and must be committed to a hospital; later, the same court was asked to find that sociopaths do not belong in mental hospitals because they are not mentally ill.[22] Thus, we arrive at the precarious point where criminals cannot be put into prison because they are mentally ill, and they cannot be put into mental hospitals because mental hospitals do not afford adequate or proper treatment for them.

The failure of deterrence led the courts into a rehabilitative position, as seen in the Robinson, Durham, Driver, Easter, and Budd cases. The failure of rehabilitation led the courts to the conclusions reached in the Kent, Gault, Powell, and Rouse cases. If deterrence is a failure, and rehabilitation is a failure, what is the role of the court in criminal justice? As Stewart said in the Gault case, we are back in the nineteenth century.

### Suggested Court Reforms

Many suggestions for reforming the judicial system have been made, including changes in sentencing procedures, reorganization of lower courts, reforming bail bond and summons procedures, changing the procedures for selecting judges and prosecutors, changes in the training of judges and prosecutors, new rules for handling evidence or other pretrial procedures, appointment of counsel for those in poverty, use of computers to process and store data and to schedule hearings, and so forth.[23] Some of these suggestions involve coordinating judicial activities at the state level through a state Department of Criminal Justice. As Lumbard notes, the move to place crime control at state rather than local levels is motivated by increased urbanization, need for state and federal tax base, problems of jurisdiction, problems associated with population growth and mobility, and need for better-trained personnel for crime control agencies.[24]

However, such plans for administrative reorganization of the court system or administration of justice system is the application of a band-aid where radical surgery is needed. The courts suffer from an excess of cases, which causes congestion and delay. It now takes years to get some cases into the court, and this encourages dropping charges, pleading guilty, settlements out of court, and other moves to avoid going into the court system. The present model is one of expanding the facilities: hiring more judges and prosecutors, building more courts and prisons, spending more money on the judicial system. Such a model is doomed to failure because, as the facilities for handling criminals expand, the number of criminals will also expand. It is comparable to the opening of mental health clinics—the more clinics you have, the more clients you have.

The answer to the difficulties facing our judicial system is to prevent the crimes *before* they occur, rather than congesting the courts with thousands of cases *after* the crimes occur. The prevention model will work, but the treatment model has not worked so far and probably never will. If we allow the air and water to be polluted, no amount of effort will ameliorate the results; we must prevent pollution before it occurs. We must prevent cancer and heart disease before they occur, since treatment after they occur is of limited success at best. Likewise, we must deal with crime in terms of a new model, rather than by building bigger courthouses and bigger prisons.

The civil liberties issue can be settled by preventing crimes. If crimes are not committed, people will not be harassed, arrested, detained by police, subject to illegal interrogations, wiretapping, or eavesdropping, and so forth. Most illegal police activity takes place after a crime has been committed.

*Summary*

The courts have failed to prevent or control crime because (1) they act after the offense has been committed, (2) they act on the basis of deterrence or rehabilitation, neither of which controls human behavior, (3) they have inadequate ways of determining who are the guilty, and (4) they are based on administrative rules and procedures rather than on scientific procedures which focus on the eventual elimination or control of crime.

Very few criminals are convicted by the courts, and, even if convicted, they receive sanctions which are weak and ineffective. The rehabilitation model has been accepted generally by our judicial system, as seen in decisions declaring alcoholics, the mentally ill, and narcotics addicts to be removed from punitive or deterrent efforts. At the same time, the courts have held that mentally ill criminals and juvenile delinquents are not receiving adequate treatment. As a result, the courts have weakened the deterrent potential of the criminal law while at the same time failing to find successful treatment alternatives.

It has been the general theme of this book that the judicial system as it now functions has sacrificed deterrence for treatment without either reforming criminals or protecting the basic civil liberties of the accused. The courts have contributed their fair share to the deterioration of the criminal law as an effective instrument of social control. The control model used is one of dealing with the *individual offender after* the crime has been committed, whereas the environmental conditions producing crime are not touched by legal procedures or the day-to-day operation of our criminal justice system.

## NOTES

[1.]  New York Times, August 12, 1969.

[2.]  President's Commission on Law Enforcement and Administration of Justice, *Science and Technology,* Washington D.C.: Government Printing Office, 1967, pp. 57-60.

[3.]  President's Commission on Law Enforcement and Administration of Justice, *The Courts,* Washington, D.C.: Government Printing Office, 1967, p. 4.

[4.]  Donald J. Newman, *Conviction,* Boston: Little, Brown, and Co., 1967; Frank W. Miller, *Prosecution,* Boston: Little, Brown, and Co., 1969.

[5.]  Walter C. Reckless, *The Crime Problem,* 4th ed., New York: Appleton-Century-Crofts, 1961, pp. 752-755; Sol Rubin, *The Law of Criminal Corrections,* St. Paul: West Publishing Co., 1963, pp. 650-671; Paul W. Tappan, "Sentencing Under the Model Penal Code," *Law and Contemporary Problems,* Summer, 1958, pp. 528-543.

[6.]  Reckless, op. cit., pp. 752-755; Rubin, op. cit., pp. 650-671; Sol Rubin, "Model Sentencing Act." *New York University Law Review,* April, 1969, p. 251 ff.

[7.]  214 F. 2nd 862 (1954).

[8.]  H.L.A. Hart, *Punishment and Responsibility.* New York: Oxford University Press, 1968, p. 194 ff; Herbert L. Packer, *The Limits of the Criminal Sanction,* Stanford: Stanford University Press, 1968, pp. 13-28.

[9.]  Packer, op. cit., p. 132.

[10.]  370 U.S. 660 (1962).

[11.]  356 F. 2nd 761 (1966).

[12.]  361 F. 2nd 50 (1966).

[13.]  392 U.S. 514 (1968).

[14.]  247A.2d 669 (1968) at 674.

[15.]  69S. Ct. 1079.

[16.]  Commonwealth vs. Fisher, 213 Pa. 48 (1905); People vs. Lewis, 260 N.Y. 171 (1932).

[17.]  383 U.S. 556 (1966).

[18.]  87S Ct. 209 (1966).

[19.]  Albert K. Cohen, "An Evaluation of Gault by a Sociologist," Symposium on Juvenile Problems: In Re Gault, *Indiana Law Journal.*

[20.]  392 U.S. 514 (1968).

[21.]  373 F: 2nd 451 (1967).

[22.]  C. Ray Jeffery, *Criminal Responsibility and Mental Illness,* Springfield: Charles C Thomas, 1967, p. 139 ff.

[23.]  President's Commission on Law Enforcement and Administration of Justice, *The Courts,* op. cit.

[24.]  Elliot H. Lumbard, "State and Local Government Crime Control," *Notre Dame Lawyer,* Volume 43, No. 6.

*Chapter 6*

# Prisons

*Prisons, Deterrence, and Rehabilitation*

Imprisonment has been the major means of punishment since the use of capital punishment fell into disrepute during the eighteenth and nineteenth centuries. Prisons have been used as institutions for penitence, deterrence, and rehabilitation, and in the twentieth century the rehabilitation ideal has been gaining in prominence, as was indicated in Chapter 2. The failure of deterrence has forced correctional officials to reevaluate the basic purpose served in our society by imprisonment. The usual argument is that ninety-five percent of those sent to prison are eventually returned to the streets and, unless they have been rehabilitated while in prison, they will return to a life of crime. Though rehabilitative ideas play a major role in correctional programs today, the use of punishment to deter criminals still has enough prominence to justify a discussion of prisons in terms of mixed goals. As in the case of the courts, prisons have been greatly modified in recent years by the rehabilitation philosophy of crime control called by some, "the new penology." [1]

*Prisons and Behavior Change*

The first fact to be faced is that less than five percent (probably two percent or less) of all known criminals are imprisoned. If we add to this the fact that the crime rate is much higher than the "crimes known to police" figure, we then have a situation where the threat of imprisonment is very weak and in the far-distant future. Correctional systems depend on the efficiency of the police and courts, and, as we have already noted, this is not an efficient system which would make deterrence a successful model for crime control.

Of those who reach prison, between thirty-three and sixty-six percent have been in prison before, depending on whose figures one uses. Myrl

Alexander, the Director of the U.S. Bureau of Corrections, has stated that "as a means of punishment and as an instrument with which to change criminal behavior, imprisonment still is a failure when it must be acknowledged that even among the best correctional institutions at least thirty percent of their inmates become repeaters."[2]

John Conrad made a survey of international corrections and concluded we have little evidence of highly successful programs. He writes that "correctional research consistently finds social restoration depends largely on attention to the social system from which the client came and to which he returns."[3] This means, of course, the community, not the prison, is the key to rehabilitation.

Conrad discusses the Scandinavian system, one of the most advanced correctional systems, and he finds a recidivist rate of seventy-five percent.

> Of the Scandinavian correctional apparatus it can be reasonably said that if good intentions and community support of humane objectives will resociate offenders, then the outcome of Scandinavian corrections should be impressively reasonable. Neither among either staff or laymen did we encounter doubt that the generous, almost lavish, program was consistent with community feeling about treatment of offenders. . . .There is a limit to what kindness can accomplish in correctional practice, but whatever the limit may be, the best place to look for it is in Scandinavia.[4]

In his survey of therapeutic communities in Denmark, Conrad found little research and no evidence of the effectiveness of modern therapeutic concepts.[5]

Some studies have shown that sixty to seventy percent of the prison inmates have been in prison before. Sutherland and Cressey state that sixty-seven percent of the offenders studied are recidivists.[6] Caldwell states that forty to seventy percent of the men in prison have been in prison before and will return later.[7] The FBI careers in crime project indicates that sixty percent of those offenders arrested for federal offenses were rearrested within four years, and this figure was as high as ninety-one percent for those cases which were acquitted or dismissed.[8]

Bailey, from a survey of one hundred reports on the effectiveness of correctional treatment, found that fifty percent reported some positive results. He concludes:

> But, when one recalls that these results, in terms of success or failure of the treatment used, are based upon the conclusions of the authors of the reports, themselves, then the implications of these findings regarding the effectiveness of correctional treatment become rather

discouraging. A critical evaluation of the actual design and the specific research procedures described in each instance would substantially decrease the relative frequency of successful outcome based upon reliable valid evidence. Therefore, it seems quite clear that, on the basis of this sample of outcome reports with all its limitations, evidence supporting the efficacy of correctional treatment is slight, inconsistent and of questionable reliability.[9]

Henry McKay made two studies of delinquent careers in Chicago. He found that fifty-eight percent of the delinquents in one study had been arrested as adults, and the second study dealing with boys committed to training institutions showed seventy-five to eighty percent of the delinquencies studied had been rearrested after release. McKay cited studies by Healy, who found that sixty-one percent of the juvenile offenders he studied went on to adult criminal careers, and by the Gluecks, who found that eighty percent of their group entered adult criminality. McKay concluded: "On the basis of the findings in this and other studies, it can be concluded that the behavior of a significant number of boys who become involved in illegal activity is not redirected toward conventional activity by the institutions created for that purpose."[10]

One consultant's paper for the President's Crime Commission concluded that "there are no demonstrable proven methods for reducing the incidence of serious delinquent acts through prevention or rehabilitative procedures."[11] A study of the California penal system revealed that the longer a man was in prison, the greater the rate of recidivism.[12]

Glaser has challenged the sixty-six percent recidivism rate as being too high, and he concluded that nearer to thirty-three percent of those in federal institutions were reinstitutionalized within five years.[13] The figures put forth by Glaser are in contrast to those of other studies, but even a sixty-six percent success rate would not prove that imprisonment was related to the postrelease behavior of inmates. Sixty-six percent of those diagnosed as mentally ill recover whether in therapy or not. Do we know whether criminals would have the same recidivist rate whether imprisoned or not? The fact that Glaser studied federal offenders might have influenced his results. The fact that he used the reimprisonment rate meant that he could not have been aware of crimes committed for which there was no imprisonment.

It is widely maintained among professional criminologists that prisons are a failure, regardless of the recidivist rate quoted. The impact of imprisonment on human behavior is more damaging than any potential benefits which might be derived from its use. For this reason, many experts are now calling for (1) rehabilitation programs within prison, and (2) substitutes for imprisonment in the form of probation and community-based remedial projects.

*Rehabilitative Programs*

Any discussion of prison and postrelease programs must be general because of the variation in the programs of various institutions. The major conflict is always custody v. treatment[14], since the primary task of the institution is the security of the institution. Most of the personnel and costs are directed at security, not at treatment.

Prisons have always served as a means of punishment; however, since the positive school of criminology gained eminence, the prison has also been used as a treatment facility. Most prisons have some treatment programs: remedial education, vocational training, individual and group therapy, recreational programs, and religious programs. The major difference in emphasis depends upon whether one believes in therapeutic intervention in the psychic lives of inmates or in the usefulness of vocational and academic training.

Street, Vinter, and Perrow, from a three-state survey of juvenile institutions, found fifty percent to be custodial—based on conformity through punishment, twenty-five percent to be reeducational—based on changing attitudes and skills, and twenty-five percent to be treatment oriented—based on psychological services to the delinquent inmates. Though they found differences in administrative policy and organization, and in staff-inmate relations, they did not draw any conclusions about the relative effectiveness of each type. However, they did conclude that "none of the institutions was truly successful at producing changes appropriate to the lives the inmates would lead on the outside."[15]

Glaser found that prison behavior is a poor indicator of postrelease success.[16] He found that only ten percent of the prisoners released benefited from prison work training. He noted that since ninety percent of the offenses were crimes against property, crime was a substitute for work. Unemployment is a major factor in the history of criminals; yet, only twenty-five percent of the releasees had jobs related to prison work experience.[17] Thirty-one percent of those released are never employed after release, and unemployment was twice as high for those who failed as for those who were successful on parole.[18] Glaser concluded that recidivism varies inversely with postrelease employment, and a lack of employment is not due to a criminal record, but to the lack of skilled work experience.[19]

So far as a prison education is concerned, Glaser found that prison education was useful in about twenty percent of the jobs inmates held during their first four months out of prison.[20] Glaser found higher recidivism rates among inmates in educational programs due to such factors as low academic achievement levels, lack of real interest in education, competition with vocational programs, and especially the fact that a small amount of education impairs postrelease prospects by inspiring inmates with unrealistic aspirations.[21]

Glaser found no significant relationship between group counseling and parole outcome.[22] He did find that work supervisors had the most influence and caseworkers the least influence on the inmates.[23]

The conclusions of the prison study by Glaser indicate a failure of prison educational, vocational, and therapeutic programs to rehabilitate inmates. The most critical factors in success on parole are those environmental factors to which the inmate is subjected after release—employment, financial resources, family, and so forth.[24]

Conrad, after a survey of the growth of group counseling, especially as it is practiced in the California institutional system, came to the conclusion that "it is hard to see that group counseling has done any harm."[25] He writes that it is too early to appraise the effectiveness of group counseling in a correctional setting, though he advocates the further extension of the concept of therapeutic institutions and therapeutic communities. Conrad places a great reservation on correctional programs when he notes that "the addition of a special program of psychotherapy, education, or industry is irrelevant unless the community itself is oriented to social restoration as an organizational goal."[26]

### Reasons for Failure of Correctional Programs

Many reasons can be cited for the high failure rate of correctional programs:

*(1) Such programs work on the model of indirect controls* over criminal behavior via education, job training, or therapy. It is assumed that because a man is unemployed or undereducated, he can be rehabilitated through training programs.

The evidence gathered by Glaser conclusively shows that prison educational programs and vocational training programs are inadequate and not related to postrelease employment. Another factor is involved—namely, the motivation of people to work. A man trained in automobile mechanics in prison may decide to "hot-wire" cars in order to steal them when he is in the open community. So long as cars can easily be stolen, car theft will exist in spite of vocational programs.

*(2) The deterrent effect of punishment is made ineffective* by the fact few criminals end up in prison. Beyond that, it may be that imprisonment is an ineffective punishment for many people. Rehabilitative programs,

especially probation and early parole, have made it possible for criminals to commit acts and to escape punishment. Since the rehabilitative philosophy does not believe in punishment, it encourages the avoidance of punishment, and thus a self-fulfilling prophecy is set in motion—we don't punish because punishment is not effective, and punishment is not effective because we don't punish.

*(3) Prisoners adjust to the environment of the prison,* not to the environment of free men. As Glaser, Conrad, Street, and others have demonstrated, prison adjustment is a poor indicator of postrelease behavior. Hardened criminals usually make a better adjustment to prison life than do first offenders, primarily because they know the rules of the game.

    The contingencies of prison life are such that a man behaves so as to gain special privileges and an early release. This would mean compliance to prison rules, conformity to prison expectations, and making it easy for the guards to maintain security and order. Such behaviors have no value in the community. Upon release, the prisoner is subjected to a new environment with new contingencies. Training in one environment will not carry over to another environment unless similar contingencies apply. Institutional programs are organized so that they must fail, since the environment to which the criminal must adjust is not the prison, but the community from which he came and to which he returns. The prison philosophy is the old philosophy we have criticized throughout—that is, changing the individual offender, and not the environment. Until the environment in which crimes are committed is changed, no great reduction in the crime rate will occur.

    It must also be noted that prisons are violent places, where murder, assault, robbery, and rape are common events. Even the security system of a prison does not prevent crimes.

*(4) The organization of the prison itself works against rehabilitation efforts.* There exists a built-in conflict between custodial staff and treatment staff, between staff and inmate, and among inmates. The major organizational issue is the influence of the informal organization of the inmates upon the correctional process.

    Inmates support a code of values; don't interfere with inmate interests, don't be nosey, don't rat on a con, play it cool, do your own time, don't weaken, be a man, never cooperate with a guard.[27] As a result of the inmate organization, an alliance occurs between inmates and prison officials which might be called accommodation. An exchange of favors occurs—the inmates' leaders guarantee a quiet and orderly prison, while the officials allow minor violations of the code. The warden does not want trouble that will bring him criticism from the outside. The inmates want special privileges such as movies, food in cells, contraband cigarettes or liquor, special hours, and so forth. Thus the inmate leaders share power with the administration in order to maximize rewards for the inmates and to ensure control by officials. Inmate cooperation is needed if a prison is to operate successfully. Such a pattern of accommodation has been cited in many studies of bureaucratic systems, including hospitals, government agencies, business concerns, and prisons.[28]

Schrag has classified inmates into four categories:

(a) prosocial—the square Johns who support a legitimate value system;

(b) antisocial—the right guys who support a criminal value system;

(c) the pseudosocial—the politicians who manipulate both the inmate and official system; and

(d) asocial—the outlaws and hoods who are isolates not supporting any normative system of group values and who are troublemakers in prison.[29]

According to Ohlin, the pseudosocial or politician emerges as the inmate leader in a custodial institution, since he deals with the administration in the sharing of power and privileges. In a treatment-oriented prison, the right guy, or antisocial inmate is the leader, since the inmate criminal code must now be protected from the reform efforts of the treatment staff. The inmate code is thus an attempt to isolate the inmate from the treatment program.[30]

The behavior of inmates and guards could be predicted from behavioral psychology, which states that men behave so as to maximize gain (pleasure) and minimize loss (pain). The inmate reacts to the prison environment so as to make it as comfortable as possible; the staff reacts so as to make the job as easy and noncontroversial as possible. In neither case is there any reward for rehabilitation. Wardens are paid for running quiet prisons, not for reforming inmates. Any attempt to establish rehabilitative programs in prison is opposed by both staff and inmates because it makes life more difficult for all concerned. One of the major lessons of organizational theory is that agencies will sacrifice ends for means; they will do the things they can do to give a good public appearance, but they will ignore tasks which will result in failure, such as rehabilitating criminals, educating ghetto children, or making welfare recipients independent of the welfare system.

*(5) Prisons violate the basic tenet of psychology*—namely, use rewards to gain the behavior you want. When a man enters prison, he is stripped of material rewards and social status; there is nothing left to take from him. How does one control a man under such circumstances except through physical force?

Glaser writes that

> It is well established in psychology that punishment usually does not change behavior patterns as effectively as rewarding alternative behavior. It follows from psychological learning theory that if a pattern of response (crime) has been gratified to a certain type of stimulus, punishment may promote inhibition of this old response, but the old response proves more rewarding.[31]

Conrad writes: "The problem, as expounded by Skinner and Homans, is to extinguish criminal behavior by seeing to it that it goes unrewarded, and to reinforce some more acceptable form of behavior."[32] Sykes[33] has analyzed the prison system in these terms:

> The New Jersey State Prison makes an initial grant of all its rewards and then threatens to withdraw them if the prisoner does not conform. It does not start the prisoner from scratch and promise to grant its available rewards one by one as the prisoner proves himself through continued submission to the institutional regulations. . . .In effect, rewards and punishments of the officials have been collapsed into one and the prisoner moves in a world where there is no hope of progress but only the possibility of future punishments. Since the prisoner is already suffering from most of the punishments permitted by society, the threat of imposing those fears remaining is all too likely to be a gesture of futility.

Imprisonment is weak because there is no way to reward good behavior. If a man has little to lose, he is harder to control than if he had a great deal to lose. Throughout the book, emphasis has been placed on rewards and punishment. To be effective, punishment must be applied, and rewards must be available for alternative behaviors. Lawful behavior must be rewarded more than unlawful behavior if we expect a criminal to engage in noncriminal behavior.

Because of the lack of positive reinforcement in a prison, many undesirable behaviors are developed by institutionalization. Such an environment, by excluding, as it does, natural contacts with females, friends, and other social and material rewards, leads to a serious deterioration of social behavior. For this reason, imprisonment usually results in more antisocial behavior after release than before incarceration.

### Suggested Reforms and New Ideas in Corrections

The "new look at corrections" involves specialized therapy and community-based programs in place of incarceration. One procedure borrowed from learning theory is to reward inmates for good behavior by giving them points which can be exchanged for money, clothing, trips, and so forth. Slack and Schwitzgebel used such techniques to get delinquents to enter into the therapeutic process.[34] At Draper Youth Center in Alabama, a programmed instructional system was established for inmates as part of the educational process. The CASE project in Washington, D.C., used reinforcement in therapy in the educational program of the National Training School. Inmates could earn points for good academic behavior, which could then be exchanged for food, clothing, rent on rooms, trips, and other such things. The control of behavior under such conditions is easy, and results are remarkable. This design depends on the "hungry rat" model of experimental psychology; a rat is reduced to eighty percent of body weight, and then food is offered as a reinforcement. The model is retained in prisons where subjects are in cages very similar to those in the psychological laboratory. An inmate who is hungry and has but one response to gain food will exhibit a high rate of responding.

The CASE project altered the educational behavior of delinquents, but not the criminal behavior. How does one know that by improving the reading scores of delinquents one is thereby reducing the delinquent behavior? The crucial point is how the delinquent responds in a free operant environment. If a delinquent pushes a lever on a teaching machine to get rewarded in prison, will he do something similar when out? The President's Commission on Law Enforcement stated about CASE: "No research has yet been conducted on the maturity of inmates in dealing with analogous discretion in a free community upon release."[35]

Alexander recommends better sentencing procedures based on the character of the offender, halfway houses, work release programs, and furlough programs.[36]

A recent issue of the *Annals* devoted to the "Future of Corrections" noted the failure of prisons and advocated community programs based on therapy, educational rehabilitation, and job placement.[37] Though the emphasis is away from prisons and toward community projects, one writer noted that "Despite the general enthusiasm with which the National Crime

Commission applauded the establishment of new community-based programs and encouraged their extension, there is little hard evidence that any
of the programs have achieved the objectives which they have
sought."[38] The President's Crime Commission likewise placed heavy
emphasis on education, job training, and guided group interaction, while
recommending avoiding institutionalization if possible.[39] Haskell and
Yablonsky[40] conclude after a survey of the California Correctional
System that "California and some other states have made enormous steps
forward in the field. The progress, however, is toward a more humanistic
approach to criminals and delinquents, not necessarily to a *truly effective
rehabilitation program.*"

The general consensus is that prisons are a failure, and new substitutes
must be found in education, job placement, and group therapy. Since
these are rehabilitative measures, we shall discuss the place of each in
crime control in the next section devoted to rehabilitation.

### Conclusions

Prisons are a failure both as deterrent and as rehabilitative devices. The
model used is the familiar one of dealing with the *individual offender after*
the crime has been committed.

(1) Very few offenders ever go to prison—so, even if effective,
imprisonment would reach very few criminals.

(2) Prisoners adjust to the environment of the prison, and prison
behavior is appropriate to that environment. The prison environment
does not control the prisoner's behavior when he is released into the
environment in which he committed his crimes in the first place.
That environment and the criminal behavior are left untouched by
our prison system.

(3) Prison programs are based on an indirect control of criminal
behavior through education, job training, and therapy. No causal
relationship exists between those variables and criminal behavior,
and by changing one set of behaviors (education, job training, group
therapy behavior), we do not cause or influence another set of
behaviors (criminal behavior).

The failure of our prisons has led to an emphasis on community-based
programs as substitutes for prisons, a further move in the direction of
using the correctional process for rehabilitation rather than for deterrence.

# NOTES

[1.] Harry Elmer Barnes and Negley K. Teeters, *New Horizons in Criminology*, 3rd ed., Englewood Cliffs: Prentice-Hall, 1959, pp. 440-464.

[2.] Myrl E. Alexander, "Corrections in Transition," *Nebraska Law Review*, January, 1966, p. 11. See also Myrl E. Alexander, "Current Concepts in Corrections," *Federal Probation*, September, 1966, pp. 3-8.

[3.] John Conrad, *Crime and Its Correction*, Berkeley: University of California Press, 1965, pp. 64-65.

[4.] Ibid., pp. 135-136.

[5.] Ibid., pp. 228-236.

[6.] Edwin H. Sutherland and Donald R. Cressey, *Principles of Criminology*, 7th edition, Philadelphia: J.P. Lippincott and Co., 1966, p. 665.

[7.] Robert Caldwell, *Criminology*, New York: Ronald Press, 1956, p. 502.

[8.] Federal Bureau of Investigation, *Uniform Crime Reports*, Washington, D.C.: U.S. Government Printing Office, 1967, p. 37.

[9.] Walter C. Bailey, "Correctional Outcome: An Evaluation of 100 Reports," *Journal of Criminal Law, Criminology, and Police Science*, June, 1966, pp. 156-157.

[10.] President's Commission on Law Enforcement and Administration of Justice, *Juvenile Delinquency and Youth Crime*, Washington D.C.: U.S. Government Printing Office, 1967, p. 107 ff.

[11.] Ibid., p. 410.

[12.] Carol Crowther, "Crimes, Penalties, and Legislatures," *Annals*, January, 1969, pp. 151-152.

[13.] Daniel Glaser, *The Effectiveness of a Prison and Parole System*, Indianapolis: Bobbs-Merrill Co., 1964, p. 13 ff.

[14.] Conrad, op. cit., pp. 11-57.

[15.] David Street, Robert D. Vinter and Charles Perrow, *Organization for Treatment*, New York: Free Press, 1966, p. 281.

[16.] Glaser, op. cit., p. 294.

[17.] Ibid., p. 251-252.

[18.] Ibid., p. 239.

[19.] Ibid., pp. 359-361.

[20.] Ibid., p. 271.

[21.] Ibid., pp. 275-283.

[22.] Ibid., p. 191.

[23.] Ibid., p. 134 ff.

[24.] Ibid., p. 311 ff.

[25.] Conrad, op. cit., p. 242.

[26.] Ibid., p. 247.

[27.] Sutherland and Cressey, op. cit., pp. 559-560.

[28.] Amitai Etzioni, *Modern Organizations*, Englewood Cliffs: Prentice-Hall, Inc., 1964, p. 61 ff.; Donald R. Cressey, ed., *The Prison*, New York: Holt, Rinehart and Winston, 1961; Donald Clemmer, *The Prison Community*, New York: Rinehart and Co., 1958; Gresham M. Sykes, *The Society of Captives*, Princeton: Princeton University Press, 1958; Howard W. Polsky, *Cottage Six*, New York: Russell Sage Foundation, 1962.

[29.] Cressey, ed., *The Prison*, op. cit., p. 347 ff.

[30.] Lloyd Ohlin, "The Theory of Individualization in Treatment and Institutional Practice." Paper presented at 9th Annual Meeting of Illinois Academy of Criminology, April 17, 1959.

[31.] Glaser, op. cit., p. 486.

[32.] Conrad, op. cit., p. 303.

[33.] Gresham M. Sykes, *The Society of Captives,* Princeton: Princeton University Press, 1958, p. 52. See also Michael Hindelong, "A Learning Theory Analysis of the Correctional Process," *Issues in Criminology,* Vol. 5, No. 1 (Winter, 1970), pp. 43-58.

[34.] Ralph Schwitzgebel, *Street Corner Research,* Cambridge: Harvard University Press, 1964.

[35.] President's Commission on Law Enforcement and Administration of Justice, *Corrections,* Washington, D.C.: U.S. Government Printing Office, p. 53.

[36.] Alexander, "Corrections in Transition," op. cit., pp. 10-21; Alexander, "Current Concepts in Corrections," op. cit., pp. 3-8.

[37.] John Conrad, ed., "The Future of Corrections," *Annals,* January, 1969, pp. 1-158.

[38.] Ibid., p. 86.

[39.] *Juvenile Delinquency and Youth Crime,* op. cit., especially pp. 416-423.

[40.] Martin R. Haskell and Lewis Yablonsky, *Crime and Delinquency,* Chicago: Rand McNally and Co., 1970, p. 467.

Part III

# THE REHABILITATION MODEL

# Chapter 7

# Studies of
# Individual Offenders

## *Positivism and the Individual Offender*

The positivist school emphasized rehabilitation through the study of individual offenders (see Chapter 2). If the offender is to be reformed, there must be an application of social science to the study of criminal behavior. From Lombroso's time (1880), theories of criminal behavior have been put forth ranging from biological to psychological to sociological. Any theory used to explain behavior in general can be and has been used to explain criminal behavior. A basic assumption is made that criminals differ from noncriminals with respect to some trait or combination of traits which cause or influence behavior. The history of professional criminology has been one of the enunciation and denunciation of theories as to why men behave as criminals. At this point in history, no one theory stands out as proven or even as acceptable to all social scientists concerned with criminality, and yet each discipline has staked out an explanation which is protected by provincial interests. The lack of acceptable explanations of criminal behavior is due to the lack of a science of human behavior in general. The methodological issues involved in science will be discussed in a later chapter, and this chapter will be devoted only to a review of the major theoretical positions taken by criminologists during the past one hundred years.

## *Biological Theories of Criminal Behavior*

Following Darwin's work on evolution, a number of attempts were made to explain behavior in terms of biological and physical traits. One school regarded criminal behavior as inherited via the genes. Studies of degenerate families such as the Jukes and the Kallikaks were supposed to prove that behavior was inherited. If the father was a drunkard, the mother was a prostitute, and the children were delinquents, did this not prove that crime was genetically inherited?

Another approach was to study identical twins and to discover the number of twins who resembled each other in criminality and delinquency. If identical twins resembled each other more than did fraternal twins, it was assumed that crime was genetically inherited.

A third approach was to study body build and relate body build to behavior. Body types have been designated by Goring, Kretchmer, Sheldon, Hooton, and others as crucial in the explanation of criminal behavior. Body types were divided into mesomorphic (muscular), endomorphic (fat), and ectomorphic (skeletal), and it has been noted that most delinquents are mesomorphic.[1]

Such explanations are faulty, in that they view behavior as a product of the physical makeup of the organism. They ignore the fact that behavior is adaptation of the organism to the environment. The question is not nature versus nurture, but rather the interaction of nature and nurture. Just because a father and son resemble one another behaviorally does not mean behavior is inherited. It means that they share the same environment and learn similar things from their experiences. The son might learn criminality from his father in some manner, or both may live in poverty, and poverty may cause criminal behavior. Studies that assume genetic inheritance to explain behavior ignore a more important process of social inheritance.

The theory of behavior to be discussed later states that the organism is equipped to receive from and to respond to environmental conditions. Body build or genetic inheritance will play a role in the way the individual will interact with his environment, but one cannot ignore the environment in this evaluation. The finding made by Hooton that Southern Europeans are more criminalistic than Northern Europeans can be explained in terms of migration patterns to the United States, age and sex variables, socioeconomic variables, and education. One need not look only at body build to explain crime.

### Psychological Theories of Criminal Behavior

After the establishment of intelligence testing around World War I, Goddard and others stated that crime was due to feeblemindedness. Goring had stated earlier that crime was due to physical and mental inferiorities, and the notion of a mental defect was in line with the idea that criminals are inferior.[2] The observation that criminals and noncriminals have the same range of IQ scores when age, social class, and education are held constant destroyed the myth that criminals have subnormal mental faculties. Some criminals are bright, and some are stupid. This observation does not rule out the fact that in any given case intellectual faculties might be an important factor. In the case of a sexually delinquent girl with an IQ of 65, the IQ and the behavior cannot be separated. This does not mean, however, that level of intelligence is a cause of criminality; quite the opposite has been demonstrated during the past fifty years.[3]

Freudian psychology is based upon the model of an innate energy system, a system that discharges energy in interaction with a given environmental situation. The id is the pleasure-seeking center of energy which is searching for release or reduction. The ego is the reality principle which directs the id to sources of pleasure and away from pain within the environment. The superego is the principle of punishment, or the evaluation of human acts by others (usually the father or mother in Freud's scheme). The superego evaluates the behavior of the individual as morally right or wrong. The Freudian system appears to be very biological in foundation and very similar to behavioral psychology in its emphasis upon reward and punishment. However, the Freudian system shifted from the external to the internal environment, the mental, not the biochemical, processes.

Freud emphasized consciousness as a vital part of his psychology, and unconsciousness thereby became a determinant of behavior. Because of conflict between the id, ego, and superego the person must repress his feelings into the realm of the unconscious, where these feelings then surface in the form of undesirable behavior. Making the unconscious a source of conscious motivation plays a major role in psychotherapy.

One of the major sources of anxiety and conflict is the Oedipus complex, the attachment and sexual feeling of a son for his mother. Such forbidden feelings can be handled by the defense mechanisms: repression, denial, reaction formation, projection, rationalization, sublimation, or regression. The Oedipus complex is regarded as the heart of neurosis, characterized by anxiety brought about by a conflict between superego and id. A neurotic has contact with reality, but he is unhappy, fearful, and anxious because of a threatening punitive situation which involves an approach-avoidance conflict. Freud did not attempt to explain psychosis, which is characterized by a break with reality as exemplified by hallucinations, delusions, depression, catatonic withdrawal, and paranoia.[4]

Crime is often explained as a product of inner psychic conflict. The Freudians, including most clinical psychologists, psychiatrists, and social workers, use this framework to interpret crime. Crime becomes symbolic. A boy steals pocketbooks which·symbolize the vagina because of penis envy; stolen objects have phallic meaning—they represent the penis or vagina (e.g., pencils, pens, purses, and the like); a man kills his wife labels such behaviors as kleptomania (compulsive stealing) or pyromania (compulsive setting of fires) and regards them as symbolic of sexual problems.[5] Thus crime is explained in terms of a mediating or intervening variable which is not verifiable empirically. Since ego, id, or neurotic defense reaction can be neither seen nor measured, one can posit that such exist without ever being proven wrong.

Psychiatry has been very concerned with labeling behavior. A person is called a neurotic, a psychotic, or a kleptomaniac. Such labels are not explanations of behavior, but descriptive categories used for classification purposes. Classification is part of scientific method, but it is not the goal or end result of science. There has never been any proof that neurotic or psychotic behavior causes or produces criminal behavior. One textbook states that one percent of criminals are psychotic, twenty percent are neurotic, thirty-five percent are psychopathic, and thirty-one percent are dyssocial.[6] More noncriminals than criminals are psychotic or neurotic. The only major psychiatric category encompassing criminal behavior is that of personality disorder or psychopathic personality. By definition, criminals are psychopaths, since the term "psychopath" means antisocial behavior. As Lady Wootton has said, "The psychopath is the model of the circular process by which mental abnormality is inferred from antisocial behavior while antisocial behavior is explained by mental abnormality."[7]

From the psychoanalytic point of view, criminal behavior is a product of abnormal psychic conflict, occurring in the mind and manifested in symbolic forms of behavior. These conflicts involve the inability of the individual to handle his sexual feelings in a way acceptable to himself or to others. The psychoanalytic view is very prevalent in psychiatry, clinical psychology, social work, and in the layman's explanation of why people commit crimes. The psychoanalytic school has been seriously challenged by sociologists and experimental psychologists.

Several attempts have been made to differentiate criminals along a psychiatric-social continuum. Hewitt and Jenkins classified delinquents according to the behavior they exhibited; the unsocialized, aggressive delinquents were assaultive, cruel, and prone to fighting. The socialized delinquents had a history of bad companions, gang membership, habitual truancy, and cooperative stealing. The overinhibited delinquents were seclusive, shy, apathetic, and sensitive. These three types might be called antisocial (psychopathic), dyssocial, and neurotic. Albert Reiss classified delinquents as (1) integrated delinquent, (2) defective superego delinquent, and (3) weak ego delinquent. The integrated delinquent comes from stable family patterns and will develop into a noncriminal adult. A defective superego delinquent has not internalized the norms of middle-class society and thus experiences little guilt, as he is a member of a delinquent subculture. The weak ego delinquents are insecure, with little self-esteem, and may be aggressive or hostile.[8]

Here we have a sociologist (Reiss) using psychoanalytic concepts to explain delinquent behavior in terms not too dissimilar from those used by Hewitt and Jenkins. There is general agreement that we must differentiate the antisocial psychopath from the dyssocial or socialized criminal from the weak ego or neurotic criminal. Coleman differentiates between the antisocial reaction and the dyssocial reaction.[9] The neurotic or weak ego criminal overconforms to the norms of society. In doing so, he is in need of love and affection, which he seeks in criminal activities. He seeks approval, but in socially unacceptable ways. The antisocial or psychopathic personality has no super-ego; he has not internalized norms of the society. The dyssocial person has internalized the norms of society, but the society to which he belongs is deviant and criminalistic, not law-abiding.

Such explanantions of criminal behavior in terms of personality traits are not really explanations as much as labels given to behavior after it has occurred. To say that someone is a criminal because of weak ego structure is not helpful if the evidence of weak ego structure is the inability to conform to the laws of society.

Halleck regards behavior as an adaptation to an environment, usually to a stressful environment. Alloplastic responses change the external environment, whereas autoplastic responses change the internal environment (mental life). Such responses are responses to aggression and feelings of helplessness. Halleck talks about belief systems and attitudes under autoplastic responses, which we can pass over here since we have no scientific way of dealing with subjective mentalistic events. Halleck, however, classifies neuroses, psychoses, and criminal activities as alloplastic responses or responses of the organism which alter the external environment. He regards neurotic responses as alloplastic rather than autoplastic, which is more consistent with the writer's framework.[10]

If we label neurotic, psychotic, and criminal behavior as adaptive and alloplastic, as does Halleck, we are in essence agreeing with the behaviorists who regard behavior as instrumental. Alloplastic behavior and instrumental behavior are the same; they alter the environment. It is crucial that we reduce the confusion existing in behavioral science by noting that different concepts are often used to refer to basically similar events.

## Sociological Theories of Criminal Behavior

Whereas Freudian psychology emphasizes the inner mental processes of the individual, the sociologist places emphasis on social interaction, social norms, role, status, and group processes. The sociologist is interested in the influences on crime rates of such variables as age, sex, ethnic background, urban residence, and subcultural value systems. The typical criminal (from official records) is a young male from a minority group living in an urban slum area. Alienation, deprivation, and anomie are terms used to explain the high crime rate of young Negro youths living in slum areas.

The theoretical position taken by sociologists is that socialization is a process by which social norms are internalized by the individual through social (symbolic) interaction with other human beings.[11] Sociology deals with *sanctioned behavior*—behavior governed by norms, mores, folkways, and laws. Durkheim regarded social norms as constraints on behavior, and his concept of anomie, or "normlessness," referred to a situation in which norms are no longer binding or forceful in controlling human behavior due to norm confusion and conflict.[12] Weber defined social action as behavior oriented toward other human beings. To interact socially, according to Weber, we must understand the subjective meaning of the behavior, and such understanding (called Verstehen) calls for putting oneself via introspection into the position of the other person and anticipating the consequences of one's behavior on the other person.[13] The core of introspection is the mental state revealed by placing oneself in the situation of another and introspecting as to how the other person feels. Verstehenism made its appearance in American sociology as subjective introspection (Charles Cooley), humanistic coefficient (Florian Znaniecki), dynamic assessment (Robert MacIver), and definition of the situation (William I. Thomas). American social psychologists, such as George H. Mead and Charles Cooley, placed great emphasis on symbolic interaction and the development of "self" or "personality" through symbolic communication, role-taking, and attitudes. Subjective terminology replaces objective behavioral referents in this school of social psychology.[14]

Emphasis on mental processes, as opposed to physical, is based on an ancient philosophical argument that will be discussed later. It should be noted here that one interpretation of behavior found in sociology, psychology, and criminology places emphasis on mental states which, according to this interpretation, cause or produce behavior. Behavior is explained in terms of intervening variables and inferential concepts drawn from behavior and then used to explain behavior. Gordon Allport expressed this viewpoint when he stated that "Nothing ever causes behavior except mental sets [attitudes and motives]. Background factors never directly cause behavior, they cause attitudes and attitudes in turn determine behavior."[15] The authors of a major textbook in social psychology state that their major concern is with what goes on within the skin of the individual as viewed from a perspective of cognitive theory.[16] "Cognitions, feelings, and action tendencies are interrelated to form a system called attitudes. . .man's social actions are directed by his attitudes. . . .By knowing the attitudes of people it is possible to do something about the prediction and control of their behavior."[17] Herman Mannheim, the British criminologist, has diagrammed this approach to behavior in this manner.[18]

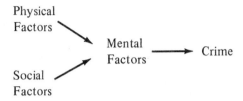

Mannheim writes that "only by producing a certain state of mind can any of the other factors lead to crime."[19] An American criminologist, Richard Quinney[20] accepts the mentalistic approach to criminal behavior, and he denies that a science of criminal behavior is possible:

> Much of criminological theory, based on positivistic assumptions, has sought to explain the causes of crime. That search continues, but the modern concept of causation employed in the philosophy of science is considerably different from that used by criminologists . . . .Thus, causation could be used substantively to explain crime in the special sense of *social causation*. To the extent that man defines situations, that is, constructs his own world in relation to others, the student of social life may conceive of a social causation as part of a social reality.

Quinney is relying on the subjective Verstehen school of sociology associated with Weber, Cooley, MacIver, Znaniecki, Parsons, and Becker.

The theory that people internalize group norms resulting in mental attitudes which cause behavior was used to explain criminal behavior by Edwin H. Sutherland. Knowing that Shaw and McKay had found the distribution of delinquency to be influenced by urban areas, socio-economic class, minority status, and employment, Sutherland put forth his theory of differential association to explain criminal behavior. Criminals are individuals who have associated differentially (including intensity, duration, priority, and frequency of associations) more with people who have criminal attitudes and values than with people who maintain law-abiding attitudes and values. The crucial element is "definitions favorable to the violation of law over definitions unfavorable to violations of law."[21] According to this statement, which is consistent with and a part of the sociological tradition, people commit crimes because of the people with whom they associate; criminal behavior is behavior learned in association with people who are criminals or who maintain criminal attitudes and values.

In a recent textbook, Gibbons restated what has been the major thrust of sociological thinking when he wrote that "our view is that criminal and delinquent activities are a function of definitions of the situation entertained by persons who engage in these acts."[22] A criminal is one who has criminal attitudes or definitions of the situation; i.e., behavior is a product of a mental process whereby a person defines a situation as one in which a criminal act is proper and acceptable.

Many criticisms of differential association have been made during the past thirty years.[23] Two attempts have been made to empirically verify the theory, one by Short, the other by Reiss. The Short study was inconclusive, and Reckless wrote about the Short data that "the crux of Sutherland's formulation. . .still remains untested."[24] The Reiss study of delinquent triads indicated that close friendship involvement in delinquency is "well below what one would expect from the learning hypothesis of differential association. Close friendship choices are more closely correlated with delinquency per se than with participation in specific patterns of delinquency presumably learned from others."[25] It is impossible to verify the statement of differential association because criminal attitudes are known only (1) if the person behaves as a criminal and is convicted, or (2) if the person behaves as to give verbal support to criminal activities. From behavior we infer criminal attitudes, and from criminal attitudes we explain the behavior; thus, the behavior to be explained is explained by concepts inferred from the behavior and not from variables operationally independent of the behavior. The assumption that human learning is limited to learning attitudes from others is too limited and is not acceptable when viewed from the standpoint of experimental learning theory as now stated by psychologists.[26] Glueck argues that criminal associations often follow, rather than precede, criminal behavior, and thus it could logically be argued that criminals associate with criminals because they are criminals, rather than arguing that criminals are criminals because they associate with criminals.[27] The difficulty of drawing causal inferences from data will be discussed in a later chapter.

Following the positivist tradition, Sutherland stated he was attempting "to explain the criminal and non-criminal behavior of individual persons."[28] Donald R. Cressey has been an outstanding and capable advocate of differential association; however, his own study of embezzlers did not support the theory of differential association. Cressey states that differential association may not explain individual behavior, but it can explain the epidemology of crime or differential crime rates.[29] If differential association was put forth to explain individual behavior, and if it fails to explain individual behavior, then it is not a legitimate theory of criminal behavior.

One of the major issues plaguing differential association is the fact that criminals associate with both criminal and noncriminal values, and criminals may even report verbally that they believe in noncriminal values. Kobrin has observed that in any slum area there are both criminal and noncriminal value systems, and the individual delinquent is in contact with both.[30] Matza and Sykes found middle-class values among delinquents, but they also found techniques of neutralization such as denial of responsibility or injury by which delinquents justify verbally their delinquent behavior.[31] Matza has attempted to resolve the problem by theorizing that delinquents drift between criminal and conventional behavior, responding to the demands of each system on the basis of a combination of free will and determinism (soft determinism as Matza labels it).[32] Matza explains everything and nothing, for from his notion of drift he can say if an individual is a delinquent, it is because he has drifted toward a delinquent value system; if he is law-abiding, it is because he has drifted toward conventional values. How do we disprove a statement that infers the explanatory concept from the behavior to be explained?

If individuals behave so as to conform to group norms, then how does one explain deviance? This is a problem posed to sociologists who explain behavior as the internalization of norms defining acceptable behavior. The answer has been to assume that norms supportive of criminal behavior are created within subcultural systems. Kobrin, Matza, and Sykes have emphasized the duality of norm systems in our society, one criminal, the other law-abiding. Albert K. Cohen explains delinquency as a rejection of middle-class norms by lower-class youths who cannot achieve middle-class goals. By a psychological process of "reaction formation," the lower-class delinquent inverts middle-class norms to emphasize masculinity and nonutilitarian acts. Delinquency is a product of status frustration found among lower-class males.[33]

Durkheim's concept of anomie has been used by Merton to mean a lack of integration of means and ends in a society. A person can use illegal means to gain a legal end (innovation); he can give up the goal, but retain the means (ritualism); or he can give up both means and goals (retreatism).[34] Cloward and Ohlin combine the Durkheim-Merton thesis with Sutherland's theory of differential association when they explain delinquency as a product of blocked legitimate opportunities (means) to obtain social goals. If criminal means exist to reach legal goals (innovation), the individual will learn criminal values and practices, and a criminal subculture will emerge. If no legal or criminal opportunities are present, the individual will either join a fighting gang (conflict subculture) or a drug-alcohol response will take place (a retreatist subculture). The emphasis is on learning the criminal code from those who are criminal. If no criminal subculture exists, the individual will not become a criminal.[35]

Lander, from a study in Baltimore, found a high correlation between delinquency, home ownership, and percentage of nonwhites in the area. He defined lack of home ownership and a low percentage of nonwhites in an area as anomie, characterized by a lack of social cohesion, a lack of community feeling, a feeling of powerlessness, and a high level of deprivation.[36] Lack of social cohesion or anomie is a popular view of delinquency, as seen in the poverty programs established recently to combat juvenile delinquency.

Lander has been critical of the Cloward-Ohlin thesis and the concept of anomie put forth by Merton, and he argues that anomie, according to Durkheim, means primarily a breakdown in moral codes and the inability of moral codes or the collective conscience to control human behavior.[37] To state that moral or social codes control behavior is to state a tautology which is unprovable, since we infer moral codes from the behavior we are explaining. We do not know the existence of moral codes independent of the behavior of the person under study.

Blake and Davis, in a discussion of norms, values, and sanctions, point out that norms are inferred from behavior, verbal or other, and that to explain behavior in terms of norms is redundant. "If norms are taken to be regulations of behavior, they have no analytical significance at all; they are merely another name for behavior itself, and cannot contribute to an understanding of behavior."[38] They emphasize the place of sanctions of punishment and reward in the enforcement of norms instead of a concept of normative causation, which they regard as a fallacy.[39]

Norms do not cause behavior, they are behavior; they state the future consequences of behaving in a given way. The crucial element is the sanction (consequence) and whether it is applied ninety percent or five percent of the time.

### Who is the Criminal?

As was noted in Chapter 2, the classical school defined criminals and crimes in legalistic terms, whereas the positive school used sociological definitions and concepts. The criminologist does not have an acceptable definition of crime from which to conduct his research. Cressey, for example, in his study of embezzlers, departed from a legal definition in search of a unified behavioral category from which causal inferences could be made, as did Sutherland in his study of white-collar crime.[40]

Another methodological issue even more damaging than the above is the fact criminologists study arrested and convicted criminals. Robison[41], Schwartz[42], Porterfield[43], Murphy[44], Wallerstein and Wyle[45], Dentler and Monroe[46], and Short and Nye[47] have all reported that the hidden rate of crime and delinquency is high, and that many citizens have committed offenses for which they could have been arrested. The President's Crime Commission reported that forcible rapes were more than 3.5 times the reported rate, burglaries 3 times, assaults and larcenies more than twice, and robberies fifty percent greater than the officially reported rates.[48] The usual conclusions drawn from such unreported crime surveys is that middle-class white citizens commit more crimes than are reported, whereas the high crime rate for lower-class people from minority groups is a product of arrest practices and court procedures as much as it is a reflection of lower-class Negro behavior. Studies which attempt to explain criminality in terms of lower-class minority group status have been challenged on these grounds.

Reiss and Rhodes[49] discovered that both the social status and the delinquency rate of an area were independent sources of variation in the rate of delinquency for an ascribed family status group. The status structure of the school is more important than the occupational position of the father in determining delinquency rates. A high-status school will have a low rate of delinquency; therefore, a low-status boy in a high-status school will have a lower rate of delinquency than a low-status boy in a low-status school. Life chances for delinquency are greater in a low-status area and a high-delinquency area; therefore, lower-class status by itself is not a necessary or sufficient condition in the etiology of delinquency.

Clark and Wenninger[50] discovered that delinquency rates vary with the type of community. In a rural farm community, few differences are found in delinquency rates between social classes, but, in an industrial urban setting, class differences do emerge. They found that more serious offenses occur in industrial cities and in lower-class urban areas than in rural farm areas or upper-class urban areas.

In recent years, studies have focused on the behavior of the police and of judges and lawyers in determining who is the criminal (see Chapters 4 and 5). The study of the individual criminal is inadequate and misleading, as the studies of unreported crimes have indicated. The crime rate is a result of deviant behavior, legal definitions of crime, police practices, judicial processes, and correctional procedures, all of which involve a great deal more than the individual offenders. Yet, theories of criminal behavior are based on studies of individual offenders, as seen above, and such an approach assumes that the causes of behavior lie in the past experiences, social and psychological traits, and the heredity of individual offenders. Criminal behavior has been explained in terms other than the criminal act itself, in terms of indirect variables such as sex, social class, subcultural groups, differential opportunities, or differential association.

The criminologist studies the criminal rather than the environment in which crimes are committed. One notable exception is an ecological study by Boggs.[51] She studies the character of the environmental opportunities specific to each crime rather than the character of the criminal. Boggs devised a crime occurrence rate based on the ecological distribution of crime targets—safes, cash registers, people, cars, and so forth. Since crime occurrence rates differ from criminal offender rates (where criminals live), the crime occurrence rate cannot be explained by the same factors that account for the prevalence of offenders.[52]

Boggs discovered that in the case of crimes against property—business robbery, nonresidential burglary, and larceny—the criminals do not live in the area where crimes are committed. In the case of residential crimes—homicide, assault, burglary—the criminal lives in the area where he commits the crime. The former she explains in terms of profitable targets for criminal acts; the latter she explains in terms of familiarity of the criminal with the victim of the crime.[53]

The Boggs' study demonstrates the value of an analysis of the characteristics of the environment in which crimes occur as compared to studies of the individual offender.

### Conclusions

Criminal behavior has been explained in terms of the individual offender and his psychological, biological, and sociological traits. Such a view of behavior ignores the environment in which crimes occur, and it ignores the fact that behavior is determined by present environmental conditions and future consequences rather than by past experiences. Although psychologists and sociologists disagree as to the crucial variables which explain behavior, they agree that the process is mentalistic, involving changes in the "mind" such as implied in concepts of the ego, self, role, norm, value, and attitude. Sutherland's theory is a culmination of the view that the cause of criminality is an "attitude," or a "norm," or a "value system." Because of the insistence of American criminology that it explain criminality in terms of the individual offender, in the manner of the positive school of criminology, there is no one acceptable or proven theory of criminal behavior, nor is there any research designed to produce such a theory. One of the major difficulties facing criminology is an acceptable theory of behavior based upon biological, psychological, and sociological findings.

In 1932, the Michael-Adler report concluded that criminology is not a science and would not be a science until a science of behavior has been established as a basis for treatment and prevention programs.[54] In 1959, Lady Wootton made a survey of criminological research and concluded there was no basis for causal statements or scientific policy concerning the prevention of crime.[55] In 1967, the President's Crime Commission concluded that

> delinquency is behavior, and until a science of human behavior matures far beyond its present confines, an understanding of those kinds of behavior we call delinquency is not likely to be forthcoming . . . .The same uncritical and unrealistic estimates of what is known and can be done that make expectation so much greater than achievement also serve to justify extensive official action and to mask the fact that much of it may do more harm than good.[56]

"There is probably no subject of comparable concern to which the nation is devoting so many resources and so much effort with little knowledge of what it is doing. It is true, of course, that many kinds of knowledge about crime must await better understanding of social behavior."[57] The future of criminology and crime control depends on the development of a scientific theory of human behavior based on experimental research. The use of science in explaining human behavior will be discussed in Part IV of the book.

## NOTES

[1.] Ruth Cavan, *Criminology*, 2nd edition, New York: Crowell Co., 1955, pp. 688-697; Edwin H. Sutherland and Donald R. Cressey, *Principles of Criminology*, Philadelphia: Lippincott Co., 7th ed., 1966, pp. 122-143; Edgar Schuler et al., *Readings in Sociology*, New York: Crowell Co., 1960, p. 40 ff., p. 56 ff.

[2.] Cavan, op. cit., pp. 692-693.

[3.] Cavan, op. cit., p. 700; Sutherland and Cressey, op. cit., pp. 162-164.

[4.] Calvin Hall and Gardner Lindzey, *Theories of Personality*, New York: John Wiley and Sons, 1957; Calvin Hall, *A Primer of Freudian Psychology*, New York: Mentor Books, 1954; Donald Ford and Hugh Urban, *Systems of Psychotherapy*, New York: John Wiley and Sons, 1965.

[5.] David Abrahamsen, *The Psychology of Crime*, New York: Columbia University Press, 1960; David Abrahamsen, *Who Are the Guilty*, New York: Grove Press, 1952; Franz Alexander and Hugo Staub, *The Criminal, the Judge, and the Public*, New York: Macmillan Co., 1931; Franz Alexander and William Healy, *Roots of Crime*, New York: Knopf, 1935; Cavan, op. cit., pp. 702-709; Sutherland and Cressey, op. cit., pp. 161-180.

[6.] James C. Coleman, *Abnormal Psychology and Modern Life*, 2nd ed., New York: Scott Foresman and Co., 1956, p. 349.

[7.] Barbara Wootton, *Social Science and Social Pathology*, New York: Macmillan Co., p. 250.

[8.] Herbert C. Quay, *Juvenile Delinquency*, New York: D. Van Nostrand, 1965, p. 150 ff.; Herbert Block and Frank Flynn, *Delinquency*, New York: Random House, 1956, p. 164 ff., p. 226 ff.

[9.] Coleman, op. cit., p. 337 ff.

[10.] Seymour L. Halleck, *Psychiatry and the Dillemmas of Crime*, New York: Hoeber Medical Books, 1967, p. 63 ff.

[11.] Don Martindale, *The Nature and Types of Sociological Theory*, Boston: Houghton Mifflin Co., 1960, pp. 339-374; Paul B. Horton and Chester L. Hunt, *Sociology*, New York: McGraw-Hill Book Co., 1964, p. 144.

[12.] Horton and Hunt, op. cit., p. 147; Martindale, op. cit., pp. 86-92; George Simpson, *Man in Society*, Garden City: Doubleday and Co., 1955, p. 51.

[13.] Simpson, op. cit., p. 52; Martindale, op. cit., pp. 385-388; John F. Cuber, *Sociology*, 6th ed., New York: Appleton-Century-Crofts, 1968, p. 36.

[14.] Cuber, op. cit., p. 233 ff.; Martindale, op. cit., p. 339 ff.; Simpson, op. cit., pp. 53-55; Everett K. Wilson, *Sociology*, Homewood: Dorsey Press, 1966, p. 45 ff.

[15.] Gordon Allport, review of *The American Soldier*, *Journal of Abnormal and Social Psychology*, XLV (1950) p. 172.

[16.] David Krech, Richard Crutchfield, and Egerton Ballachey, *Individual in Society*, New York: McGraw-Hill Book Company, 1962, Preface.

[17.] Ibid., p. 139.

[18.] Hermann Mannheim, *Comparative Criminology*, New York: Houghton Mifflin Co., 1965, p. 202.

[19.] Ibid., p. 202

[20.] Richard Quinney, *The Social Reality of Crime*, Boston: Little, Brown and Co., 1970, pp. 5-15.

[21.] Sutherland and Cressey, op. cit., p. 81.

[22.] Don C. Gibbons, *Society, Crime, and Criminal Careers,* Englewood Cliffs: Prentice-Hall, Inc., 1968, p. 499.

[23.] Sutherland and Cressey, op. cit., pp. 84-94.

[24.] Walter C. Reckless, *The Crime Problem,* New York: Appleton-Century-Crofts, 1961, p. 403.

[25.] Ibid., p. 408.

[26.] C. Ray Jeffery, "Criminal Behavior and Learning Theory," *Journal of Criminal Law, Criminology, and Police Science,* Vol. 56, No. 3, pp. 294-300; Robert L. Burgess and Ronald L. Akers, "A Differential Association-Reinforcement Theory of Criminal Behavior," *Social Problems,* Vol. 14, No. 2, pp. 128-146.

[27.] Sheldon Glueck, "Theory and Fact in Criminology," *British Journal of Criminology,* October, 1956, p. 95 ff.

[28.] Sutherland and Cressey, op. cit., p. 83.

[29.] Ibid., p. 60, pp. 93-97.

[30.] Solomon Kobrin, "The Conflict of Values in Delinquent Areas," *American Sociological Review,* October, 1951, pp. 653-661.

[31.] Gresham Sykes and David Matza, "Techniques of Neutralization: A Theory of Delinquency," *American Journal of Sociology,* December, 1957, pp. 664-670.

[32.] David Matza, *Delinquency and Drift,* New York: John Wiley and Sons, Inc., 1964.

[33.] Albert K. Cohen, *Delinquent Boys,* Glencoe: Free Press, 1958.

[34.] Robert K. Merton, "Social Structure and Anomie," in *Social Theory and Social Structure,* Glencoe: Free Press, 1957, pp. 131-160.

[35.] Richard Cloward and Lloyd Ohlin, *Delinquency and Opportunity,* Glencoe: Free Press, 1961.

[36.] Bernard Lander, *Towards an Understanding of Juvenile Delinquency,* New York: Columbia University Press, 1954. See criticism by Travis Hirschi and Hanan C. Selvin, *Delinquency Research,* New York: Free Press, 1967, p. 146

[37.] Bernard Rosenberg, Israel Gerver, and F. William Howton, *Mass Society in Crisis,* New York: Macmillan Co., 1964, pp. 140-141.

[38.] Judith Blake and Kingsley Davis, "Norms, Values and Sanctions," in *Handbook of Modern Sociology,* edited by Robert E.L. Faris, Chicago: Rand McNally and Co., 1964, p. 464.

[39.] Ibid., pp. 456-484.

[40.] Donald R. Cressey, "The Criminal Violation of Financial Trust," *American Sociological Review* (December, 1950), p. 740; C. Ray Jeffery, "The Structure of American Criminological Thinking," *Journal of Criminal Law, Criminology, and Police Science,* Vol. 46, No. 5 (February, 1956), pp. 658-672.

[41.] Sophia M. Robison, *Can Delinquency Be Measured?,* New York: Columbia University Press, 1936.

[42.] Edward E. Schwartz, "A Community Experiment in the Measurement of Juvenile Delinquency." *Yearbook,* National Probation Association, 1945.

[43.] Austin Porterfield, *Youth in Trouble,* Fort Worth: Leo Patishman Foundation, 1946.

[44.] F.J. Murphy, M.M. Shirley, and H.L. Witmer, "The Incidence of Hidden Delinquency," *American Journal of Orthopsychiatry,* Vol. 16 (1946), pp. 686-689.

[45.] James S. Wallerstein and C.J. Wyle, "Our Law Abiding Law Breakers," *National Probation* (March-April, 1947), pp. 107-112.

[46.] Robert A. Dentler and Lawrence J. Monroe, "Social Correlates of Early Adolescent Theft," *American Sociological Review,* Vol. 26, No. 5 (October, 1961), pp. 733-743.

[47.] F. Ivan Nye and James F. Short, "Scaling Delinquent Behavior," *American Sociological Review,* Vol. 22 (June, 1957), pp. 326-331.

[48.] President's Commission on Law Enforcement and Administration of Justice, *Crime and Its Impact – An Assessment,* Washington, D.C.: U.S. Government Printing Office, 1967, p. 17.

[49.] Albert J. Reiss, Jr., and Albert Lewis Rhodes, "Delinquency and Social Class Structure," *American Sociological Review,* Vol. 26, No. 5 (October, 1961), pp. 720-732.

[50.] John P. Clark and Eugene P. Wenninger, "Socio-Economic Class and Area as Correlates of Illegal Behavior Among Juveniles," *American Sociological Review,* Vol. 27, No. 6 (December, 1962), pp. 826-834.

[51.] Sara Boggs, "Urban Crime Patterns," *American Sociological Review* (December, 1965), pp. 899-908.

[52.] Ibid., p. 900.

[53.] Ibid., pp. 907-908.

[54.] Jerome Michael and Mortimer J. Adler, *Crime, Law, and Social Structure,* New York: Harcourt Brace, 1933.

[55.] Barbara Wootton, *Social Science and Social Pathology,* New York: Macmillan Co., 1959.

[56.] President's Commission on Law Enforcement and Administration of Justice, *Juvenile Delinquency and Youth Crime,* Washington, D.C.: U.S. Government Printing Office, 1967, p. 8.

[57.] President's Commission on Law Enforcement and Administration of Justice, *The Challenge of Crime in a Free Society,* Washington, D.C.: U.S. Government Printing Office, 1967, p. 273.

# Chapter 8

## Therapy and Group Processes

### Introduction

Psychiatric and sociological studies of individual offenders, as outlined in Chapter 7, had implications for the treatment and rehabilitation of offenders.

(1) It was assumed the focus of rehabilitation would be the individual.

(2) It was assumed that the scientific knowledge needed to rehabilitate the offender was available.

(3) It was assumed that service rather than research was the key to the rehabilitative process, i.e., therapy, casework, and group processes could be used to change the behavior of criminals and delinquents.

The impact of psychiatric and sociological concepts has been significant on our legal and correctional systems; rehabilitation has replaced deterrence or revenge as the formalized goal of the justice process. As a consequence of the development of behavioral science, two major schools of thought developed as to how criminals can be rehabilitated. One school which developed out of Freudian psychology advocates therapy for offenders—individual, group, milieu. The other school, sociological in background, advocates resocialization through group dynamics and group interaction (which looks a great deal like group therapy from psychiatry), or it advocates increasing legitimate opportunities for legal goals through reeducation and job training programs. In this chapter, we shall be concerned with the therapeutic approach as developed by psychiatrists, psychologists, social workers, and sociologists.

### Crime and Mental Illness

The early positivists of the nineteenth century placed great emphasis upon mental disease, denial of responsibility and free will, psychic

determinism, and psychiatric interpretations of criminal behavior. Mauds-
ley, Ray, and Doe were pioneers in the application of psychiatry to
criminal law. The work of Ray and Doe led to the rejection of the
McNaghten Rule in New Hampshire, and the New Hampshire rule was
adopted by the District of Columbia in 1954 as the Durham Rule.[1] The
emergence of Freudian psychology in the early twentieth century
produced a major theoretical framework for the analysis and treatment of
offenders.

By accepting the Freudian approach to human behavior and behavior
change, the psychiatric criminologist has accepted the basic tenets of this
school.

(1) Behavior is a product of internal mental conflict and anxiety.

(2) Mental illness exists and can be defined.

(3) Mental illness causes or is a factor in criminal behavior.

(4) The physician treats illness; therefore mental illness (behavioral
problems) is best treated by the physician, not the behavioral
scientist.

(5) Mental illness can be treated by means of psychiatric therapy
and social casework.[2]

Mental illness has never been defined satisfactorily, and, as a result, a
labeling process is used whereby certain types of behavior are classified as
psychotic, neurotic, or character disorders. What goes into each category is
a matter of discretionary judgment, since there is in nature no such thing
as a "psychosis" or a "neurosis." The investigator does not observe
"psychosis," but behavior, and from the behavior he abstracts a concept of
a psychotic condition. "Psychosis" and "behavior" are one and the same
thing; we only know a person is psychotic if he behaves, and labeling his
behavior "psychosis" is of no value in explaining or understanding the
behavior. Thomas Szasz, a psychiatrist, has denied that there is such a
thing as mental illness[3], and he has noted:

> disregarding even the most obvious doubt concerning exactly what
> the expression "mental illness" is supposed to denote, it denotes a
> theory and not a fact. . . .To believe that one's own theories are facts
> is considered by many psychiatrists as a symptom of schizophrenia.
> Yet this is what the language of the *Durham* decision does. It reifies
> some of the shakiest and most controversial aspects of psychiatry,
> those pertaining to what is "mental disease" and the classification of
> such allied diseases, and by legal fiat seeks to transform inadequate
> theory into judicial fact. . . .Is Durham an improvement if it merely
> changes the "criminal" to "patient"?[4]

Hollingshead and Redlich state that "mental illness is defined socially, that is, whatever a psychiatrist treats or is expected to treat."[5] Hartung writes that "one must conclude that when people use the term 'mental illness' they literally do not know what they are talking about. Psychiatrists are even divided on the crucial issues as to whether there can be such an entity as mental disease."[6]

The term "mental illness" is often used to refer to psychosis, though in recent years under the Durham decision, the notion of mental illness has been expanded to include such behaviors as neurosis, alcoholism, drug addiction, and sociopathic personalities.[7] The law allows mental disease to be used as a defense against criminal responsibility, though the court has never defined "mental illness" in any manner approaching scientific reliability. The law has used the concept of mental illness as a means of introducing "treatment" and "therapy" in a situation where a criminal conviction would result in death or imprisonment. When the court says alcoholism or drug addiction is a disease, what it means is that we want to establish a policy whereby alcoholics and addicts are treated, not punished. It should be obvious, however, that we can treat a behavioral problem without calling it illness, and it is also obvious that by calling behavior "illness" we do not automatically cure it.[8]

The relationship of crime to mental illness is even more difficult to establish. Guttmacher and Weihofen[9] quote figures indicating that 1.5% of the criminal population are psychotic; 2.4% are mentally defective; 6.9% are neurotic; and 11.2% are psychopathic. East[10] states that less than 1.0% are insane and 1.2% are neurotic. A study of 10,000 men in Sing Sing[11] indicated that the prison population could be divided into the following five groups: psychotic, 1%; mental defectives, 13%; psychoneurotic, 20%; psychopathic, 35%; and dyssocial, 31%.

Guttmacher and Weihofen state[12]:

> There are some radical theorists who go so far as to say that all criminals are mentally disordered, otherwise they would not engage in criminal behavior. . . .Although an appealing brief can be written on behalf of this thesis, it is wholly impractical. It reduces the meaning of mental disorder to a point where it has no discriminatory significance.

W. Norwood East, after making a survey of 4,000 British delinquents, concluded[13]:

> These figures disprove the assertion of those who declare that crime is a disease, for it is difficult to believe, and contrary to experience. . .that the number of boys who are mentally, temper-mentally, or morally abnormal at the age of thirteen is nearly double

the number at the age of nineteen, and there appear to be no facts to prove that eight men are abnormal in the above direction to one woman. No single place has been found for crime in any psychiatric scheme.

Paul Tappan [14], in reviewing the growth of the rehabilitation ideal in psychiatric criminology, wrote:

The focus upon mental pathology has resulted in a conception of criminals as sick people. . . .The prevalent idea of criminal illness is highly misleading. Criminals are not generally neurotic, psychotic, or psychopathic. . . .worse, by merely attaching a general label to the offender, one may be led to assume quite erroneously that the problem has been solved thereby or that it is necessary only to provide some vague psychotherapy to resolve the difficulty.

### Psychotherapy and the Treatment of Crime

Since the Freudian model of behavior holds that crime is a product of inner drives, mental conflict, and unconscious motivation, and criminal behavior is symbolic of these mental states, the cure for crime is not to deal directly with the criminal behavior, but rather to treat the unconscious motivation for the crime. David Abrahamsen [15], a psychiatrist/criminologist, has summarized this position when he stated:

Freud's contributions to general psychopathology were the greatest of all, particularly his idea that unconscious motivation is the drive for most of our actions. This has allowed the application of psychoanalysis to psychiatric criminology which paved the way for a better understanding of the mind of the criminal and his act.

In contrast to the psychotherapeutic philosophy outlined above by Dr. Abrahamsen, an experimental psychologist, Albert Bandura, views therapy in this manner [16]:

The inner disturbing agents, comprise a host of unconscious psychodynamic forces and psychic complexes—warded off ego-alien impulses, oedipal, castration, and inferiority complexes, ancestoral [sic] unconscious and primordial images, latent instinctual tendencies, self-dynamisms, counter-instinctual energies, wills and counterwills, and ego instincts and apparatuses—somewhat akin to the hidden demonic spirits of ancient times. Thus, the prevailing theories of psychopathology essentially employ an amalgam of the medical and demonology models, which have in common the belief that the underlying pathology and not the symptomatic manifestations must be treated. Consequently, therapeutic attention is generally focused not on the deviant behavior itself, but on the presumably influential internal processes. Indeed, direct modification of so-called symptomatic behavior is considered not only ineffective, but actually dangerous, since the removal of the symptom may lead to even more serious forms of symptom substitution.

The major technique of therapy is verbal communication of feelings and problems, "a condition where two people sit privately in an office and talk about the thoughts and feelings of one of them."[17] Middle-class Americans believe in a "talking cure" or "getting it out by discussing it" approach to behavioral problems. We are verbal, we are accustomed to talking, and we have great faith in the healing powers of talk.

The major techniques for therapy are catharsis—eliminating a problem by bringing it to consciousness and affording it expression; insight—seeking the origin of one's problem in the past; transference—transferring feelings for parents to the therapist; love—acceptance and giving affection and acceptance at an emotional level; and free association—talking about one's feelings as a stream of consciousness.[18]

> Psychoanalysis is aimed at enabling the patient to achieve insight into his unconscious mind, and analysis avoids all other methods of psychiatric relief. It is the only major form of therapy which has clearly established ground rules, though in practice the rules have to be played by ear. The patient lies on a couch and reports his feelings through free association, while the psychiatrist relies on interpretation to bring the patient to an awareness of these feelings. In short, psychiatry today is a remarkable profession wracked by dissension, lacking established rules or practices, unsure of its proper role in society—and flourishing anyway.[19]

Halmos argues that psychiatry is a matter of religious faith, a belief in the healing power of love and empathy. The solution to human problems is sought in interpersonal dynamics, sensitivity training, and group processes.[20] Ehrenwald states that psychotherapy is based as much on myth as on scientific method.[21]

Many major issues are involved in talking therapy. The fact that middle-class people attempt to manipulate behavior through verbal interaction is in itself of interest. The control of verbal behavior by its

environmental contingencies is in no way different from the control of
other behaviors, though it is often assumed that verbal behavior is
different in that it represents or reflects the mind and mental processes. As
Boring has remarked, "Introspection is still with us, doing business under
various aliases, of which verbal report is one." [22] Though the psychiatrist and psychologist may rely heavily on verbal reports, such reports
should not be regarded as having the same scientific status as direct
observations of behavior under discussion. It is known that the psycho-
therapist determines the content of the verbal interview by his responses
to the patient's statements.[23] What the therapist does, of course, is to
shape the verbal behavior of the patient, whereas the behaviors for which
the person is in therapy go untouched.

### Failure of Psychotherapy

Berelson and Steiner concluded their inventory of scientific findings on
behavior by stating that

> There is no conclusive evidence that psychotherapy is more effective
> than general medical counseling or advice in treating neurosis or
> psychosis. Strictly speaking, it cannot even be considered established
> that psychotherapy, on the average, improves a patient's chances of
> recovery beyond what they would be without any formal therapy
> whatsoever.[24]

The British psychologist H.J. Eysenck discovered that patients receiving
psychoanalytic treatment showed an improvement rate of forty-four
percent, while patients who received other forms of therapy showed an
improvement rate of sixty-four percent, whereas those who received no
psychotherapy showed an improvement rate of seventy-two percent.[25]
"These data fail to prove that psychotherapy facilitates the recovery of
neurotic patients. They show that roughly two-thirds of a group of
neurotic patients will recover or improve to a marked extent within two
years of the onset of their illness, whether they are treated by means of
psychotherapy or not."[26] Eysenck regards the basic difficulty of
psychoanalysis to be its lack of commitment to scientific methodology
and procedures.

> Psychoanalysis in my view is trying to *understand* rather than to
> explain; that, consequently, it is essentially non-scientific and to be
> judged in terms of faith and belief, rather than in terms of proof and
> verification; and that its great popularity among non-scientists

derives precisely from its non-scientific nature, which makes it intelligible and immediately applicable to problems of understanding other people.[27]

In the first place, then, psychoanalytic conclusions are based on unreliable data. Its data are introspections [of the analyst] and verbalized statements [of the analyzed]. Data of this kind are essentially subjective, and therefore present special difficulties to the scientist.[28]

Ernest Hilgard[29], in an appraisal of psychoanalysis as a science, noted:

Anyone who tries to give an honest appraisal of psychoanalysis must be ready to admit that, as it is stated, it is mostly very bad science, that the bulk of articles in its journals cannot be defended as research publications at all. If psychoanalysts are themselves to make a science of their knowledge they must be prepared to follow some of the standard rules of science.

The application of psychotherapy to the rehabilitation of criminals and delinquents has not been successful. The Judge Baker Guidance Center in Boston offered casework placement and social services to disturbed (delinquent) children. According to a survey by Sheldon and Eleanor Glueck, the clinic was a failure because of the eighty-eight percent recidivism rate of the subjects. The director of the clinic wrote off the experiment as a failure and "the close of another chapter in criminology."[30]

The Cambridge-Somerville project assigned to counselors for guidance and social services three hundred predelinquent boys. Two separate evaluations at the end of the project found the project to be a failure, since the treatment group had a higher delinquency rate (29.5 to 28.3) than the control group.[31]

The Highfields project, which used group therapy and job experiences to rehabilitate delinquents, showed a fifty-six percent recidivism rate compared to a seventy-nine percent recidivism rate for the reformatory group after sixty months' exposure to the Highfields' program.[32]

A study of the effectiveness of social work intervention in treating female delinquency found that social work was ineffective in preventing delinquency.[33] Szasz has questioned the basic assumptions of psychiatry, and he argues that in many cases the psychiatrist deprives the patient of his freedom and liberties without effectively treating the concept "mental illness."[34] Lady Wootton found no reason to feel confident about the psychiatrist's contribution to criminal law and to the issues of treatment and responsibility.[35] Halmos concluded that therapists labor without evidence of success.[36]

Recently, due to the Baxtrom decision in New York State, over 900 patients were released from hospitals for the criminally insane and either placed in civil hospitals or released into the community. The experts were very shocked to discover that most of these patients adjusted beautifully after their release from the hospitals.[37] The Matteawan story in New York reminds one of the situation in France during World War II when 153 incurable patients fled a mental hospital. A postwar survey revealed that fifty-seven percent of them were in communities and had apparently recovered.[38]

Rehabilitative prison programs based on a therapeutic model have been used throughout the nation's penal system, but without any measurable impact on the recidivism rate. Prison therapy is generally handicapped by a lack of trained personnel, conflict between custodial and treatment concepts, the failure of psychotherapy in the treatment of standard psychiatric categories, and the lack of any real relationship between psychotic and neurotic behavior on the one hand, and crime on the other hand. The only psychiatric category of importance in prison is the sociopath, and the sociopath is a sociopath because he is antisocial: he is a criminal because he is sociopathic. The circularity of the definitions prevents any meaningful statement as to the relationship between sociopathic personality and criminal behavior. In addition, the sociopath is not amenable to treatment.[37] Lindner[40] has reported success in treating sociopaths with hypnotherapy, though most efforts to work with the sociopath have been unsuccessful.

### Reasons for the Failure of Therapy

The failure of therapy can be related to several factors.

*(1) In talk therapy, the verbal behavior of the client is manipulated and controlled,* but the behavior for which he is in therapy is not.[41] A patient who is an alcoholic or is unhappily married talks about his problems, but this does not control the behavior he wishes to eliminate. We do not cure cancer by talking about it; neither do we cure behavioral disorders by talking about them.

*(2) The patient is under the control of the therapist only in the therapeutic setting.* The behavior modified is that related to the therapeutic environment.[42] The control of behavior depends upon the

proper modification of the environment in which the behavior occurs. The patient returns to the same environment that produced his drinking problem or sexual problem, and he thus responds to this environment in the same or similar manner. The therapist *does not modify the environment in which the problem behavior occurs.*

*(3) The therapist has faith in love, acceptance, and supportiveness* as cures for the problems of his client.[43] Often the therapist will reinforce the behavior of the patient by his love, acceptance, and encouragement. Such social reinforcement may actually encourage the behavior which the therapist wishes to eliminate. It has been observed that mental hospitals and prisons encourage the development of deviant behaviors. If a person is expected to behave as a psychotic, he will develop psychotic responses. If a patient is fed by his ward attendant, he will become dependent on the attendant and will refuse to feed himself. If a nurse pays attention to a patient who refers to herself as the Virgin Mary, then such behavior will be strengthened.[44]

### Group Treatment

The failure of traditional middle-class therapy for treating criminality has led to the use of groups as treatment agents. Although a variety of names and procedures are employed—group therapy, guided group interaction, encounter groups, T-training, and applied human relations—the major thrust of the concept involves the use of groups to alter human behavior.

Durkheim's concept of *anomie* is essentially a statement that people behave in response to group norms and pressures. Cooley's concept of the primary group is another major contribution to the literature of groups and human behavior. The study of group influence has been either positive—when the group is present, the individual member behaves thus and so—or negative—in the absence of group cohesiveness, the individual behaves thus and so.

Sherif and Asch have shown that verbal responses to visual stimulation (the autokinetic effect) can be conditioned to conform to group norms; that is, subjects judge the length of a line in terms of a group norm.[45] Janowitz and Shils found that in a military organization during wartime, strong primary group ties are more important than organizational norms in controlling human behavior.[46] Festinger, Schacter, and Back found that the physical structure of a housing project determined the extent to which graduate students who lived in the project interacted socially.[47]

On the other hand, the breakdown of group cohesiveness (Durkheim's anomie) has been related to deviant behavior and social alienation. Faris and Dunham found in Chicago that schizophrenia rates were high in areas of social isolation and alienation.[48] Kohn, Clausen, and Jaco likewise found social isolation, anonymity, few personal friends, and interpersonal alienation as characteristics of behavioral disorder.[49] The Sterling County Study by Leighton et al. revealed the same relationships between social disorganization and behavioral disorders.[50] Langner and Michael found in Manhattan a high relationship between lack of friends and behavioral disorders.[51]

Experiments with animals have given even more conclusive experimental evidence of this pattern. Harlow found that infant rhesus monkeys isolated from other monkeys during the first six months of life were incapable of normal behavioral development.[52] The Harlow studies remind one of the studies by Rene Spitz who found a lack of normal physical and social development in human infants reared in hospitals or orphanages, and thus isolated from social contact.[53]

The influence of the group on criminal behavior is contained in Sutherland's theory of differential association. If criminals are criminals because they associate with criminals, then the rehabilitation of criminals is a matter of bringing criminals under the influence of noncriminal groups.

The use of group therapy or guided group interaction has been used widely in New Jersey and California penal systems, especially after the Highfields experiment in New Jersey.[54] The objective of guided group interaction is "the use of free discussion in a friendly, supportive atmosphere to reeducate the delinquent to accept the restrictions of society."[55] Such group interaction is to force the inmate to face the facts of life, to gain insight into his criminal behavior, and to gain acceptance of the general restrictions of society.[56]

The results of the Highfields experiment was a fifty-six percent recidivism rate for delinquents sixty months after release[57], and though this was lower than the seventy-nine percent recidivism rate for Annandale releasees, it is too high to be regarded as significant, since the selection process in itself would account for this difference. The Pinehills experiment showed a seventy-three percent success rate for probation and Pinehills subjects, and a forty-two percent rate for state school releasees, thus again raising questions as to the effectiveness of probation versus guided group interaction versus state schools. The President's Crime Commission concluded that Highfields was at least as successful as the reformatory.[58] Cressey states that "it is not certain as yet that guided group interaction, group counseling, and similar group-therapy programs

are more efficient than self-government and honor systems in accomplish-
ing transfers of allegiance from criminal to anti-criminal values."[59]
Arthur Pearl concludes that "the inadequacies of Highfields also need to
be clearly stated and universally understood. Highfields did not provide a
reintroduction to society."[60]

Cressey advocates the use of differential association theory to rehabilitate criminals.[61] "The two general processes in reformation are the
alienation of the criminal from groups which support values conducive to
criminality, and concurrently, the assimilation of criminals into groups
supporting values conducive to law-abiding behavior."[62]

Two ideas seem to run throughout group therapy:

(1) the use of the group as an agent for allowing the individual to
express his feelings and to work out his problems;

(2) the use of the group as an agent for socializing the individual
through a new code of conduct—that is, a new group norm for
governing behavior.

The first model is more therapeutic in nature, using the group as the
therapist would be used in individualized therapy. The second model is
more social, using the group as the source of experiences essential to
socialization and norm acceptance. The one model can look to psychiatry
as its father, the other to sociology and social psychology.

The group model is plagued by all the shortcomings of the individual
model.

(1) It deals with the individual offender, and it does not change the
environment in which crimes are committed.

(2) It is based on unproven theories of behavior, be they derived
from Freud or from Sutherland.

(3) Group therapy does not concern itself with criminal behavior,
but with verbal behavior directly, and, indirectly and by implication,
with personality development, criminal values, group norms, and
other such concepts. The model assumes that criminal behavior can
be controlled indirectly by means of the manipulation of the
individual's verbal behavior.

(4) Though it is true that a person's behavior will change depending
on the group context of the behavior, there is no reason to assume
that when he leaves the group his behavior will continue to be
controlled by the group. The ability of the group to control behavior
depends both on the presence of the group and the desire of the
individual to remain in the group, neither of which is realized

through group therapy. The group must be able to reinforce the individual for his membership to a higher degree than that reinforcement found in the commission of an illegal act. The individual may not find the noncriminal group reinforcing enough to maintain the behavior which the group is attempting to strengthen. The group still functions within an environment in which alternative responses are available to the criminal.

### Nonprofessional Aides in Therapy

One of the major developments in the handling of behavioral disorders is to have ex-criminals or ex-addicts act as the therapists. Charles Slack, a former Harvard University clinical psychologist, discovered that if he acted as a therapist in a patient-therapist relationship the patient did not get well. However, if he acted as a scientist in a scientist-subject experimental relationship, the patient was cured. From this, Slack concluded that the patient must be able to identify with the therapist. A concept of a "self-help" model was thus developed—a person who helps others help himself. If a criminal tries to rehabilitate another criminal, then he usually changes his own behavior in the process.[63]

It has often been noted that nonprofessional personnel have a greater degree of influence on inmates of prisons and mental hospitals than do the professional staff of psychologists, psychiatrists, and social workers. Glaser concluded from his study of the federal correctional system that the work supervisors had the greatest influence, while the prison psychologists had the least influence, on releasees from federal institutions.[64] An experiment at the University of California revealed that untrained psychiatric aides scored better in "curing" mental patients than psychiatrists, clinical psychologists, and psychiatric social workers.[65] The observation that nonprofessionals can "cure," whereas the professional cannot, has been reinforced by such self-help groups as Alcoholics Anonymous and Synanon (for drug addicts). In these programs, addicts and alcoholics help themselves by helping others like themselves. One can interpret the results as due to better communication and empathy between one addict and another, or greater ability to detect deceit and rationalizations by an addict in a fellow addict. The artificial barrier between professional and client is removed in the case of an addict working with another addict.

The failure of professional therapy to reach addicts, alcoholics, and delinquents, and the greater degree of success which self-help groups have, needs some sort of theoretical explanation. The crucial factor present in the case of self-help groups is that they attach consequences to the behavior they are attempting to control. As was noted above, the professional psychiatrist or social worker usually reinforces sick behavior with his sympathy, love, and understanding, whereas the ex-addict shows no mercy to the addict. As Synanon has demonstrated, when an addict goes to a hospital he is given drugs and sympathy, whereas when he enters Synanon he is given verbal abuse and the "cold turkey treatment." Remarkable as it may seem, the Synanon addict has fewer behavioral symptoms than the hospital addict.[66] The reason is obvious—Synanon punishes rather than reinforces addict-like behavior. The ex-addicts of Synanon by pure accident used the same techniques to eliminate undesirable behavior that Professors Ayllon and Lovaas used in their treatment of psychotic patients. A study in 1954 by Whitehorn and Betz found that psychiatrists who set limits on the amount of obnoxious behavior they would tolerate were much more successful in treating psychotics than were passive or accepting therapists.[67]

In organizations such as Synanon and Phoenix House (a new treatment center in New York City), the group reacts to reinforce honesty, responsibility, and cooperation, whereas failure to obey the rules and to stay clean of narcotics leads to verbal lashings in therapy sessions or even to eventual expulsion from the project.

The use of ex-addicts or criminals as agents of rehabilitation has been merged with the "guided group interaction" programs, as seen in the writings of Cressey, Grant, Empey, Riessman, Pearl, and others.[68] Not only do criminals help themselves when they attempt to help other criminals, but the "new careers for the poor" model calls for the use of unskilled people in subprofessional positions as aides to social workers, teachers, recreation directors, and health services personnel.

The Joint Commission on Correctional Manpower and Training has published a pamphlet on the use of offenders as a correctional manpower resource, although there is no attempt therein to evaluate the overall effectiveness of such programs.[69] Empey did write in the series that

> Instead of proceeding systematically to define and then solve our correctional problems, we have made sweeping changes in correctional programs without adequate theoretical definitions of the causes of crime or the development of strategies to deal with them. The New Careers movement threatens to do the same. I feel strongly, therefore, that the previous strategy of activity should not be followed in this case, but should be replaced by a strategy of search. A strategy of search should be a part of the movement.[70]

### Probation

Probation casework can be considered an aspect of a therapeutic approach to criminality, since most probation officers who are academically trained are trained in social casework.[71] Dressler has outlined probation services in terms of three functions: (1) manipulation—job-finding, home-finding, and education; (2) community resources such as medical care, legal care, and vocational guidance; and (3) guidance and leadership.[72] Probation work involves presentence investigations and supervisory control over probationers, based primarily on concepts from social casework. Such casework is designed to provide social and psychological services to strengthen the individual. Supervision uses such techniques as treating each individual as unique, giving understanding and acceptance, and allowing each individual to find the solutions to his own problems.[73]

The success rate for probation has been put at between eight and seventy-five percent. The Gluecks found a success rate of forty-two percent in one study and an eight percent success rate in another.[74] The FBI study showed a forty-eight percent success rate for men on probation.[75] In light of these findings, and also taking into consideration the number of variables involved in trying to measure a recidivism rate, Korn and McCorkle[76] stated that "stripped to their essentials, these instructions boil down to exhortations to treat, to befriend, and to encourage. In effect, our treatment personnel are often told little more than to go out there and rehabilitate." Sutherland and Cressey[77] evaluate probation casework in these terms:

> The psychiatric school of criminology has a conception that the primary value to be attained in treatment is insight by the probationer into the reasons for his delinquent behavior. This school argues that a probationer who attains this insight will be likely to violate the law in the future. The probation officer who attempts to use this method should be trained in psychiatry and should generally be a psychiatrist or at least a psychiatric social worker. . . .Although this school of thought and treatment has an extensive vogue in the United States at the present time, the value of the techniques has not been demonstrated by objective studies and the validity of the theories is open to question. The principle reason for scepticism is that the procedure is based on a mistaken assumption that criminality can be treated in an office or a clinic just as an infectious disease can be.

The major dilemma facing probation is that no one has even defined the "probation process" in meaningful terms. The probation officer is told to use the casework method to rehabilitate offenders, with no general understanding of the means for producing behavior change. The social casework/therapeutic approach to probation is subject to all the limitations of an individualistic case method approach to criminal behavior, discussed above.

*Summary*

The use of psychotherapy to rehabilitate criminals has not been successful. First, the object of therapy is to change the individual offender, not the environment in which he lives. Second, therapy does not deal directly with criminal behavior, or with behavior in general, since it regards behavior as a symptom of some underlying mentalistic cause. The effect of therapy, therefore, is to create better-adjusted people, with the assumption that if ego conflict or neurotic anxiety is reduced, criminal behavior will be reduced. Changing one class of behaviors (psychoses, neuroses, character disorders) will not change another class of behaviors (criminal, delinquent, deviant). Behavior does not *cause* behavior; it has to be explained in terms other than other behavior.

The failure of traditional therapy has led to the development of group therapy, which combines psychiatric and sociological concepts. Group pressure to change must still compete with the environmental pressures reinforcing criminal acts, and changes in behavior brought about in group interaction sessions will not be maintained by the more general environment in which the criminal lives.

One of the most hopeful developments in recent years has been that of behavior therapy and reality therapy, which will be discussed in Part IV of the book.

## NOTES

[1.] Hermann Mannheim, ed., *Pioneers in Criminology*, London: Stevens and Sons, 1960, pp. 113-167.

[2.] Franz Alexander and Hugo Staub, *The Criminal, the Judge, and the Police*, New York: Macmillan and Co., 1931; Franz Alexander and William Healy, *Roots of Crime*, New York: Knopf, 1935; David Abrahamsen, *Who Are the Guilty*, New York: Grove Press, 1952; David Abrahamsen, *The Psychology of Crime*, New York: Columbia University Press, 1960; M. Guttmacher, *The Mind of the Murderer*, New York: Farrar, Straus, and Cudahy, 1958; Philip Q. Roche, *The Criminal Mind*, New York: Farrar, Straus, and Cudahy, 1958; Gregory Zilborg, *The Psychology of the Criminal Act and Punishment*, New York: Harcourt, Brace, and Co., 1954; Seymour L. Halleck, *Psychiatry and the Dilemmas of Crime*, New York: Harper and Row, 1967; Karl Menninger, *The Crime of Punishment*, New York: Viking Press, 1968.

[3.] Thomas Szasz, *The Myth of Mental Illness*, New York: Haefer-Harper, 1961. See also Michael Hakeem, "A Critique of the Psychiatric Approach to Crime and Corrections," *Law and Contemporary Problems*, Autumn, 1958.

[4.] Thomas Szasz, "Psychiatry, Ethics, and the Criminal Law," *Columbia Law Review*, Vol. 58 (1958) pp. 182 ff.

[5.] A.B. Hollingshead and F.C. Redlich, *Social Class and Mental Illness*, New York: John Wiley, 1958; pp. 11-12.

[6.] Frank Hartung, "Manhattan Madness: The Social Movement of Mental Illness," *The Sociological Quarterly*, Autumn (1963), pp. 264-265.

[7.] C. Ray Jeffery, *Criminal Responsibility and Mental Disease*, Springfield: Charles C Thomas, 1967; see also Hartung, op. cit.; Earl Parsons, "Recent Changes in Psychiatric Diagnoses in the Correctional Field," *Federal Probation*, September (1969), pp. 39-43.

[8.] Jeffery, op. cit., pp. 193-206.

[9.] M.S. Guttmacher and Henry Weihofen, *Psychiatry and the Law*, New York: W.W. Norton, 1952, p. 382.

[10.] Sir W. Norwood East, *The Adolescent Criminal*, London: Churchill, 1952, pp. 233-234.

[11.] James C. Coleman, *Abnormal Psychology and Modern Life*, 2nd ed., New York: Scott, Foresman, and Co., 1956, p. 349.

[12.] Guttmacher and Weihofen, op. cit., p. 24.

[13.] East, op. cit., p. 300.

[14.] Paul W. Tappan, ed., *Contemporary Correction*, New York: McGraw-Hill Book Co., 1951, p. 11.

[15.] Abrahamsen, *The Psychology of Crime*, op. cit., p. 12.

[16.] Arthur W. and Carolyn K. Staats, *Complex Human Behavior*, New York: Holt, Rinehart, and Winston, 1963, pp. 488-489.

[17.] Norman L. Munn, L. Dodge Fernald, and Peter S. Fernald, *Introduction to Psychology*, 2nd ed., New York: Houghton Mifflin.

[18.] Coleman, op. cit., Donald H. Ford and Hugh Urban, *Systems of Psychotherapy*, New York: John Wiley and Sons, 1965; Paul Halmos, *Faith of the Counselors*, New York: Schoeken Books, 1966; Munn, Fernald and Fernald, op. cit.,

p. 544 ff.; David Kretch, Richard S. Crutchfield, and Norman Livson, *Elements of Psychology*, New York: Alfred Knopf, 1969, pp. 781-783.

[19.] Richard Lemon, "Psychiatry: The Uncertain Science," *Saturday Evening Post* (August 10, 1968), pp. 38-39.

[20.] Halmos, op. cit.

[21.] Jan Ehrenwald, *Psychotherapy: Myth and Method*, New York: Grune and Stratton, 1966.

[22.] Arthur Bachrach, ed., *Experimental Foundations of Clinical Psychology*, New York: Basic Books, 1962, p. 309.

[23.] Bachrach, op. cit., Urban and Ford, op. cit., pp. 14 ff., pp. 681 ff., Leonard Krasner and Leonard P. Ullman, *Research in Behavior Modification*, New York: Holt, Rinehart, and Winston, 1966, p. 211 ff.

[24.] Bernard Berelson and Gary A. Steiner, *Human Behavior*, New York: Harcourt, Brace and World, 1964, p. 287.

[25.] H.J. Eysenck, *Handbook of Abnormal Psychology*, New York: Basic Books, 1961, pp. 712-713.

[26.] Ibid. p. 712.

[27.] H.J. Eysenck, *Uses and Abuses of Psychology*, Baltimore: Penguin Press, 1953, p. 226.

[28.] Ibid., p. 235.

[29.] Ernest Hilgard, ed., *Psychoanalysis as a Science*, Stanford: Stanford University Press, 1952, p. 44.

[30.] Helen L. Witmer and Edith Tufts, *The Effectiveness of Delinquency Prevention Programs*, Washington, D.C.: Children's Bureau, U.S. Department of Health, Education, and Welfare, 1964, pp. 37-39.

[31.] Edwin Powers and Helen L. Witmer, *An Experiment in the Prevention of Delinquency*, New York: Columbia University Press, 1951; William and Joan McCord, *Origins of Crime: A New Evaluation of the Cambridge-Somerville Study*, New York: Columbia University Press, 1959.

[32.] Lloyd W. McCorkle, Albert Elias, and F. Lovell Bixby, *The Highfields Story*, New York: Henry Holt and Co., 1958, p. 143.

[33.] Henry J. Meyer, Edgar Borgatta, and Wyatt Jones, *Girls at Vocational High*, New York: Russell Sage Foundation, 1966.

[34.] Szasz, *The Myth of Mental Illness*, op. cit.; Thomas S. Szasz, *Psychiatric Justice*, New York: Macmillan Co., 1965; Thomas S. Szasz, *Law, Liberty and Psychiatry*, New York: Macmillan, 1963.

[35.] Barbara Wootton, *Social Science and Social Pathology*, New York: Macmillan Co., 1959.

[36.] Halmos, op. cit., p. 146 ff.

[37.] New York City Bar Association, *Mental Illness, Due Process, and the Criminal Defendant*, New York: Fordham University Press, 1968, pp. 221-228; Grant H. Morris, "The Confusion of Confinement Syndrome Extended: The Treatment of Mentally Ill Non-Criminals in New York," *Buffalo Law Review*, Vol. 18, No. 3 (1968), pp. 393-439.

[38.] Lemon, op. cit., p. 53.

[39.] Tappan, op. cit., pp. 191 ff.

[40.] Vernon C. Branham and Samuel Kutash, eds., *Encyclopedia of Criminology*, New York: Philosophical Library, 1949, pp. 490 ff.

[41.] Ford and Urban, op. cit., pp. 14 ff.; Krasner and Ullman, op. cit., pp. 211 ff.

[42.] Ford and Urban, op. cit., pp. 681 ff.

[43.] Halmos, op. cit., pp. 49 ff.

[44.] Teodoro Ayllon and Jack Michael, "The Psychiatric Nurse as A Behavioral Engineer," in *The Control of Human Behavior,* ed. by Roger Ulrich, Thomas Stachnik, and John Mabry, New York: Scott, Foresman and Co., 1966, pp. 170 ff.

[45.] Muzafer and Carolyn Sherif, *An Outline of Social Psychology,* 2nd ed., New York: Harper and Brothers, 1950, pp. 250 ff.

[46.] Robert E.L. Faris, *Handbook of Modern Sociology,* Chicago: Rand McNally and Co., 1964, p. 224.

[47.] George C. Homans, *Social Behavior and Its Elementary Forms,* New York; Harcourt Brace and Co., 1961, p. 120 ff.

[48.] R.E.L. Faris and H.W. Dunham, *Mental Disorders in Urban Areas,* Chicago: University of Chicago Press, 1939.

[49.] Melvin L. Kohn and John A. Clausen, "Social Isolation and Schizophrenia," *American Journal of Sociology* (June, 1955), pp. 567-573; E. Gantly Jaco, "The Social Isolation Hypothesis and Schizophrenia," *American Sociological Review* (October, 1954), pp. 567-577; See also, C. Ray Jeffery, "An Integrated Theory of Crime and Criminal Behavior," *Journal of Criminal Law, Criminology, and Police Science* (March, 1959), pp. 533-552. John Clausen, "The Sociology of Mental Illness," Robert Merton, Leonard Broom, and Leonard Cottrell (eds.), *Sociology Today,* New York: Basic Books, 1959, pp. 485-508.

[50.] Alexander Leighton, *My Name is Legion,* New York: Basic Books, 1959; Charles C. Hughes et al., *People of Cove and Woodlot,* New York: Basic Books, 1960; Dorthea Leighton et al., *The Character of Danger,* New York: Basic Books, 1963.

[51.] Christopher Alexander, "The City as a Mechanism for Sustaining Human Contact," William R. Ewald (ed.), *Environment for Man,* Bloomington: Indiana University Press, 1967, p. 69.

[52.] Ibid., p. 71.

[53.] Rene Spitz, "The Role of Ecological Factors in Emotional Development in Infancy," *Child Development* (Vol. 20), pp. 145-156.

[54.] Edwin H. Sutherland and Donald R. Cressey, *Principles of Criminology,* 7th ed., Philadelphia: J.P. Lippincott Co., 1966, pp. 554-557; Tappan, op. cit., p. 211 ff.; Frank Riessman, Jerome Cohen, and Arthur Pearl, *Mental Health of the Poor,* New York: Free Press of Glencoe, 1964.

[55.] Sutherland and Cressey, op. cit., p. 554.

[56.] Ibid., p. 555.

[57.] McCorkle, Elias, and Bixby, op. cit., p. 143.

[58.] President's Commission on Law Enforcement and Administration of Justice, *Corrections,* Washington, D.C.: U.S. Government Printing Office, 1967, p. 39.

[59.] Sutherland and Cressey, op. cit., p. 557.

[60.] Riessman, Cohen, and Pearl, op. cit., p. 484.

[61.] Sutherland and Cressey, op. cit., pp. 373-380, 675-680.

[62.] Ibid., p. 677.

[63.] Arthur Pearl and Frank Riessman, *New Careers for the Poor,* New York: Free Press, 1965, p. 88, p. 234.

[64.] Daniel Glaser, *The Effectiveness of a Prison and Parole System.* Indianapolis: Bobbs-Merrill Co., 1964, p. 141 ff.

[65.] Kretch, Crutchfield, and Livson, op. cit., p. 790.

[66.] Lewis Yablonsky, *The Tunnel Back: Synanon,* New York: Macmillan Co., 1965.

[67.] Lemon, op. cit., p. 53.

[68.] Riessman, Cohen, and Pearl, op. cit.; Pearl and Riessman, op. cit.

[69.] *Offenders as a Correctional Manpower Resource,* Washington, D.C.: Joint Commission on Correctional Manpower and Training, 1968.

[70.] Ibid., p. 19.

[71.] Herman Piven and Abraham Alcabes, *The Crisis of Qualified Manpower for Criminal Justice,* Volume I: Probation/Parole, Washington, D.C., Office of Juvenile Delinquency and Youth Development, 1969, p. 11.

[72.] David Dressler, *Probation and Parole,* New York: Columbia University Press, 1951, pp. 154-156.

[73.] Tappan, op. cit., 384-396; Robert G. Caldwell, *Criminology,* New York: Ronald Press, 1956, pp. 444-453; Ruth Cavan, *Criminology,* 3rd ed., New York: Thomas Y. Crowell Co., 1962, pp. 522-528; Charles L. Newman, *Sourcebook on Probation, Parole and Pardons,* 3rd ed., Springfield: Charles C Thomas, 1968, pp. 205-331.

[74.] Caldwell, op. cit., pp. 453-456; Sutherland and Cressey, op. cit., pp. 495-499.

[75.] Federal Bureau of Investigations, *Uniform Crime Reports,* Washington, D.C.: U.S. Government Printing Office, 1967, p. 37.

[76.] Richard R. Korn and Lloyd W. McCorkle, *Criminology and Penology,* New York: Holt and Co., 1959, p. 593.

[77.] Sutherland and Cressey, op. cit., p. 495.

# Chapter 9

## Poverty: Community Action Programs

### Poverty and Crime

Sociological criminologists have emphasized such variables as poverty, urban areas, unemployment, minority group status, and undereducation when they attempt to explain crime rates or criminal behavior. The official statistics reveal that the average offender is young, unemployed, a high school dropout, and a minority group member living in a slum area.

The thesis that poverty causes crime has been an important one in criminology since the nineteenth century, as seen in the works of Quetelet, Guerry, Bonger, and others who found that the distribution of crime varied with geographical and social conditions. From studies of individual offenders, high correlations have been found between criminality and poverty (unemployment, minority group status, slum areas, lower socio-economic status). The conclusion is thus reached that the cure for crime is to do away with poverty.

The President's Crime Commission placed emphasis on "insuring opportunity as the basic goal of prevention programs."[1] The Commission recommended improving the quality of family life, community life, educational opportunities, and employment opportunities of those living in poverty.[2] The National Commission on the Causes and Prevention of Violence found that crime is centered in large cities, is committed by males fifteen to twenty-four years of age, and stems from the ghetto slums in which most Negroes live. "When poverty, delapidated housing, high unemployment, poor education, overpopulation, and broken homes are combined, an interrelated complex of powerful criminogenic forces is produced by the ghetto environment."[3]

One major issue is whether lower-class people commit more crimes, or whether lower-class people are arrested, convicted, and imprisoned to a greater extent than are the middle class, because of the way in which the criminal justice system is administered (see Chapter 7). Is the lower class more criminalistic (a) because they commit more crimes, or (b) because the justice system defines crimes and enforces the criminal law in such a way as to involve more poverty-stricken people? Reckless writes,

> all that can be said in the present state of reporting offenders is that in the United States males, younger persons, and Negroes are disproportionately arrested and imprisoned in comparison to females, older persons, and whites, and that lower-class individuals as well as members of certain foreign nationality groups have more chance to be brought to the attention of police, courts, and prisons for offenses than native-born individuals who belong to the middle and upper classes.[4]

Wilkins has criticized criminologists for using prison populations as a sample from which to draw inferences concerning the nature of crime.

> Certainly any information about the personalities of offenders or recidivists and inferences regarding their environmental situation cannot be determined on the basis of factors that merely change the probability of the offender finding himself within the catchment area of the net used by the research worker as a sampling frame, whatever that net might be. Studies of inmates in selected prisons or selected types of offender are unsatisfactory.[5]

A related issue is that of organized and white-collar crime, both of which are committed by middle- or upper-income people without the social or psychological characteristics of the lower-class criminal. Anyone who argues that crime is related to poverty or psychopathology must recognize that such theories arise from studies of a given group of individuals, not from those of a population which commits criminal acts.

Another defect in the poverty theory is that crime does not vary with economic cycles in any meaningful way. Serious property offenses may be slightly higher during a period of depression than prosperity, though this relationship is not firmly established. Several studies have shown a positive correlation between delinquency and prosperity.[6] Glaser and Rice found a direct relationship between adult crime and unemployment, whereas an inverse relationship exists between juvenile delinquency and unemployment.[7] The reason delinquency is higher during periods of prosperity may be the absence of parental supervision if the parent or parents are employed.

Toby has argued that crime is related to economic conditions via affluence. In an affluent society, where the differences between classes are great, the crime rate will be high.[8] This is a case of differences between expectation and achievement. If one is surrounded by mass media urging one to live expensively, then one might feel deprived even though one's income is $20,000 a year. Many white-collar criminals are in this category, and the concept of "relative deprivation" has some merit here.[9]

The view that poverty causes crime has been seriously challenged in recent years. Sutherland and Cressey state that

> criminal behavior is related consistently to poverty and low economic status according to studies which compare residential areas of criminals and non-criminals, but it is related inconsistently or not at all to poverty and low economic status when chronological periods are compared. . . .Poverty, may, therefore, be significant because of the social accompaniments of poverty. The general conclusion is that poverty affects crime and criminality as it determines associations with criminal behavior patterns or isolation from anti-criminal behavior patterns.[10]

The theory of differential association which they advocate in this statement has been discussed above (see Chapter 7).

Vold concludes that

> from the earlier studies to the present, the conclusion has usually been taken for granted that poverty and unemployment are major factors producing criminality.[11]

> It would be more logical to conclude that neither poverty nor wealth, as these are experienced in modern society, is a major determining influence in crime and delinquency.[12]

> In the objective data reviewed, assumptions involving either *positive* or *negative* relationships with economic conditions may be supported with some show of statistical significance. The obvious inference is that the general relations of economic conditions and criminality are so indefinite that no clear or definite conclusion can be drawn.[13]

The British criminologist Leon Radzinowicz is a leading opponent of the idea that poverty causes crime. Speaking of the heavy investment by the Ford Foundation in action projects, he has stated that

> these schemes are primarily concerned with social policy, social welfare and social services and it is essential to emphasize that. . . they should not be identified too closely in the public mind with programs of crime prevention. Their true function is to raise the standard of living and the status of the underprivileged and to help eradicate poverty. . . .If these grants are intended to help reduce crime, a much larger portion of them should be devoted to objectives more specifically connected with combating it.[14]

Radzinowicz is especially critical of the Cloward-Ohlin opportunity thesis which supports the view that poverty causes crime.

When Cloward and Ohlin speak of criminal opportunities, they are thinking primarily of the chance to learn criminal attitudes and techniques. It seems to me, however, that in trying to account for crime in an affluent society we cannot ignore criminal opportunities in another sense—the sheer frequency with which situations present themselves which make crime both tempting and easy.[15]

The American sociologist-criminologist, Marshall Clinard, is also an opponent of the idea that poverty causes crime. Clinard criticizes the Cloward-Ohlin hypothesis for confusing justification with causation. Opportunity structures may be blocked because of gang activities, rather than delinquent activities resulting from blocked legitimate opportunities.[16] Clinard concludes that the evidence for the poverty-anomie-deviant behavior thesis is lacking. Mannheim comments that the Cloward-Ohlin thesis lacks firsthand data, and Bloch and Geis conclude the theory "suffers from a lack of data."[17]

At the 1968 annual convention of the American Bar Association Lord Justice John Passmore Widgery of England stated that, based on the British experience with poverty programs, "anyone here who believes the relief of poverty will bring a decrease in crime is in for some kind of disappointment."[18]

### Poverty: Interaction of Variables

Poverty is not a simple variable but is the product of the interaction of several variables: unemployment undereducation, family structure, income, poor housing, and so forth. These variables interact with one another. Education influences employment and is influenced by employment. Income influences education and is influenced by education. Employment influences income, which influences education, which influences employment. A cycle of causation is set up, which was referred to in the Moynihan Report as "the tangle of pathology," by which Moynihan meant the interrelatedness of poverty, unemployment, education, illegitimacy, desertion, family structure, poor housing, poor health, and welfare.[19]

Where do we break into the cycle of poverty? If we have a twenty-three-year-old black female with three illegitimate children who is supported entirely by welfare, do we

(a) educate the mother and place her in a job;

(b) educate her unemployed boyfriend who is fathering her children and place him on a job, hoping he will support the family;

(c) place the children in Headstart projects, and hope that by the time they are twenty years of age they will be employable and self-sufficient;

(d) start massive welfare and housing programs with which to support future generations of uneducated and unemployed people; or

(e) start massive projects to restructure the urban environment, including the housing, educational system, and welfare system, so as to produce in the future fewer welfare cases and more healthy and productive citizens?

We have many options open to us as to how we fight poverty, poor schools, the welfare system, and unemployment. The question is how we can accomplish what we set out to do.

The relationship between poverty and crime is not causal, to say the least. One relationship that stands out is that between delinquency and income. Fleisher found that *income* was much more crucial than *unemployment* in his analysis of the economics of delinquency.[20] The HARYOU project also found the same relationship; the relationship of social pathology (juvenile delinquency, aid to dependent children, venereal disease, and homicide) to income is $-.60$, to education is $-.78$, but to male unemployment is $+.07$. The authors conclude "the low correlation with male unemployment is surprising."[21] Likewise, Dentler found unemployment was unrelated to dropout rates, whereas low income was highly related to dropout rates.[22]

We thus can hypothesize that low income, not unemployment, housing, medical care, or the like is the crucial variable we must manipulate to reduce crime and delinquency. Crime, within this framework of analysis, is a means to money or to material goods. Glaser observes that crimes against property are a substitute for work.[23] Liebow, in his study of Tally's Corner, observed that the black male was paid only $35.00 a week because his employer expected him to steal another $35.00 to $40.00 a week from the firm.[24]

Fleisher points out that unemployment and income are not directly related due to sources of income other than employment—namely crime and welfare.[25] A Columbia University study of riots discovered that, in Harlem, welfare and crime are important sources of income. "Such activities [hustling] remain officially unreported because of society's disapproval, yet they are important sources of sustenance for poor urban groups throughout the world, and they offer opportunities which in many cases present an attractive alternative to legitimate menial jobs."[26]

Three means are available for obtaining income: legitimate work, crime, and welfare. The problem of solving poverty is to raise income through legitimate work, while reducing the amount of income available through crime or welfare. The thrust of the poverty program has been to raise income through educational and employment projects, while at the same time leaving untouched the environmental opportunities for committing crime.

### Failure of Total Community Programs

The main thrust of the poverty program has been in the area of community action projects. From 1954 to 1957 a total community action project was in operation in Boston, involving the community, the family, and the gang. The Mid-City program followed the now-familiar design of strengthening citizen participation in local affairs, the so-called "participatory democracy" ideology of action projects. Miller concluded that the Boston project failed to control delinquency, since major offenses for males increased by 11.2%.[27] Court appearance for major offenses increased by 12.9%. Miller found a "negligible impact" of the community project on delinquency.[28] Yet as Miller points out in footnote 1, the total community attack on delinquency is the model used by several large-scale projects, and he cites Mobilization for Youth as his prime example.[29] It is interesting to ask, if the Mid-City project was regarded as a failure in 1960, why heavy funding by the Ford Foundation and the Office of Juvenile Delinquency was forthcoming from 1963 for the Mobilization for Youth Project.

The Cloward-Ohlin thesis that delinquency was a product of blocked opportunities was accepted by the federal administration as the basis for its delinquency control program, as seen in the establishment of Mobilization for Youth in New York City.[30] Mobilization for Youth was an action program to increase opportunities through education, employment, and involvement of the poor in the political affairs of the community. The basic thesis was that the way to fight delinquency was through poverty: "A year after the project had entered its action phase reducing poverty was given first priority in order to prevent and control delinquency."[31] Several other projects, similar in nature, were funded through the Ford Foundation and the Office of Juvenile Delinquency. Though the results of such efforts are not generally available, some reports are now starting to be published.

Marris and Rein made a comprehensive survey of these efforts, and they concluded that

> while projects could claim many individual successes, and may well have increased somewhat the range of opportunities they did so at great cost, and without benefit to perhaps two-thirds of those who sought their help.[32]

> Eager to take advantage of new appropriations voted by Congress, the projects evolved their plan opportunistically leaving research to hasten after money with as coherent an evaluative design as could be put together. . . .The projects expanded according to the grants they could obtain, rather than the logic of an experimental progression.[33]

> Under the second title of the Economic Opportunity Act $340 million were appropriated until June 1965. . . .For the second year the sum was doubled. After four years of doubtful achievement, many frustrations, and a few precarious triumphs, the endeavor was rewarded by a fifty-fold increase in its funds.[34]

Concerning the use of the poverty program to fight delinquency, Marris and Rein state that the President's Commission on Juvenile Delinquency

> was never primarily concerned with delinquency and crime. It was less an instrument to advance the study and control of a threatening social problem than a movement of reform, attacking both within the federal and local government bureaucratic fragmentation and conservatism. . . .They inclined more towards a preventive strategy than to measures of professional training or experiments in the treatment of delinquents.[35]

> If your elder brother has a better chance of a job, your younger sister a better chance in kindergarten, and your mother can get better advice on how to deal with the landlord, rheumatism, and father, then you will be less inclined to vex your years from twelve to sixteen with illegitimate protest. . . .Every component of the proposal then is to be evaluated according to its influence on delinquency, through some related aspect of behavior.[36]

> The poverty program could afford to neglect theory, since the relevance of employment, training, health and education to economic opportunity scarcely needed to be argued. A delinquency program which virtually ignored delinquents called for a more elaborate justification than the same program presented as a means to end poverty.[37]

Research, planning, and evaluation were passed over lightly by the poverty program.

> The leaderless, ill-educated, dispirited people of a city slum, if they could find their voice, would hardly speak to the brief of a nationally-minded elite of university professors and foundation executives. Research, planning, coordination, must seem remote answers to a rat-infested tenement. . . .Yet, at least in principle, the reformers were ready to jeopardize their carefully laid strategy for the sake of grass-roots participation.[38]

> The act passes lightly over experimentation, research, and planning. The allotment of resources is governed by need, not by the knowledge a proposal promises to add to our understanding of social problems. . .programs are to relieve poverty where it prevails, and not merely show how it might be relieved. Research, training, and demonstrations are not to absorb more than fifteen percent of the annual appropriation. . . .Experimental innovation gives place to the dissemination of a new convention of social service.[39]

> [They conclude that] after five years of effort the reforms had not evolved any reliable solutions to the intractable problems with which they struggled. . . .Given the talent and money they had brought to bear, they had not even reopened very many opportunities.[40]

### Politics and Poverty

Not only did the poverty program lack a research and evaluation base, as well as being ineffective in reducing poverty or crime, but it became entangled in local politics to the extent that more harm than good came of it in many instances. The Office of Economic Opportunity made appropriations which bypassed state and local governmental powers in order to destroy or combat the conservatism of the establishment, which social reformers in charge of the program felt necessary. Programs such as HARYOU and Mobilization for Youth were established to fight the local power structure, to give the poor political control over local institutions.[41] In Philadelphia, New Haven, Chicago, Los Angeles, Cleveland, Boston, and New York, conflict broke out between various local groups.[42] Competition for funds by local groups not only placed universities against poverty agencies, but poverty agencies opposed one another in their struggle for power. Whites opposed blacks; blacks opposed blacks; blacks opposed Puerto Ricans. The New York State Commission for Human Rights found that a poverty group in New York City had discriminated against a white man by refusing to name him as assistant director because he was white.[43] Two borough presidents in New York City had to intercede in a struggle between blacks and Puerto Ricans over the control of a local poverty program.[44] The late Robert Kennedy stated that in one program in the Bronx Puerto Ricans were kept off the community board after they had won a local election.[45] Bertram Beck, executive director of Mobilization for Youth, stated that neighborhood antipoverty elections had led the poor to fight each other.[46] In Detroit, the Model City program was subjected to bitter political fighting which all but excluded whites from membership on the governing board.[47] A struggle between blacks and Puerto Ricans had a similar impact on a Model Cities project in New York.[48]

The Moynihan Report on the structure of the black family received so much adverse criticism from black civil rights leaders and the permanent federal bureaucracy that its effectiveness was undermined.[49] Whereas Moynihan had attempted to objectively discuss the black family structure as a reality, he was criticized for being a racist, for pointing to the illegitimacy and desertion rate among lower-class blacks, and for ignoring the role of unemployment, jobs, and white racism in the black problem. One controversial aspect of the Moynihan Report was a chart showing that, while unemployment among black males had declined since 1962, AFDC recipients had increased during the same period.[50] Moynihan was concerned with the breakdown in the black family and the resulting increase in welfare dependency, and he recommended programs geared to strengthening the black family. Again, as we noted above, unemployment is not the answer, as income can be gained via AFDC as well as can employment. The fact that employment and AFDC can both increase at the same time supports our thesis that *income*, not *employment*, is the crucial variable.

Moynihan, in a recent book, has argued that the federal administration did not know what it was doing when it initiated community action programs controlled by the poor.[51] "Maximum feasible participation" of the poor in poverty programs is required by law. Moynihan is especially critical of Richard Cloward, and of Mobilization for Youth for its effort to use the poor to bring down the political structure of New York City.[52] Community action programs created racial hostility—blacks versus Puerto Ricans and blacks versus whites—as well as political conflict between local groups advocating community control and the formal city administration. The cycle of radicalization as Moynihan describes it is (1) radicalization of the project by middle-class whites who were initially involved in setting up the program, (2) black radical antagonism, (3) retaliation by the white community, and (4) bitterness, failure, and defeat.[53]

Moynihan is especially critical of social scientists who became involved in the poverty program and who did not have the knowledge to alleviate poverty or delinquency but who pretended or thought they possessed such knowledge. They (social scientists) became advocates of social reform based on questionable social science theories, rather than acting as critics of the basic thinking of the poverty program. Moynihan states, and quite rightly, that the role of the scientist is not to formulate social policy but to evaluate its results.[54]

Adam Yarmolinsky, a major architect of the poverty program, stated in 1967 that he did not anticipate that the phrase "maximum feasible participation" would mean that the poor would make policy and operate programs.[55]

The poverty program was established on a crash basis, with the objective of producing dramatic results within six months to a year.[56]

> They were under great pressure to produce results, and reluctant at the outset to run too great a risk of failure; so they accomplished first the programs which came easiest—a summer camp, vacation jobs for high school students, training courses for well-qualified applicants, holiday tasks for college volunteers—rather than those which mattered most.[57]

The writer was a consultant to an electronics corporation which received a contract from OEO in mid-April and was told to be in operation by June 1.

In the haste to put programs together, some frauds took place. In New York City, between $300,000 and "millions" were stolen through the Neighborhood Youth Corps, and the fiscal director, Mrs. Helynn Lewis, was arrested for embezzling $22,900 while on her $19,000-a-year job.[58]

In January 1969, an investigation revealed that millions had been lost by the Human Resources Administration of New York City through fraud, inefficiency, and mismanagement. More than $1 million was transferred to a Switzerland bank account, and $1.7 million was stolen by a group of young employees called the "Durham Mob." Federal officials are now threatening to withdraw financial support for neighborhood youth projects wherein, one memorandum within the Human Resources Administration stated, "management failures had more than negated the impact of the anti-poverty program in local communities."[59] How much money has been embezzled by individuals while employed by the poverty program is unknown, but the facts support Moynihan's contention that the program was poorly managed and administered.

One of the major complaints arising out of the poverty effort has been the high salaries paid to the middle-class staff members. The executives of UPO in Washington, D.C., received $22,000 to $25,000 a year.[60] These men in most cases were not professional scientists, but social reformers. The Deputy Director of Human Resources Administration in New York City was a Negro Congregational minister who received a salary of $32,500.[61] Salaries of OEO officials were often over $25,000 a year.[62]

Some of the officials were controversial not only because of their salaries, but because of their militant activities. In Washington, D.C., a local black militant was a consultant to UPO, and his assistant was Catfish Mayfield, a young man with an active delinquent career.[63] Herman Ferguson, a principal in a public school in Queens, was sentenced to prison for conspiring to murder Roy Wilkins and Whitney Young, Jr.[64] In July 1968, 1,500 youngsters went on a rampage outside City Hall in New York, destroying property and cars belonging to government officials. They were protesting a cutback in funds for summer jobs, and their leader was Willie Smith, an $18,000-a-year city official, director of the Neighborhood Youth Corps in New York City.[65] Smith was suspended from his job, but a week later reinstated by the mayor. The Mobilization for Youth Project has sponsored protest action against both the educational and welfare systems of New York City. Likewise, HARYOU became a project devoted to protest and social unrest.[66]

In Cleveland, four men charged with the murder of three policemen had received money from a poverty project called NOW.[67] In Delaware, a project to strengthen black businessmen ended after a year because of losses to "young hoodlums," whose criminal activities frightened away customers and bankrupted the business operations.[68]

The creation of poverty programs does not guarantee either the success of the program or the reduction of the crime rate. Haggstrom, after a review of existing programs, wrote, "At this point *all* solutions to poverty have failed. Public housing, public welfare, casework, job training, educational programs, the trickle down from affluence—all these have failed at least as dismally as the organization of the poor to achieve their originally announced objectives."[69]

### Conclusions

The thesis that poverty causes crime has been around for many years, and, though no empirical verification has ever been found for the thesis, it has been made the major assumption of recent crime prevention programs by the federal government and the Ford Foundation.

In order for poverty programs to reduce delinquency it is necessary (1) to reduce poverty, and (2) to have a causal relationship between poverty and delinquency so that when poverty is reduced, delinquency is reduced.

The community action programs initiated recently to reduce poverty and delinquency have failed to demonstrate any major breakthroughs. Such programs were politically inspired; poorly conceived, without an adequate research base; hastily implemented and made operational; plagued by racial conflict, fraud, and political protest; and often manned by reformers dedicated to a political ideology rather than to scientific objectivity.

Poverty does not cause crime; poverty and crime are correlated with many other variables, such as employment, income, family stability, housing, illegitimacy, education, and welfare dependence. The crucial factor appears to be income, since income has a more significant relationship to crime than do the other variables. However, we cannot deal with income without also dealing with employment, job training, education, and welfare.

The poverty and crime thesis is based on studies of the characteristics of individual offenders caught in the web of justice, and, from the characteristics of individual offenders, we construct rehabilitation programs. It is another example of a crime prevention program set up to work through the rehabilitation of the individual offender, an assumption which runs throughout positivistic criminology. So long as we insist on designing crime control programs around the characteristics of individual offenders, rather than around the environment in which crimes are committed, we are going to emphasize changing the individual offender and not changing the environment.

Poverty programs are an indirect approach to crime control, since they operate through education, job training, and community involvement. As in the case of therapeutic approaches (see Chapter 8), the community-action approach does not deal directly with crime, but with poverty and its several correlates. We assume that, if we change one behavior system, we will change another behavior system.

The distinction between environmental opportunities to commit crimes and individual opportunities to receive an education or a job is ignored by Cloward and Ohlin and by those who have financed projects designed to extend the opportunity structure for participation in American life. The desire to reduce poverty via increased opportunities is a noble, ambitious and worthwhile goal, but it should not be confused with crime prevention and control.

## NOTES

[1.] President's Commission on Law Enforcement and Administration of Justice, *Juvenile Delinquency and Youth Crime,* Washington, D.C.: U.S. Government Printing Office, 1967, p. 41.

[2.] Ibid., pp. 41-56.

[3.] New York Times, November 24, 1969.

[4.] Walter C. Reckless, *The Crime Problem,* 4th ed., New York: Appleton-Century-Crofts, 1961, p. 98, pp. 438-440.

[5.] Leslie T. Wilkins, *Evaluation of Penal Measures,* New York: Random House, 1969, p. 52.

[6.] Edwin H. Sutherland and Donald R. Cressey, *Principles of Criminology,* 7th ed., Philadelphia: J.B. Lippincott and Co., 1966, p. 246; George B. Vold, *Theoretical Criminology,* New York: Oxford University Press, 1958, pp. 159-182.

[7.] Daniel Glaser and Kent Rice, "Crime, Age, and Employment," *American Sociological Review* (October, 1959), pp. 679-686.

[8.] President's Commission on Law Enforcement and Administration of Justice, op. cit., pp. 132-144.

[9.] Robert Merton, *Social Theory and Social Structure,* revised ed., New York: Free Press, 1957, pp. 234-235.

[10.] Sutherland and Cressey, op. cit., pp. 241-242.

[11.] Vold, op. cit., p. 169.

[12.] Ibid., p. 172.

[13.] Ibid., p. 181.

[14.] Leon Radzinowicz, *The Need for Criminology,* London: Heinemann, 1965, pp. 30-31.

[15.] Leon Radzinowicz, *Ideology and Crime,* New York: Columbia University Press, 1966, p. 98.

[16.] Marshall Clinard, *Sociology of Deviant Behavior,* 3rd ed., New York: Holt, Rinehart and Winston, Inc., 1968, pp. 157 ff., p. 238 ff.

[17.] Hermann Mannheim, *Comparative Criminology,* New York: Houghton Mifflin Co., 1965, p. 512; Herbert A. Block and Gilbert Geis, *Man, Crime, and Society,* New York: Random House, 1962, p. 135.

[18.] New York Times, August 8, 1968, and August 11, 1968.

[19.] Lee Rainwater and William L. Yancey, *The Moynihan Report and the Politics of Controversy,* Cambridge: MIT Press, 1967, p. 75.

[20.] Belton Fleisher, *The Economics of Delinquency,* Chicago: Quadrangle Press, 1966, pp. 112-115.

[21.] Harlem Youth Opportunities Unlimited, *Youth in the Ghetto,* New York: Orans Press, 1964, p. 159.

[22.] Robert A. Dentler and Mary Ellen Warshauer, *Big City Dropouts,* New York: Center for Urban Education, 1965, pp. 16-21.

[23.] Daniel Glaser, *The Effectiveness of a Prison and Probation System,* Indianapolis: Bobbs-Merrill Co., 1964, p. 230.

[24.] Elliot Liebow, *Tally's Corner,* Boston: Little, Brown and Co., p. 37.

[25.] Fleisher, op. cit., pp. 112-115.

[26.] The Academy of Political Science, *Urban Riots: Violence and Social Change,* Montpelier: Capital City Press, 1968, p. 76.

[27.] Walter B. Miller, "The Impact of a Total Community Delinquency Control Project," *Social Problems* (Fall, 1962), p. 181.

[28.] Ibid., p. 187 ff.

[29.] Ibid., p. 169.

[30.] George A. Braeger and Francis P. Purcell, *Community Action Against Poverty*, New Haven: College and University Press, 1967.

[31.] Ibid., pp. 88-89.

[32.] Peter Marris and Martin Rein, *Dilemmas of Social Reform*, New York: Atherton Press, 1967, p. 89.

[33.] Ibid., p. 192.

[34.] Ibid., p. 208.

[35.] Ibid., p. 132.

[36.] Ibid., p. 195.

[37.] Ibid., p. 213.

[38.] Ibid., p. 165.

[39.] Ibid., p. 211.

[40.] Ibid., p. 222.

[41.] Ibid., p. 39 ff.; Braeger and Purcell, op. cit.; Shirley Scheibla, *Poverty is Where the Money Is,* New Rochelle: Arlington House, 1968.

[42.] Marris and Rein, op. cit., p. 94 ff.

[43.] New York Times, November 9, 1967.

[44.] New York Times, October 8, 1967.

[45.] New York Times, February 8, 1968.

[46.] New York Times, February 12, 1968.

[47.] Wall Street Journal, February 20, 1968.

[48.] New York Times, February 25, 1968.

[49.] Rainwater and Yancey, op. cit.

[50.] Ibid., p. 59.

[51.] Daniel P. Moynihan, *Maximum Feasible Misunderstanding,* New York: Free Press, 1968.

[52.] Ibid., p. 102 ff., p. 46 ff.

[53.] Ibid., p. 134.

[54.] Ibid., p. 193.

[55.] New York Times, October 29, 1967.

[56.] Scheibla, op. cit.

[57.] Marris and Rein, op. cit., p. 341.

[58.] New York Times, October 2, 1968, October 4, 1968, September 14, 1968.

[59.] New York Times, January 12, 1969.

[60.] Washington Post, March 23, 1965.

[61.] New York Times, November 8, 1968.

[62.] Scheibla, op. cit.

[63.] Washington Post, July 25, 1967.

[64.] New York Times, October 4, 1968.

[65.] New York Times, July 11, 1968.

[66.] Braeger and Purcell, op. cit., p. 269 ff.; Marris and Rein, op. cit., p. 48 ff.

[67.] New York Times, April 21, 1969.

[68.] New York Times, February 15, 1969.

[69.] Irwin Deutscher and Elizabeth J. Thompson, ed., *Among the People,* New York: Basic Books, 1968, p. 68.

# Chapter 10

# Poverty: Education, Job Training, and Welfare

## Education and Delinquency

As was pointed out in Chapter 9, the belief that poverty causes delinquency is a major assumption upon which delinquency prevention programs are based. The assumption is made that either community action programs or education/job training programs should be used to increase legitimate opportunities to social goals.

A statistical relationship has been noted many times between under-education, unemployment, and delinquency. Fleisher notes that the peak age for arrests, school dropouts, and unemployment is the same—namely, age 16.[1] This suggests a process whereby a student drops out of school, becomes unemployed, and commits a delinquent act.

Cervantes discovered that ten times the incidence of delinquency exists among dropouts than among stay-ins.[2] Burke and Simons found that ninety percent of the Lorton Youth Center population were high school dropouts, and Amos and Southwell found a high correlation between dropping out of school, unemployment, and related social and personal maladjustments.[3] Shore and Mannino suggest the need for new types of intervention in the lives of those who have or are about to drop out of school.[4] Daniel Glaser observed that "the growing number of youths who are both out of school and out of work are the hard core of America's delinquency problem, regardless of the type of delinquent subculture in which they are involved."[5]

Daniel Schreiber, director of the School Dropout Project, notes the high correlation between unemployment and dropping out of school. He also notes that ninety percent of the inmates under twenty-five years of age are high school dropouts.

The importance of these statistics is clear. But it is imperative to be extremely precise in their interpretation, since with the increase of concern about the dropout problem, there is developing a tendency to equate the dropout with the delinquent. They state—nothing more than this—that the sentenced delinquent is much more likely to be a dropout than an in-school student or a graduate. Beyond this, it would probably be impossible to establish any strictly causal relationship between the two phenomena, e.g., that a youngster is delinquent *because* he was a dropout, or a dropout because he was a delinquent.[6]

Though the experts agree that education, employment, and delinquency are interrelated, they disagree as to the nature of the relationship and as to the role of delinquent subcultures in the delinquent process. If, as Schreiber argues, and as the author would argue, there is no causal relationship between delinquency and dropping out of school, then how does one attack crime and delinquency through education projects? Two basic assumptions must be made if one argues that educational programs can reduce delinquency. (1) The techniques for educating ghetto youths exist; and therefore the educational level of dropouts can be raised. (2) An increase in the educational level of delinquents will reduce the delinquency rate. This chapter shall be concerned with attempts to improve education, welfare, and employment opportunities for the disadvantaged in the hope that, by increasing legal opportunities, one will thereby decrease illegal activities.

### *Policy for Increased Educational Opportunity*

The Coleman Report on Educational Opportunities concluded that racial and ethnic groups are segregated in public schools, and that black students perform below the level of performance of white students.[7] The surprising finding of the Coleman project was that schools attended by blacks are equal in most respects to schools attended by white students when compared for facilities, faculties, equipment, special programs, textbooks, counseling, and so forth. The *school* itself made little or no difference in determining the performance of the students.

What did make a difference was the family and community background of the students. Black students attending schools with middle-class white students do much better than those in all-black schools. The aspirations and motivational level of fellow students, along with a sense of control over one's environment (over one's future destiny) are crucial to the achievement level of the students.

What the child brings with him to school as strengths or weaknesses determined by his social class is the prime correlate of school achievement. It is influenced most substantially not by facilities, curriculum, or teachers but by what other pupils bring with them as class-shaped interests and abilities. In practical terms as the proportion of white pupils increases in a school, achievement among Negroes and Puerto Ricans increases...desegregation does affect factors of immediate relevance to student achievement. These factors are individual academic motivation and peer environment.[8]

The U.S. Commission on Civil Rights concluded that compensatory educational programs are not successful with racially isolated groups, and the Commission recommends desegregation as the best or only answer to black schools.[9] Coleman, in a subsequent article, wrote that school integration was *not* the total answer to the educational problems. "The aim of racial integration of our schools should be recognized as distinct from the aim of providing equal opportunity for educational performance."[10]

Dentler and Warshauer found no significant relationship between dropouts and illiteracy, on the one hand, and the quality of school and welfare programs, on the other hand.[11] Dentler concludes that the general economic opportunity and development of the community was crucial.

Health, education, and welfare expenditures...are generally related *unfavorably* to current levels of educational attainment. In other words, cities with higher levels of non-white school dropouts and adult illiterates...are cities with higher than average per pupil and per family AFDC expenditures. They are also cities that spend relatively *more* on health services....That is, cities with higher proportions of dropouts and illiterates than expected tend to be cities with *higher* than average educational, health, and public welfare expenditures. Secondly, we have concluded that no observable association obtains between character of educational or welfare programs and levels of school withdrawal and adult illiteracy.[12]

[They conclude] the burden of our research is that existing welfare and education programs in the big cities do not affect levels of school withdrawal....The new era seems to be one in which we will disabuse ourselves, by virtue of the problems of our major urban centers, that educational programs can resolve welfare or employment problems, or vice versa.[13]

Also, as Dentler and Warshauer noted, the differentiation between the high school dropout and graduate so far as employment is concerned is disappearing; that is, the graduate is in many instances no better off than the dropout. Added to this is the fact that twenty-nine percent of the white dropouts are unemployed, compared with thirty-one percent of the black graduates.[14]

The general conclusion of such studies is that educational programs do not educate, community forces can offset the advantages of an educational system, and educational programs are not going to solve welfare or employment problems. Though the federal policy is one of integrating the public school system, as seen in the U.S. Office of Education and the U.S. Commission on Civil Rights, the local policy in many instances is one of segregated education, due to the fact that blacks and whites are geographically and socially segregated. To bring about educational intergration without residential, economic, and social integration is a difficult, if not impossible, task.

As a result, we today have a strong black militant movement supporting racial segregation, coupled with the argument that black schools must be run by black teachers, principals, and community boards. The experience in New York City, where the public school system has been shut down by teacher strikes, parent boycotts, and controversy over desegregation of the school system is a good example of the political consequences of recent educational policy.[15]

The issues have become racial and political, not educational. The end sought is better education for black children, but the means used hold slight promise of success. Psychological and educational research have been replaced by racial politics, both black and white, which seeks segregation or integration, neither of which in and of itself will educate white or black students. New techniques must be developed for educating the lower class, be they black or white, and such techniques must be based on *behavior* principles, not racial or political policies.

## *Failure of Educational Programs*

The failure of the urban ghetto school has been so well documented elsewhere that there is no further need to do so here. Kohl, Kozol, Goodman, Friedenberg, Henry, Holt, and others have written extensively on the plight of the urban school system.[16] Herein the focus will be on several major urban educational projects; rather than on resorting to a more general survey of such programs, since no means exist at present to even know the total variety of effectiveness of such programs in existence.

The Model School program in Washington, D.C., was established as an experiment on curriculum, teacher training, utilization of teachers, and management of urban ghetto schools. The Model School program was designed to make use of the latest in teaching techniques, educational theory, and programmed instructional technology. The Model School division was established in June 1964, and by December 1965 the chairman of the advisory committee, Judge David Bazelon, declared the program a "near total failure."[17] In March 1966, Bazelon resigned his position, and his advisory committee issued a report documenting the failure of the Model School division.[18] The program was opposed both by the local poverty agency and by the Superintendent of Education, Carl Hansen. As a result of the failure of the educational system, Hansen was forced to resign; however, there is no evidence as of today that the educational system of Washington, D.C. has improved. An article in the *Washington Post* declared in 1966 that "the war on poverty is a dud in the Capital's schools, due primarily to bureaucratic infighting and doctrinal confusion."[19] A literacy program operated by UPO in Washington, D.C., had only twenty-five students enrolled in a program designed for 500.[20]

One of the most promising educational programs, Project Headstart, was found by Professor Wolff of the Center for Urban Education to be a failure, since the effects faded away in six to eight months. Another study of Headstart by a Johns Hopkins team also found few benefits from the program. Professor Bronfenbrenner, although criticizing the above studies of Headstart results, also concluded that the gains were small, and he emphasized the need for follow-through by the elementary school system.[21]

A New York University special project in the Bedford-Stuyvesant area of Brooklyn was discontinued because "it was a shattering experience and defeat for the university and for the school system." A film of the school project, made by National Educational Television and shown nationally under the title "The Way It Is" depicted the school as bedlam, where little education took place.[22]

The More Effective Schools program in New York City was proposed and sponsored by the United Federation of Teachers. An evaluation of MES by the Center for Urban Education found the program did not have a significant impact on the academic skills of the student body.[23]

The Ocean Hill-Brownsville demonstration project, which led to several serious strikes by the UFT in 1967 and 1968, has been labeled "bedlam and a model mess" by Martin Mayer and others. A review of compensatory educational programs by Roger Freeman of Stanford University mentioned no noticeable exceptions to this pattern of failure.[24] As noted above, the U.S. Commission on Civil Rights, after a review of many such programs, concluded "the evidence reviewed here strongly suggests that compensatory programs are not likely to succeed in racially and socially isolated school environments."[25]

The failure of our schools has been documented and analyzed in many places, including the President's Commission on Law Enforcement and the Administration of Justice.[26] The reasons given are many and varied: the performance of teachers, the middle-class values of school systems, the irrelevance of education for the black student, the lack of "payoff" or reward for going to school, the lack of motivation on the part of students, the lack of proper materials and supplies, and the need for community control of ghetto schools. For our purpose, the two questions raised earlier are (1) can we improve the educational level of the dropout, and (2) if we improve education, will we decrease crime and delinquency?

The answer to the first question is a tentative "no" at present, with some few exceptions. Without attempting to go into detail as to all the possible reasons for such failure, it may be helpful to go back to a point made consistently throughout this book—that is, our failure to make use of a *science* of human behavior. Education is basically the application of learning theory. B.F. Skinner, the father of modern learning theory and teaching machines, writes that we fail to educate because we fail to apply scientific principles of learning.[27] Education, according to Skinner, is carried out in an aversive, punitive environment where punishment is used much more often than reward. An aversive environment creates a withdrawal or escape response in the form of tardiness, truancy, lack of attentiveness, lack of motivation, and dropping out. If we look at undermotivation, truancy, and leaving school as responses to an environment, then we must conclude the environment is not conducive to learning. If children do not learn, it is because the environment is not engineered so as to produce learning. Buckminster Fuller, the environmental engineer who invented the geodesic dome, expressed it thusly: "given the right environment and thoughtful answers to his questions, the child has everything he needs educationally right from birth. . . .I have learned to undertake reform of the environment and not to try to reform man. If we design the environment properly, it will permit man and child to develop safely and to behave logically."[28]

If we redesign the environment so as to make learning possible, it must include educational materials designed from behavioral principles. It will also include teachers trained in reinforcement theory, teachers who will know how to shape behavior.

Coleman has suggested restructuring the environment by allowing parents to choose from a variety of private contractors who would undertake the teaching of reading and arithmetic. Sizer has made a similar recommendation in his plan to give public money to children and allow them to select the school they wish to attend, thus creating competition among several schools in a district.[29] These proposals suggest what has been argued herein: students and teachers must be *rewarded* for learning and teaching. We now either do not reward learning and teaching or we reward neither process to the extent needed to maintain the behavior we wish to encourage. If we give money indiscriminately, however, we will not produce better students or teachers. A flat across-the-board payment to students (as is often given via poverty programs) or an across-the-board salary increase (as is negotiated by teachers' unions) will reward the poor student and teacher as well as the competent one. New techniques of reinforcement within our educational system must be developed.

Any educational program in the future must be based upon *research,* not upon *service.* Coleman, Dentler, and others have found no differences in physical facilities and expenditures for black schools, and they found no correlation between money spent and educational results obtained. We are spending millions for educational *services,* whereas we should be finding answers to how one educates a child.

As for the second question, there is no evidence that increasing the educational level of dropouts will make them less delinquent. The assumption is that if the dropout is educated, he becomes employable, and if employed, he will not be delinquent. This argument for increased legal opportunities was discussed above and rejected as unsound. Poverty does not cause crime. The relationship between education, employment, and crime is not causal, and by educating a person we may make him employable, but the behavior involved in education is not that needed for employment. Educated, employed people are behaviorally able to commit crimes. As we have noted above, we cannot expect educational programs to solve our welfare, employment, and delinquency problems.

### The Washington, D.C., Dropout Project

One study that did attempt to answer the question of the relationship between education and delinquency was conducted by the writer in Washington, D.C., over a three-year period. The project was conducted under grants from the U.S. Army, the U.S. Office of Education, and the Public Welfare Foundation (private agency in Washington, D.C.), and it worked with up to forty black high school dropouts who had a history of delinquency.[30] The students were given points for good behavior, both academic and social, and these points were redeemable for money at the end of the week. Each student could earn up to $40.00 a week for regular attendance, passing examinations, and so forth. Family counseling and job preparation programs also were part of the project.

The academic program made use of programmed instructional materials, teaching machines, ungraded classrooms, and invidualized instruction. Each student started at his level of performance and moved at his own pace with the use of instructional materials. Rewards for correct responses were immediate, and a student was corrected immediately if he made an error. No student was allowed to move to more difficult materials until he had mastered the basic materials. As much control as possible was exerted over the environment in which learning took place.

The results of the academic program were encouraging, as students moved from the third- or fourth-grade level to the tenth- or twelfth-grade level in reading, English, mathematics, science, and social studies. Significant gains in academic achievement could be documented in the space of six months.

The major difficulties in the project pertained to nonacademic behaviors. Widespread cheating on examinations occurred, as well as singing, cursing, and fighting at the project center. Stealing of typewriters, supplies, clothing, checks, and so forth was so widespread that it seriously challenged the future operation of the project. Drug use was also found among the students.

In spite of the fact that students were paid to go to school, only twenty-five percent of those who were contacted by the project remained with it. A dropout rate of seventy-five percent destroyed the effectiveness of the project. At the end of the project, twenty-two students took the General Educational Development Test (for a high school equivalency diploma) and fifty-nine percent (thirteen) passed the examination. However, there was no significant correlation between passing the GED examination, number of weeks in program, or number of programmed units completed in program. The delinquency rate was not reduced for the subjects in the program; and those who passed the GED test were more delinquent than those who failed.

The family counseling and job preparation programs were total failures in terms of any measurable impact on family, community, or employment problems. Though many jobs were found for the group, few of them were interested in menial work, and they would not remain on a job for more than a day or two.

The failure of an educational project to reduce delinquency can be discussed in several ways. The relationship between delinquency and education is correlational, not causal. The jobs available to dropouts, even with a GED diploma, were not attractive enough to motivate them. The money offered for going to school could not compete with money available through crime and welfare. The family and community problems of these youths were so great as to destroy a great deal of whatever behavior change the program produced.

The major point to remember is that the environment created by the project was not the environment in which crimes, family problems, unemployment, and so forth occurred. The environment which produced crime was *untouched* by the project. A student could study, go to classes, take drugs, and hustle all within the same twenty-four-hour period. There is nothing about reading an English text that prevents armed robbery or larceny. The control over crime via education is *indirect*; that is, it depends on decreasing one class of behaviors (delinquent) by increasing another class of behaviors (academic), and it might be concluded that it is most difficult to alter behavior indirectly through other behavior. The therapist attempts it through *verbal* behavior; the sociologist through *educational* or *employment* behavior. The thesis presented in this book is that criminal behavior can be controlled only by *direct* controls designed to control criminal behavior, not through therapy, antipoverty programs, or other such indirect measures.

### Job Training Projects

Job training projects have been plagued by high dropout rates, little success in job placement, and low levels of academic and vocational skills of the unemployed. The modern technological world has created an economy in which unskilled people are in abundant supply and little demand. Youths who are dropouts cannot be placed in jobs, and, under our current system, they are not being educated. Education is not the answer to unemployment, but a given level of education is a necessary, if not a sufficient, condition for employment. People must be motivated (1) to complete a training program, and (2) to accept a job once they are trained.

The President's Commission on Law Enforcement emphasized job training as a means of fighting delinquency.[31] The federal poverty program created many such programs through the Job Corps and Manpower Development and Training Act. Such programs have been expensive, with the cost of training a Job Corps enrollee averaging between $7,000 and $15,000 a year.[32]

Facts on federal training projects are hard to come by because OEO has the power to withhold publication of the results of studies on the effectiveness of such programs.[33]

Amos found from his study of thirty black males, ages sixteen to eighteen, who were placed in jobs, that *none* remained employed as long as three months. He concluded that keeping a job is more crucial than finding one.[34] The United Planning Organization of Washington, D.C., found 2,000 jobs for 12,000 applicants, and these jobs were at a very menial level.[35]

In New Haven, trainees for a job training program were selected from highly qualified and motivated applicants—high school graduates who had held jobs and had earned more than $3,000 the year before. The success of the program can be attributed to the fact that it did not deal with applicants who were dropouts with delinquent careers but without prior employment.[36]

In New York State, five work-training projects had no impact on the trainees, since, when compared with a control group which had not received special services, the trainees demonstrated no differences in employment. Half of both groups were unemployed, and thirty-three percent out of both groups had jobs. A gasoline station attendant project placed only one of forty-six in a job. Another project placed twenty-five percent of the work-crew trainees.[37] The operation of the Opportunities Industrialization Center in Philadelphia was more successful, though the results have not as yet been made available. Since thirty-three percent of the trainees were over thirty, this suggests that men over twenty-one were the primary target, and a much more manageable target than the sixteen- to twenty-one-year-old group.[38] Cloward and Ontell report that the Mobilization for Youth project placed only twenty-five percent of the applicants for employment. "For the bulk of those placed, the jobs are in marginal occupations at relatively low wages, and then subsequent job histories are not characterized by much stability or continuity."[39]

An MDTA project for young offenders was established by Clyde Sullivan at Rikers Island in New York City. The project gave training to 137 trainees in an experimental group, compared to 127 in the control group who received no training.[40] An IBM training program was established for the experimental group. The results after the three years show that fifty-two percent of the experimental subjects remained out of jail for one year after release, compared to thirty-four percent of the controls. These figures indicate that forty-eight percent were recidivists, a high rate even though better than the figure of sixty-six percent for those who did not have the advantage of the MDTA program.[41] However, these figures are based on 112, not 137 subjects. Sullivan does not explain this discrepancy in his charts, but he does state that 119 out of 222 subjects were back in jail within two years, both control and experimental. Sullivan *does not* include in his figures 25 who dropped out of the training program, and thus his figure is inaccurate. If we include the dropouts as failures (which they are), then the failure rate is 79 out of 137 or fifty-eight percent, not forty-eight percent. Since sixty-six percent of the control group were failures, we can conclude that no significant differences existed between the two groups. Also, Sullivan's figures are for twelve months, though in another place he tells us that forty percent of the study group recidivated within nine months, whereas ninety-two percent recidivated within twenty-one months; in other words, the second year is as crucial as, if not more so than, the first. [42]

Job Corps Centers have been plagued by a high dropout rate, though the exact rate has not been published to my knowledge. [43] A Louis Harris poll found that twenty-nine percent of the Job Corps graduates were unemployed compared to twenty-six percent for the general population of nonwhite teenagers. [44] John Carmody estimated that there were 6,500 job placements out of 62,000 attempts at a cost of $600 million. [45] Though we do not know the extent of the success or failure of the Job Corps, we can assume that it is not too successful, since no one has published any hard data indicating otherwise. Many articles have appeared discussing the failure of the program. [46]

Absenteeism in a project to train unemployed heads of households resulted in higher costs and cutbacks in training efforts. [47] Over 1,000 persons trained to be hospital aides in New York City were reported unemployed in spite of a critical shortage of health personnel. [48] A $4.3 million youth program in New York City was terminated because of a high ratio of dropouts, poor administration, and failure to graduate or find a job for a single youth. This project (TRY) was a major investment by the federal government in the Bedford-Stuyvesant district of Brooklyn. [49] A project to train unemployed men for jobs in the trucking industry was declared a failure when, out of 190 workers trained, only 4 remained on the job. [50]

On the other hand, it was estimated that in New York City over 20,000 jobs remained unfilled, while there were 135,000 unemployed in the city. [51] Employers complain that they cannot find people to fill low-skill, low-paying jobs, or to fill skilled jobs in construction which pay well. [52] Unemployed men are reported to say that they would rather be on welfare than take a job which pays $1.70 an hour. [53]

Charles Silberman has noted an increasing psychological reaction of young blacks to menial jobs, which they regard as "slaving for the white man." [54]

One of the defects of job training programs is that they allow individuals alternative behaviors to gain income (crime, welfare). So long as a man can earn more via a life of crime than by a life of work, he will continue in a life of crime. When a delinquent was asked by a HARYOU staff member why he did not get a job, he responded, "Oh, come on. Get off that crap. I make $40.00 a day selling marihuana. You want me to go down to the garment district and push one of those trucks through the street for $40.00 or $50.00 a week?" [55]

The following story is reported by Rainwater and Yancey:

> Perhaps the best indication of the estrangement of the urban Negro is the experience of Bayard Rustin who after the Harlem riots of 1964 found jobs for 120 teenagers in Harlem. A few weeks later only twelve of them were still working. One boy told Rustin he could make more playing pool than the $50 a week he had been earning; another could make more than his $60 salary by selling "pot"; another turned down a four-year basketball scholarship to a major university because he preferred to be a pimp.[56]

Stewart Alsop reported the following story in his column in *The Saturday Evening Post.*[57] "Catfish" Mayfield, the head of Pride, a poverty program in Washington, D.C., had left his job to return to stealing cars. During his questioning, it became obvious that the world of legitimate work could not compete with the excitement of the streets:

> To many wellmeaning, liberal-minded whites the solution of Negro unemployment is obvious. Find jobs for the hard-core unemployed . . . .The whole life style of Catfish and his friends has nothing at all in common with the nine to five life style of the middle classes. . . .Most of the groups on the street are simply not interested in working eight hours a day or five days a week in dull, menial jobs. The fact is that a great many of Catfish's friends are already, or soon will be, unemployable. . . .Jobs, in short are not the whole answer to hard-core unemployment, any more than education is the whole answer to functional illiteracy, or money the whole answer to poverty.

A Senate investigation of an OEO project in Chicago with the Blackstone Rangers revealed that the project center was used for gambling, smoking marihuana, and cleaning guns. The president of the Rangers, hired at $6,500 as an assistant project director, was convicted of soliciting a fourteen-year-old to commit murder. Between seventy-five and ninety percent of the checks drawn for trainee payments were fraudulently drawn or cashed.[58]

Robin, from an analysis of antipoverty programs and delinquency, concluded[59]:

Separate analyses of the police records of year-round and summer-only enrollees who worked in the in-school Neighborhood Youth Corps programs in Cincinnati and Detroit compared with those of control youths who applied to the program revealed that NYC participation, among both males and females, was unrelated to delinquency prevention or reduction. Examination of the gross and net effects of program participation disclosed no evidence that working in the program made enrollees with a previous offense record less likely to continue to commit offenses while they were working in the program, in any way had a positive effect on particular types of offenders, or reduced overall the number of police contacts or specific kinds of offensive behavior. Nor, among enrollees who had no previous offense record prior to enrollment, did the program dissuade them from entering the ranks of delinquency more so than was the case with the controls in the absence of program participation. In neither city was there any indication that NYC participation had an effect on reducing criminality on the part of enrollees while the youths were working in the program or after they left it.

Thus we have a situation in which young employed youth are unskilled, uneducated, and unwilling to take nonskilled or semiskilled jobs. Programs to train them have not been highly successful. As a result, a hard core of unemployed youths exists in our society and depends on criminal activities and welfare for its economic existence.

### Welfare Programs

No area is more charged with emotionalism than that of welfare. The Christian ethic demands that one work for a living, that the poor are responsible for their inferior position, and that we must show faith, hope, and charity to the unfortunate. We are thus caught in a dilemma of blaming the poor on the one hand and giving them sympathy and charity on the other hand. The field of welfare is dominated by good hearts, but it needs strong minds.

The crisis in social work was the theme of the 1968 annual meeting of the National Association of Social Workers, which concluded that "the profession has concentrated on how to deliver services with little regard for whether it is delivering anything of real significance to the people most in need of help. Largely because of this tendency social work now faces a major crisis: the crisis of its relevance to the human condition."[60]

A casework project in New York State found that casework service to 50 multiple-problem families was of little or no benefit.[61] Brown concluded that you cannot casework people out of poverty. In New York City, a plan to encourage AFDC mothers to take jobs or training had placed only 144 out of 130,000 eligible recipients in jobs.[62]

The major failure of the welfare policy is that it has been *service*-oriented rather than *research*-oriented. As has been noted throughout this book, service professions have failed to change behavior and alleviate human social problems.

Our welfare system has created a cycle of dependence and poverty which has grown tremendously over the past thirty years. Today we have over 8 million welfare recipients in the United States, with over 1 million in New York City alone, an increase from 694,000 in 1967. The welfare budget for New York City alone is $832 million or 26% of the city budget. More is currently spent for welfare than for education in New York City.[63]

An examination of welfare roles reveals that 2 million are over the age of 65; 500,000 are physically disabled; and 3.5 million are children on AFDC rolls for aid to families of dependent children. To these figures must be added the many people on welfare who are marginally employed and whose wages are too low to allow them to exist above the poverty level.

The rise in welfare rolls is especially prominent for AFDC cases. Several studies by Cloward, Piven, and Podell in New York City revealed that up to twenty-five percent of the welfare families contained employable males. The major reason given for the growth in welfare recipients is the fact that more people are applying, and more applications are now being approved by welfare workers.[64] Many welfare recipients are now organized into militant groups, who engage in political demands for greater benefits, which might account for the higher rates of applications and acceptances.

The fact that many welfare recipients are deserted mothers with children has created the major problem for reducing welfare caseloads. One British correspondent was pleased to hear a ten-year-old black American girl say she wanted to "draw" when she grew up, until he discovered she meant "drawing" welfare like mother and was not referring to artistic skill.[65] At the same time that employment for blacks has been increasing, welfare costs have also increased. Moynihan discovered this fact and included it in a controversial chart in his report.[66]

The new slogan in welfare is "stop swatting flies and start draining swamps."[67] The other version of this philosophy is

"You give a man a fish—he eats for one day. You teach a man to
fish—he eats for the rest of his life."

The current effort is to remove individuals from welfare rolls by making
them self-sufficient. If welfare is a degrading, dehumanizing process, why
do we have anyone on welfare?

For the aged, the obvious answer is a productive work history that
produces social security and pension funds adequate for a decent living
after sixty-five. For the physically handicapped, the answer is training and
employment. These categories of the poor can be handled within the
present social structure.

The hard-core problem is the deserted mother and her children. Since
around five million of those on welfare are in this category, we must be
most concerned with the AFDC cases. Whenever it is suggested that
welfare recipients be given meaningful jobs, the issue is raised as to how
one can expect mothers to work when they have small children at home.
One of the fallacies of the official statistic is that it neglects the fact that
most of the women on relief are or may be supporting men with their
relief checks. So far as I know, no study has been made to determine the
financial support of males by females on relief. In the terminology of the
ghetto, "Mother's Day" is the day the female receives her relief check, and
one can assume that men's presence when the check arrives is for a
purpose.[68]

The answer to AFDC cases is to see (1) that all able-bodied men are
gainfully employed, and (2) that these men support the children they
father. If we wish to have these fathers employed, we must first establish
effective educational and training projects. So long as relief money is
available without work, the job programs will fail.

How we make the biological fathers socially responsible is the most
difficult issue in handling AFDC cases. The middle-class girl knows how to
play the sex game so as to avoid pregnancy, to get an abortion, or to get
married. She exchanges sex favors for protection and security. The
lower-class girl cannot use sex in the same manner.

The issue is again one of social welfare policy establishing behavior we
wish to eliminate—namely, illegitimate children. How can we prevent
illegitimacy, or how can we control the parents without punishing the
illegitimate or abandoned child? We can continue to pay mothers for
illegitimate children, thus reinforcing the AFDC problem. We can take the
children from the mother, thus creating new problems while we might not
discourage illegitimacy. We can attempt to find some way to make the
males responsible for the financial support of the child, which is, of

course, the best solution. It would be foolish to suggest that just because men are employed they will volunteer to support a child which they may not want to acknowledge or may not know is their own.

Better efforts at creating family cohesion and responsibility are necessary, but this involves behavior control we now do not possess. It is obvious that social casework and counseling (verbal behavior) are not going to achieve the creation of parental responsibility. Perhaps we can solve the problem of unemployment of young ghetto males, and, if the female knows her boyfriend has financial resources, she may become more demanding in her relationship, at least to the extent of ensuring support for her children. The least we can do is to change the welfare system so that (1) men are not forced out of families, and (2) welfare payments are not cut if a member of the family works. If we follow the behavioral principles of learning, we will reinforce men for being in the family, and we will reinforce people for working, not for going on relief.

The Nixon Administration has recently announced a new welfare reform program wherein "workfare" replaces "welfare." "It removes the present incentive not to work, and substitutes an incentive to work; it removes the present incentive for families to break apart, and substitutes an incentive for families to stay together." As announced, the program relies heavily on job training and employment, and it would make employment a prerequisite to receiving welfare benefits.[69] Any proposal to make welfare recipients self-supporting individuals is a step in the right direction, providing that the behavioral means for training and motivating people to work are first found.

### Education, Welfare, and Crime

Crime is not directly related to education or welfare in the sense that undereducation or poverty causes crime. As was discussed above in Chapter 9, income seems to play a very crucial role in crime, and to the extent that undereducation contributes to lack of employment and low income, then education is a crucial variable. Income becomes a mediating variable between employment, education, family structure, and sub-cultural groups and crime. From this perspective, crime can be viewed as a substitute for employment and a means to income. Likewise, welfare is a means to income without working.

Using a basic learning theory model, we can hypothesize that behavior is a method of manipulating or adapting to the environment. There are three possible responses by which an individual can alter the environment so as to gain money: crime, welfare, or work. So long as alternatives to income are available, we will have educational and job training programs, which are weak at best. It is difficult to hold a nineteen-year-old boy in a training program if he can make $100 a day selling drugs or can defraud a poverty program for $5,000 or $10,000. Before any educational or training program is to be successful, *alternative opportunities* for money must be controlled. The poverty program has emphasized increasing legitimate opportunities, whereas it has done nothing to reduce illegal opportunities. As was noted above, delinquents are aware of the alternatives available to them, and, as Rustin observed, they select the easiest means to the greatest reward.

In the next section of the book, some ideas concerning how the environment can be altered so as to control crime and to put unemployed people in meaningful, constructive tasks will be developed.

*Summary*

The control of crime through education and jobs depends upon a theory that (1) undereducation and unemployment cause crime, and (2) we have the means to educate and make employable our hard-core ghetto youths. Neither proposition has much support in the way of empirical evidence. The argument is a social reform, moralistic argument and not a scientific argument supportable by behavioral data.

Though we have spent millions to alleviate poverty under the guise of delinquency prevention, we have neither alleviated poverty nor reduced delinquency. The model used calls for controlling criminal behavior *indirectly via* education and employment of individual delinquents. The control of crime through education demands that we influence the individual via education, which then influences his criminal behavior. We go from Z to X to Y. The model proposed herein is one of direct control over crime through environmental engineering. Such a model states that we change Y by changing X, thus gaining control over the variable we wish to change.

Programs for educating and training delinquents do not change the environment within which crimes are committed. Neither do these programs sufficiently change the environment within which education and training occur so as to significantly alter the educational, skill, and motivational levels of delinquent youths. Learning occurs only if the subject is in an environment which makes learning possible, and only when we change the environmental situations of our schools will we change the learning patterns of our school population. A science of education and training must replace a service-oriented educational and vocational training policy.

The rehabilitative ideal as expressed in educating and training delinquent youths has been a failure up to this point, and the use of these techniques as rehabilitative means holds little promise in the future as a means of crime control and prevention.

# NOTES

[1.] Belton Fleisher, *Economics of Delinquency,* Chicago: Quadrangle Press, 1966, pp. 79-81.

[2.] The President's Commission on Law Enforcement and Administration of Justice, *Juvenile Delinquency and Youth Crime,* Washington, D.C.: U.S. Government Printing Office, 1967, p. 148.

[3.] Nelson S. Burke and Alfred E. Simons, "Factors Which Precipitate Dropouts and Delinquency," *Federal Probation* (March, 1965), pp. 28-32; William E. Amos and Marilyn A. Southwell, "Dropouts: What Can Be Done," *Federal Probation* (March, 1964), pp. 30-35.

[4.] Milton F. Shore and Fortune V. Mannino, "The School Dropout Situation: An Opportunity for Constructive Intervention," *Federal Probation* (September, 1965), pp. 41-44.

[5.] Herbert C. Quay, *Juvenile Delinquency,* Princeton: D. Van Nostrand Co., 1965, p. 58.

[6.] Daniel Schreiber, "Juvenile Delinquency and the School Dropout Problem," *Federal Probation* (September, 1963), p. 18.

[7.] James S. Coleman et al., *Equality of Educational Opportunity,* Washington, D.C.: U.S. Government Printing Office, 1966; See also review symposium in *American Sociological Review* (June, 1967), pp. 475-483; Robert Dentler, "Equality of Educational Opportunity: A Special Review," *The Urban Review* (December, 1966), pp. 27-29.

[8.] Dentler, op. cit., p. 29.

[9.] U.S. Commission on Civil Rights, *Racial Isolation in the Public Schools,* Washington, D.C.: U.S. Government Printing Office, 1967, pp. 115-140.

[10.] James S. Coleman, "Toward Open Schools," *The Public Interest* (Fall, 1967), pp. 115-140.

[11.] Robert A. Dentler and Mary Ellen Warshauer, *Big City Dropouts,* Center for Urban Education, 1965, p. 64.

[12.] Ibid., p. 65.

[13.] Ibid., p. 68.

[14.] Ibid., pp. 8-9.

[15.] Committee for Economic Development, "Education in the Ghetto," *Saturday Review* (January 11, 1969), p. 33 ff.; Wallace Roberts, "The Battle for Urban Schools," *Saturday Review* (November 16, 1968).

[16.] Peter Schrag, "Education's Romantic Critics," *Saturday Review* (February 18, 1967), p. 80 ff.; Edgar Z. Friendenberg, "Requiem for the Urban School," *Saturday Review* (November 18, 1967), p. 77 ff.

[17.] Washington Post, December 19, 1965, Susan Jacoby, "National Monument to Failure," *Saturday Review* (November 18, 1967), p. 71 ff.

[18.] Washington Post, March 16, 1966; Model School Division, *Strategy for Change,* Washington, D.C., 1966.

[19.] Washington Post, October 15, 1966, and March 6, 1966; Jacoby, op. cit., p. 71 ff.

[20.] Washington Post, June 11, 1966.

[21.] Washington Post, February 11, 1967, and March 26, 1967; New York Times, April 14, 1969; See also Martin Deutsch, et al., *Social Class, Race, and Psychological Development,* New York: Holt, Rinehart, and Winston, 1968, p. 337 ff., p. 381 ff.

[22.] New York Times, November 26, 1967.

[23.] New York Times, August 20, 1967 and October 10, 1967; "The Controversy over the More Effective Schools," *Urban Review* (May, 1968), pp. 15-29.

[24.] Wall Street Journal, July 8, 1968.

[25.] *Racial Isolation in the Schools,* op. cit., p. 140; Edmund W. Gordon, "Programs of Compensatory Education," in *Social Class, Race, and Psychological Development,* op. cit., pp. 381-410.

[26.] *Juvenile Delinquency and Youth Crime*, op. cit., pp. 222-304; Bernard Bord, "Why Dropout Campaigns Fail," *Saturday Review* (September 11, 1966), p. 78 ff.

[27.] B.F. Skinner, "Why Teachers Fail," *Saturday Review* (October 16, 1965), p. 80 ff.

[28.] Buckminster Fuller, "What I Have Learned," *Saturday Review* (November 12, 1966), p. 70; Buckminster Fuller, *Education Automation,* Carbondale: Southern Illinois University Press, 1962.

[29.] James S. Coleman, "Toward Open Schools," *The Public Interest* (Fall, 1967), p. 20 ff.; Theodore Sizer, "The Case for a Free Market," *Saturday Review* (January 11, 1969), p. 34 ff.

[30.] C. Ray Jeffery, Director, "Development of a Program to Prepare Delinquents, Disadvantaged Youths, and Slow Learners for Education," U.S. Office of Education grant No. 6-85-355; C. Ray Jeffery and Ina A. Jeffery, "Delinquents and Dropouts: An Experimental Program in Behavior Change." Paper read at Annual Society of Criminology, Toronto, Canada, November, 1968; C. Ray Jeffery and Ina A. Jeffery, "Delinquents and Dropouts: An Experimental Program in Behavior Change," *Education and Urban Society,* Vol. 1, No. 3 (May, 1969), pp. 325-336.

[31.] *Juvenile Delinquency and Youth Crime,* op. cit., p. 54 ff.

[32.] Shirley Scheibla, *Poverty is Where the Money Is,* New Rochelle: Arlington House, 1968, p. 95 ff.

[33.] Washington Post, April 3, 1966.

[34.] William E. Amos, "Job Adjustment Problems of Delinquent Minority Group Youth," *Vocational Guidance Quarterly* (Winter, 1964-65), p. 87 ff.

[35.] Washington Post, April 3, 1966.

[36.] Peter Marris and Martin Rein, *Dilemmas of Social Reform,* New York: Atherton Press, 1967, pp. 73-75.

[37.] Ibid., pp. 78-79.

[38.] Ibid., pp. 83-85.

[39.] Ibid., p. 88.

[40.] Clyde E. Sullivan and Wallace Mandell, "Restoration of Youth Through Training," New York: Wakoff Research Center, 1967, p. 61.

[41.] Ibid., pp. 136-137.

[42.] Ibid., p. 137.

[43.] Washington Post, June 13, 1965; New York Times, February 4, 1968.

[44.] New York Times, February 4, 1968.

[45.] Washington Post, November 17, 1966.

[46.] Ben B. Seligman, ed., Poverty as a Public Issue, New York: Free Press, 1965; Scheibla, op. cit.

[47.] Washington Post, March 30, 1966.

[48.] New York Times, August 2, 1967.

[49.] New York Times, January 7, 1968.

[50.] New York Times, August 20, 1967.

[51.] New York Times, May 6, 1968.

[52.] Wall Street Journal, May 1, 1968, and October 8, 1968.

[53.] Wall Street Journal, October 8, 1968.

[54.] Lee Rainwater and William L. Yancey, The Moynihan Report and the Politics of Controversy, Cambridge: MIT Press, 1967, p. 441.

[55.] Harlem Youth Opportunities Unlimited, Youth in the Ghetto, New York: Orans Press, 1964, pp. 16-17.

[56.] Rainwater and Yancey, op. cit., p. 12.

[57.] Stewart Alsop, "A Conversation with Catfish," Saturday Evening Post (February 24, 1968).

[58.] Hearing before the Permanent Subcommittee on Investigations, Riots, Civil and Criminal Disorders, Washington D.C.: U.S. Government Printing Office, 1968, Parts 9, 10, 11, 12, 13.

[59.] Gerald D. Robin, "Anti-Poverty Programs and Delinquency," Journal of Criminal Law, Criminology, and Police Science, Vol. 60, No. 3 (September, 1969), pp. 323-331.

[60.] New York Times, May 27, 1968.

[61.] Gordon Brown, The Multiple Problem Dilemma, Metuchen: Scarecrow Press, 1968.

[62.] New York Times, October 4, 1967.

[63.] New York Times, October 16, 1968; November 1, 1968.

[64.] New York Times, November 12, 1968; November 29, 1967; January 11, 1969; New York Times Magazine, January 26, 1969.

[65.] New York Times, August 15, 1967.

[66.] Rainwater and Yancey, op. cit., p. 59.

[67.] George A. Brager and Francis P. Purcell, Community Action Against Poverty, New Haven: College and University Press, 1967, p. 120.

[68.] Lee Rainwater, "Crucible of Identity: The Negro Lower-Class Family," in Education and Social Crisis, edited by Everett T. Keach, et al., New York: John Wiley and Sons, 1967, pp. 98-127.

[69.] New York Times, August 9, 1969.

A NEW MODEL: CRIME CONTROL

THROUGH ENVIRONMENTAL ENGINEERING

*Chapter 11*

## Environmental Control of Behavior

*Introduction*

Behaviorism and environmentalism have emerged in recent years to challenge earlier theoretical approaches to the study of human behavior. The newer behavioral sciences include such fields as information theory, cybernetics, game theory, decision theory, and systems analysis. These newer analytic approaches share certain basic assumptions.[1]

(1) Scientific methodology is emphasized, in contrast with an ethical or clinical approach, limiting observations and conclusions to objective, observable behavior which can be empirically verified.

(2) The approach is interdisciplinary, cutting across old academic boundaries and borrowing freely from each. The human being is regarded as a total system—biological, psychological, and social.

(3) The human being is regarded as an input-output system, capable of receiving messages from and responding to the environment. Communications, cybernetics, and feedback are critical concepts.

(4) Adaptation of the organism to the environment is the key process. Behavior is viewed as the means by which the organism adapts to an environmental system.

(5) A systems approach is used wherein emphasis is placed on the interrelatedness of parts, structural-functional analysis, and the consequences of action in one component of the system for the system in general.

(6) Future consequences of action, rather than past experiences or variables, is emphasized in behaviorism and in decision theory.

Such a model of behavior is dynamic rather than static; i.e., the impact of the past as contained in living in an urban area as a young adult Negro can be explained only in terms of a decision theory model where the future consequences of action are considered.

*Behavior: Physical or Mental*

Since the time of Plato, Western man has divided the world into physical and mental, body and mind. Those philosophers who placed primacy on the mental became rationalists; those who placed primacy on the physical became empiricists.

Rationalism held sway in philosophy until the seventeenth century, with its emphasis on logic, formal proof, ideas, deduction, and rational processes. Empiricism developed from the seventeenth century on, with its emphasis on sensory data, experience, induction, and scientific method. The physical sciences developed empirically through the methods of science. The social sciences (sociology, psychology, anthropology, history, government, economics) developed two methodologies, one following the mentalistic approach, one following the physical. The mentalistic approach was given prominence in the German social science movement by Dilthey and Weber who used an introspective (Verstehen) approach to social sciences. The core of introspectionism is mental states revealed by placing oneself in the situation of another and imagining how the other person must feel.[2] Hilgard[3] has summarized these schools in this manner:

> In the nineteenth century before experimental psychology proper began, two theories of the mind competed for psychologists' support. The one, known as *faculty psychology,* was a doctrine of mental powers. According to this theory, the mind had a few principal faculties such as thinking, feeling, and willing, that accounted for its activities. . . .Careful students were dissatisfied with the doctrine of faculties because it explained nothing, but merely classified mental activities.

> The association psychologists held a second, opposing theory. They denied inborn faculties of the mind; instead, they limited the mind's content to ideas coming by way of the senses. They explained all mental activity through this association of ideas. . .much of learning theory, especially the theory of conditioned responses, is similar to earlier association theory, except that now we believe that stimuli and responses rather than ideas are associated.

> In order to make psychology a science, Watson said, its data must be open to public inspection like the data of any other science. When a rat runs a maze you can take a motion picture of its movements and any competent person can check your statement about the order in which it entered the blind alleys. So long as you study what the animal or person does or what he accomplishes, then you have an *objective science* distinct from the *subjective science* to which introspection limits you. Behavior is public; consciousness is private.

Science should deal with public facts. . . .The advantage of the S-R formulation is that it repeatedly reminds the psychologist that he must anchor his explanations of behavior in the real world—in the world of stimuli, at the beginning of the causal chain, and in the world of responses, at the end of the chain. He thus shares with behaviorism the desire to relate psychological principles to the same sort of events that are studied in other sciences.

Handy and Kurtz[4] write:

Under this interpretation of behavioral science emphasis is on both *behavior* and *science,* and when the behavioral scientist maintains that he is studying man's behavior, he is saying that he will use systematic observation as the basic method of his investigation. . . . Rather what is essential is the rule that all hypothesis be experimentally confirmed by reference to publicly observable changes in behavior.

Introspectionism is found in the work of Cooley, G.H. Mead, W.I. Thomas, MacIver, Znaniecki, Freud, and most clinical and social psychologists.

The empirical tradition is found in the positivism of Comte and Durkheim, and today in the writings of Lundberg, B.F. Skinner, and Homans. The core of empiricism is the study of behavior as a physical phenomenon.[5]

The mentalistic approach emphasizes man as a thinking, feeling, and willing animal. Cognition, affection, and volition are key concepts in mentalistic psychology. As a result, many concepts (intervening variables) are used to explain behavior, such as ego, id, super-ego, self, attitudes, and values.

The behaviorists want to establish a science of behavior based on objective rather than subjective introspective events which are private in nature and not subject to scientific verification. Behavior, rather than inferred mental states, is the object of study. This view regards man as a *receiving, processing,* and *responding* system.

Introspectionist psychology is related to the traditions of philosophy and humanism. It regards behavior as a product of an internal mental state of cognition, emotion, or volition. Some psychology departments are joined with philosophy, thus showing the historic origins of this tradition.

Behavioristic psychology is related to the biological sciences. Such psychology regards behavior as a product of the interaction of organism and environment via the nervous system. Laboratory work is emphasized, and, in some universities, the psychology department is a part of the division of biological sciences, rather than of philosophy.

Freud, the father of modern clinical psychology, was an M.D. trained in neurology. He became interested in behavioral disorders as part of his clinical practice in neurology, and one of the most interesting facts is that he shifted from the nervous system to the psyche to explain many of these disorders. If he found a brain lesion or other organic defect, he assumed that behavior was caused by physical conditions; if he found no physical defect, he assumed the condition was functional, not organic—i.e., a product of mental conflict and anxiety. We now have two classes of diseases—mental diseases and physical diseases. We can now talk about a "sick mind" as if the mind exists as an entity and is subject to illness or disease.

As was pointed out above, we now have the "myth of mental illness," and some writers have argued that the analogy between mental and physical illness is a poor one at best (see Chapter 8).[6] When the brain surgeon operates on the brain, he finds nerve tissue and a blood supply, not an ego or self or cognitive process. The organization of behavior as a neurological product is now well recognized in physiology and neurology, though not in most aspects of psychology and sociology. McCulloch and Pitts[7] have written

> both the formal and the final aspects of that activity which we are wont to call mental are rigorously deductible from present neurophysiology. . . .Certainly for the psychiatrist it is more to the point that in such systems "mind" no longer "goes more ghostly than a ghost." Instead, diseased mentality can be understood without loss of scope or rigor, in the scientific terms of neurophysiology.

McConnell[8] in a most critical article, has noted:

> A hundred years ago, the biological sciences were still caught up in a similar kind of spiritualism. In those days it was thought that you got sick not because there were germs in your body, but because you had somehow fallen from grace. Biology could not become a science, nor medicine, a successful art, until we got the animus out of animals, until we were ready to accept the revolutionary idea that man's body was nothing more than a biological machine whose workings could pretty well be understood without reference to a spiritual motivating force. All of the magic of modern medicine stems from this one small but radical belief in biomechanics. As long as physicians believed the body to be merely the temple of the soul and hence inviolable, there could be no heart transplants, no antibiotics, no cure for cancer.

But until very recently we have still insisted that man's behavior, his mentality, his personality, could not be explained in purely objective terms. Our language, our laws, our pattern of morality are all based on spiritual, nonscientific concepts. No wonder we have huge mental hospitals. No wonder we still have wars, riots, and murders. In most respects, we are still in the dark ages as far as the science of psychology is concerned. This almost unnoticed revolution now underway in the behavioral science is the same one that took place three centuries ago in astronomy and physics, a hundred years ago in biology and medicine. Today's revolutionary concept is that man's behavior can be studied and explained, in objective terms without any necessary reference to supernatural or spiritual or mentalistic entities. "Mind" is as useless an explanatory concept to today's scientific psychologist as the mystical element "phylogestion" that chemists once believed caused fires. . . .Indeed my own prediction is the fields of psychiatry and psychology will change as much in the next twenty years as the field of transportation has changed in the last fifty.

### Physical Basis of Behavior

From a scientific point of view, behavior is a product of the interaction of organism and environment. A biologist has defined behavior:

> The bulk of the functioning of any enduring system is displacement-correcting responses. Here is the negative feedback of engineering or the adaptive or self regulating or homeostatic response of physiology. All organisms maintain themselves in a dynamic or flux equilibrium by mobilizing internal reserves to oppose environmentally imposed change; or, more vigorously, each unit responds to loads imposed on it by its environment.[9]

The organism is so constructed as to receive signals or messages from the environment and to respond to these signals via behavior. Behavior is a mediating process, or the way in which the organism adjusts or adapts to the environment. Through behavior, the organism eats, drinks, reproduces, breathes, avoids extreme temperatures, creates pleasant sounds, colors and forms, communicates with other human beings, and so forth.

The human organism is an input-output process. There are three essential aspects to the process: input or receptors, organization or connections, and output or effectors. The input system consists of specialized sensory organs which are sensitive to specific properties of the environment. The eye is sensitive to light, the ear to sound, the skin to pressure, the nose to gases, and so forth. Through these receptor systems we make contact with the environment. The sensory organs are energy converters in that they convert stimulation from the environment into chemical processes that in turn produce nervous impulses. Light striking the eye produces a chemical change in the retina which then produces a nerve impulse in the optic nerve to the brain.

The connectors, or nervous system, consist of three classes. The afferent nerves carry impulses from the sense organs to the central nervous system. The nerve cells or centers store impulses, organize impulses, and in some biochemical manner fire or activate outgoing nerve impulses. This is the least understood process of the nervous system; however, we do know that it is a biochemical process. The glial cells manufacture protein in reaction to stimulation and are thereby the source of memory and future behavior. New brain proteins are formed whenever the human being learns from experience, and these proteins are behavior-sensitive; that is, these proteins produce nerve impulses which in turn produce muscle changes (behavior). Today serious research is being conducted into the biochemistry of learning, the process by which physical events from the environment are transmitted to the brain, produce protein in brain cells and then activate neural activity to muscles. A new brain protein called taraxein has been found in the cerebrospinal fluid of schizophrenic patients.

Kretch and others have been working on the biochemical foundations of learning.[10]

> The major hypothesis concerning intraneuronal chemical changes states that individual memory is carried by the structure of the RNA within the neurons. This hypothesis assumes that neural activity can change the detailed chemical structure of the RNA within the neurons involved in a given learning experience. Experience of the individual would thus be laid down in the details of the chemistry of the RNA in his neurons, much as the experience of his ancestors is reflected in the chemistry of the DNA.

The efferent nerves carry impulses from the central nervous system to the muscles and glands, the effectors. The efferent system consists of the corticospinal and extrapyramidal motor systems. The central nervous system controls the striated or large muscles involved in voluntary activities; the autonomic nervous system controls the smooth muscles and glands: the heart, visceral organs, and the like. The responses in which social scientists are interested are those involving the central nervous system and the striated muscles.[11]

*Models of Behavior*

The model of behavior herein developed is empirical and physical, and it places emphasis upon adaptation of the organism to the environment. Communication with the environment is possible via an input system (nervous system) and an output system (muscular reponses). The two models of behavior discussed above can be diagrammed as follows:

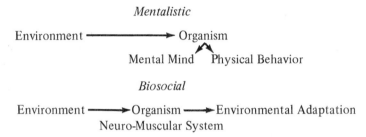

*Mentalistic*

Environment ⟶ Organism

Mental Mind    Physical Behavior

*Biosocial*

Environment ⟶ Organism ⟶ Environmental Adaptation
Neuro-Muscular System

We have placed the environment at both ends of an E–O–E arc because the behavior of an organism is a product of both past environmental conditions and future environmental conditions as modified by or as a consequence of the behavior. The emphasis is on the future consequences of behavior, not the past. A great deal of behavioral science thinking concentrates on past experiences and ignores future consequences of behavior.[12] Psychoanalytic theory has traditionally interpreted behavior as a present response to past experiences (a problem at age twenty-five is a result of a traumatic experience at age five). Sociological theory, as we reviewed it above, explains criminality in terms of past environmental experiences (urban areas, poverty, broken homes, delinquent subcultures, criminal associations). Lawyers typically are oriented to past decisions and traditions rather than to future consequences of legal processes.

Behavior is a decision process, based on past and present experiences, which are used to adapt to the environment through changing the environment of the future. The goal-oriented aspect of behavior is often described as will, thought, or values. Here, however, the term "goal-oriented" only means empirically observable consequences of behavior. Bently[13] discussed this issue: "The behaviors are present events conveying pasts into futures. They cannot be reduced to successions of instants nor to successions of locations. They themselves span extensions and duration. The pasts and the futures are rather phases of behavior than its control."

G. Sommerhof, in an article on purpose and adaptation, uses the following diagram:

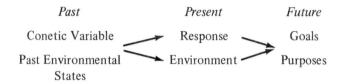

|  |  |  |
|:---:|:---:|:---:|
| *Past* | *Present* | *Future* |
| Conetic Variable | Response | Goals |
| Past Environmental States | Environment | Purposes |

Sommerhof[14] makes it clear that in discussing behavior in relation to future goals, he is not reintroducing a teleological argument. "There is nothing teleological in the sense of the future determining the present through some form of final causation. Its mode of operation is strictly mechanical and deterministic." Kretch, Crutchfield, and Livson[15] write that

> developmental determinants or antecedents of any given behavior never operate at a distance magically bridging the chasm in time. At any point in a person's life there necessarily exists some current representation of each developmental process. Whatever can influence our behavior and experience at a particular moment—whether nature or nurture, genes or early childhood events—can do so, in theory and in practice, only because these developmental determinants have some real, current existence in the organism.

### Behavioral Psychology

Throughout the history of human thought, the idea of pain and pleasure as determinants of human behavior has been prominent. Bentham expressed this idea in his political philosophy, and Freud made it a part of twentieth-century psychology in his theory of the id (the pleasure principle) and super-ego (the punishing principle).

Modern experimental psychology has developed the beginnings of a science of human behavior by studying under controlled conditions the relationship between behavior and the environment. Behavior is adaptation of the organism to the environment. Such adaptive behavior is called *operant* or *instrumental* behavior, since it operates on the environment or is instrumental in changing or controlling the environment.[16]

Environmental conditions related to a given response can be viewed as cues or signals for behavior (called discriminative conditions or stimuli) or as consequences which follow as a result of behavior (rewarding or punishing conditions).

If the interaction between organism and environment produces an *increase* in the behavior of the organism, the process is called *reinforcement* (reward), since it strengthens behavior. If the interaction between organism and environment produces a *decrease* in behavior, the process is called *punishment,* since it weakens behavior.

Behavior can be positive or negative; positive if it produces a stimulus to affect the organism, negative if it removes a stimulus which was affecting the organism. Taking food into the mouth or turning on an electric light are examples of positive reinforcement; taking an aspirin to remove a headache or closing a window to keep out cold air are examples of negative reinforcement. Receiving a shock from touching a wire is an example of positive punishment; losing money or food are examples of negative punishment. We use positive punishment when we spank a child; we use negative punishment when we take away candy or ice cream from a child (see chapter 3 for a discussion of punishment).

The relationship between behavior and environment can be placed in a paradigm as follows:

| Response Rate | Environmental Change | Label |
|---|---|---|
| Up | $S^r$ | positive reinforcement |
| Up | $S^{\bar{a}}$ | negative reinforcement |
| Down | $S^{\bar{r}}$ | negative punishment |
| Down | $S^a$ | positive punishment |

In this paradigm, $S^r$ represents a reinforcing stimulus (reward), $S^a$ an aversive stimulus, and $S^{\bar{r}}$ or $S^{\bar{a}}$ represents the removal of a stimulus.

The difficulty of defining the stimulus independent of the response has been a cause of concern, since a stimulus is reinforcing only if the response rate increases, and what increases a response rate is a reinforcing stimulus.[17] This tautological dilemma can be resolved if we refrain from defining stimuli and behavior as independent variables, but rather define punishment and reinforcement as the resultant interaction of the organism and the environment. The behavior can be viewed as approaching or withdrawing from the environment, or as initiating or terminating given environmental conditions.[18] The crucial concept is that of contingencies, or the rules that specify the consequences behavior will have for the behaving individual.[19]

*Reinforcement of Criminal Behavior*

If we regard reinforcement as a critical aspect of learning, and if we regard the future consequences of behavior likewise as critical, then we must look for the future reinforcements contingent upon criminal behavior. Rather than interpreting criminal behavior indirectly in terms of variables other than the behavior itself (ego frustration, self-concepts, subcultural systems, differential association), we feel it preferable to explain behavior directly in terms of the behavior itself. When a person behaves criminally, it is because of the immediate consequence of the behavior. The usual consequence is property, such as money, jewelry, or cars. Up to ninety-five percent of the felony offenses are property offenses, emphasizing the material reward component of criminal behavior. Such a consequence has been labeled *positive reinforcement.* The material consequences of most criminal acts are obvious, and the advantage of viewing criminality in terms of its direct consequences is that two variables (behavior and environmental changes) can be directly linked in a scientifically sound manner. This theoretical approach also allows one to explain the criminal behavior of the wealthy (white-collar and organized crime), or of those who are normal by psychiatric classification, of those who are educated and employed, and of those who do not belong to a delinquent subcultural group.

Crimes against the person, such as murder, assault, and rape, do not fit the *positive* reinforcement model. Although rape has the component of positive sexual gratification, in some instances rape also includes the component of aggression and anger. Rape cases should be differentiated as to (1) those instances involving a friend or relative, where opportunity plus enticement by the victim are involved, and (2) those instances involving a stranger, where brute force is used. Studies have shown that in many cases rape involves people known to one another, is planned, and little force or resistance is offered.[20] Rape involving a friend who may be a contributor to the behavior of the criminal is a case of positive reinforcement. Where force and violence are used, negative reinforcement may be involved.

In cases of murder and assault, negative reinforcement is obviously involved. An aversive stimulus can lead to a withdrawal response or an aggressive response. Azrin and Holz[21] differentiate two types of aggression. Operant aggression occurs when the aggression is directed toward a punishing individual or situation. Elicited aggression occurs when the aggression is directed blindly at the environment as a general response to aversive stimulation. (We kick a chair or the dog when we are angry.)

Such aggression is generalized to the environment rather than being focused on a specific individual.

Many murders are committed by friends or relatives of the victim and are often precipitated by the victim.[22] These acts (except for murder committed for money) are a response to a punishing or aversive stimulus. Aggression is a response to punishment, since it removes or terminates the punishing stimulus.[23]

The commission of a criminal act also involves the potential consequence of punishment. The gain from the criminal act must be weighed against the risk of punishment, and, as has been emphasized above, the risk factor is low in most instances.

Criminal behavior, then, involves four elements:

(1)  the reinforcement available from the criminal act;

(2)  the risk involved in the commission of the crime;

(3)  the past conditioning history of the individual involved;

(4)  the opportunity structure to commit the act.

The basic proposition of gain minus risk is not enough, for the response of the individual to a stimulus situation is dependent upon his past experience with the stimulus. A car is not a reinforcing stimulus to a teenager in the absence of a certain conditioning history with respect to automobiles. Stealing a car is not a risky situation unless the individual has experienced risk in such a situation. The argument that behaviorism is faulty because individuals do not respond in the same way to the same stimulus is based on a misconception of behaviorism. Individuals do respond differently to similar situations (the so-called differential response pattern) because each individual brings to a situation a different history of conditioning. The stimulus does not determine the response (as the critics are prone to argue), but, rather, the response is a result of the anticipated consequences of the response in the future based on past experiences.

The fourth variable, the opportunity to commit the crime, also relates to differential response patterns, since an individual will not behave criminally until a criminal opportunity presents itself in the environment. Whereas criminologists are inclined to regard criminal behavior as something carried around within the criminal, a more accurate presentation would be to say that crime is located in the environment, not in the individual. There are no criminals, only environmental circumstances which result in criminal behavior. Given the proper environmental structure, anyone will be a criminal or a noncriminal.

Criminal behavior can be represented as gain (G) minus risk (R) plus interaction with conditioning history (CH) plus interaction with environmental opportunity (EO). In order to change criminal behavior, we must change the environment (not rehabilitate the criminal) by (1) decreasing the reinforcement available from criminal acts, and (2) increasing the risk involved in criminal acts. The prevention of crime depends upon these two aspects of environmental engineering, especially the first.

### Social Rewards versus Material Rewards

As was discussed in Chapter 7, the sociologist views crime as a product of differential association with people who support antisocial behaviors. Interpersonal relations are regarded as the crucial element in behavior. This argument ignores the material reinforcement available from a criminal act, and it also ignores the extent to which social reinforcement is secondary reinforcement—e.g., dependent on primary reinforcement for its effectiveness.

The delinquent gang can reinforce criminal behavior (1) by not punishing the delinquent act, and (2) by giving verbal approval of the delinquent behavior. The major issue is whether criminal behavior is maintained (1) by the response of other people to the behavior, or (2) by the consequences of the criminal act itself—i.e., money, car, or sexual gratification resulting from the crime. Placed in the terminology of behavioral psychology, is a *material* reward more or less effective than a *social* reward in maintaining and controlling behavior? Human beings act as agents by which reinforcement takes place. Krasner and Ullman refer to this as *social* reinforcement.[24] A mother feeds her baby; a father gives his son an allowance or use of the family car; an employer gives money to an employee; a male and female exchange sex, money, and affection. Homans has developed the theory that all social interaction is based on an exchange model; that is, one party behaves in a certain way in order to get a certain response from another party. We do things for others in anticipation that they will do things for us.[25]

The argument, then, is to what extent social reinforcement (interaction with other human beings) is in itself reinforcing (primary reinforcement) or to what extent social reinforcement depends on other reinforcement (material-physical rewards). In organizational theory, the Human Relations School of Mayo, Dewey, Lewin, Roethlisberger, and Dickson emphasized social rewards—prestige, status symbols, friendship, and social groupings; whereas the Scientific Management School of Taylor and others emphasized material or economic rewards—salaries, lighting, heating, physical surroundings.[26]

The Human Relations School bases its judgment of the superiority of social to material rewards on the classical Hawthorne studies in Chicago from 1927 to 1932, wherein it was discovered that while increasing illumination did not increase productivity, social groupings and informal group norms did. From this study, the investigators concluded that social rewards of affection and respect were more crucial in altering behavior than were economic rewards of money.[27] This study has so colored behavioral science thinking that we now have what is known in research as the "Hawthorne effect," the effect of the experimenter's interest and concern on the outcome of the research; that is, a person may change not because of therapy but because someone has shown interest in him. In other words, any program would produce the same results regardless of procedures, simply because the program itself is rewarding via attention and concern.

The argument can be raised whether social rewards (attention and concern) rather than material rewards govern the behavior of human beings. Etzioni[28] has written that:

> for symbolic rewards to be effective the recipient must first identify with the granting organization and, even more important, the symbols must be appreciated by the recipient's significant other—by his wife, friends, neighbors. For these reasons, social rewards are less effective in controlling blue-collar than white-collar workers, and low ranking than high ranking employees. . . .Although social rewards have been proven important in organizations, this does not reduce the importance of material rewards. A survey conducted by the federal government of 514 plants where wage incentive plans were introduced showed that, on the average, production increased 38.99 percent and labor costs decreased 11.58 percent. In another case, an hourly wage differential of about 30 percent led many steel workers to exchange their comparatively non-repetitive, skilled, autonomous jobs for assembly line jobs which lacked these qualities but paid more.

Etzioni[29] divides the means of control into physical punishment, material rewards, and symbolic social rewards. Though Etzioni states that social rewards generate more commitment than material rewards, his statement quoted above must be regarded as crucial, since there he notes that social rewards are not too effective with lower-class individuals, the population most involved in the criminal process, and social rewards for middle- and upper-class individuals in all likelihood are effective only when material rewards are retained at the same time and at a given level.

Douvan[30] found that material rewards are more effective than social rewards with lower-class children when compared to middle-class children.

In a recent review of the Hawthorne studies, Alex Carey notes that the evidence reported by the investigators supports the view that material and financial reward is the principal influence on behavior. Carey presents evidence that output was not increased by presentation of friendliness and free supervision, but only by increments in the monetary rewards. Carey[31] asks, "How is it possible for studies so nearly devoid of scientific merit, and conclusions so little supported by evidence, to gain so influential and respected a place within scientific disciplines and to hold this place for so long?"

The belief in social rewards has been furthered not only by Human Relations Management, but by psychoanalytic therapy, especially as practiced by social caseworkers and by permissive educators. Today we are not only beginning to question the scientific evidence for the Hawthorne effect, as did Carey, but also the scientific evidence suggesting the value of permissive education and love therapy. Certainly the treatment of delinquents with kindness has failed to make an impression on changing delinquent behavior.

### Behavior Therapy

There has developed in recent years an approach to behavioral change based on learning theory and the principles of reinforcement. As McConnell[32] has stated:

> For more than a century now, psychology has been defined as the science of the mind. And, of course, those people who have psychological problems are those people who suffer, we say, from "mental illness." But stop and think about it for a moment: the mind is a very elusive quality. You cannot see it, feel it, or measure its functions directly. People get into insane asylums not because they have a "mental" illness but because they have started acting pretty peculiarly. We say they have a sick "mind" but that is just an inference we make, an explanantion we offer for their "sick" behavior. It is the behavior that bothers us, not the mind. Psychiatrists often state that they try to cure a mental condition they presumed caused the "sick" behavior, but it's clear none of their techniques work very well. So a new viewpoint, a very simple but a very radical viewpoint, has developed. If we cannot cure the

"mind" maybe we can cure the behavior. In fact, maybe that's all there is to "cure." Maybe "mental illness' is a myth—maybe what is wrong with most patients is that they have learned bad or "sick" behavior patterns. And if they have *learned* those patterns, they can be induced to *unlearn* them if we go about things in the right way.

The prime reason that the new behavioral therapies work is that they are based on scientific experimentation rather than on the humanistic speculation that underlies most other forms of therapy. Physicists made one of their greatest breakthroughs when they stopped hunting for "spirits" and began looking at the behavior of the objects in the physical world, for the laws of mechanics are incompatible with spiritualism. The biologists made their greatest breakthrough when they realized that the workings of the human body were explainable in purely mechanical terms, that the physiological "behavior" of the liver, or the brain, can be understood without resort to spiritualism. If we take a lesson from physics and biology, if we begin to focus our attention on the *behavior* of the human organism rather than on the *mind,* our whole perspective changes. We begin to realize that while we cannot see "mind" or measure it directly in any way, we can see behavior, we can touch it and measure it—and we can control it.

Sherman and Baer have succinctly summarized the differences between traditional therapy and behavior therapy as follows[33]:

If psychology is the study of behavior, then psychotherapy is the modification of problem behavior, usually through environmental manipulation. In most conventional psychotherapies this environmental manipulation has been attempted in regularly repeated therapy sessions during which the therapist and patient interact. Traditionally this interaction is verbal; its purpose is to establish a "relationship" between the two through which the deviant behavior of the patient eventually will be changed. The techniques of traditional psychotherapy, in general, are based upon four assumptions: (1) Deviant problem behavior grows out of a maladaptive personality state (commonly anxiety). (2) The maladaptive personality state is a result of faulty early interpersonal relationships. (3) Since the personality state is causal to behavior, durable modification of the behavior cannot be obtained without prior changes in this state. (4) Verbal behavior is an expression of the underlying personality state and also can serve as a medium for the modification of it.

Recently, unconventional psychotherapies have appeared under the label of "behavior therapy" or "behavior modification." Many of these therapies result from the work of investigators who are students primarily of what people do, not what they think, feel, or wish. Consequently, a very different set of assumptions underlies the behavior therapies: (1) An individual may be viewed simply as the sum total of the behaviors which he emits. (2) There are general principles which describe the relationship of those behaviors to the environment; these principles emphasize the power of current environmental events. (3) Deviant, problem behavior is not different in quality than [sic] behavior in general, and thus it can be changed by the techniques already known to be applicable to other more ordinary behaviors. (4) Somewhat redundantly with the preceding three assumptions, it is neither necessary nor realistic to hypothesize a deeper level of behavioral function than the environmental events known to operate in current behavioral techniques. Behavior modification thus is a changing of overt behavior, not of an underlying personality state; the environmental manipulations applied typically are performed directly upon the deviant behavior.

In summary, then, it appears that there are five basic environmental manipulations which can be applied to the development, maintenance, or change of operant behavior: two reinforcement contingencies, two punishment contingencies, and extinction. Thus, operant therapy is primarily an enterprise in programming reinforcing consequences for desirable behaviors and eliminating the reinforcement for or punishing the undesirable behaviors. Correspondingly, the bulk of this review of behavior therapy studies will be organized in terms of these elemental contingencies, as they encompass the most functional logic of operant behavior therapy available.

Behavioral therapy works by rewarding desired behavior and by punishing undesired behavior. Reinforcement principles have been used to treat schizophrenics in a mental hospital. Ayllon treated a patient who hoarded towels by saturating her with towels, that is, giving her towels throughout the day. Nurses were instructed not to reinforce patients who engaged in psychotic talk; rather the patients were reinforced for normal talk. Patients were also reinforced for cleaning their rooms, getting to the dining room on time, or taking care of their personal needs.[34] Neurotic behaviors such as tics, enuresis, hysterical blindness, and stuttering have been controlled by such behavioral procedures. Eysenck[35] and his associates have engaged in behavioral therapy in England for a number of years now. Wolpe[36] has developed behavioral therapy in terms of what he calls "reciprocal inhibition." This system of conditioning uses the concept of an incompatible response, that is, it replaces the undesired response with one that is incompatible with it. Wolpe treats neurotic fear or anxiety in this manner. A persons who is afraid of a given thing (a cat, for example) will be placed in a situation where the cat is present, but also present is an inhibiting stimulus, such as music or food or the voice of the therapist. Wolpe also used the principle of successive approximation. He may at first use the word "cat" or a picture of a cat, then next a piece of fur-like material, then a cat in the room, then the subject approaches the cat gradually over a period of days, and finally the patient may actually touch the cat. In this way a new response to cats is established through gradual experiences of a positive nature toward cats. The patient relearns to respond to his environment. We use these principles in training children who are afraid of water to swim. We take the child to the pool, allow him to touch the water, to place his feet in the water, to stand in water, and finally to place his face in the water. Professor Lovaas of UCLA has used behavioral therapy to reshape the behavior of autistic children. He uses food to reinforce the child who otherwise avoids contact with adult human beings. Lovaas also uses punishment, an electric shock, to develop human contact—i.e., human contact removes the electric shock. Professor McConnell[37] has stated in regard to the work of Lovaas:

How shall we view the use of punishment in psychotherapy? Who was right about Greg? The kind and gentle persons who gave him love and affection and understanding and thereby kept him strapped to a bed for seven long and horrible years—or the seemingly heartless scientist who stopped Greg's self-destructive tendencies in seven short, painful minutes. Is it kind to keep patients locked up for years in bleak, grey wards when being momentarily strict or even cruel to them will help get them out of hospitals in weeks or days or even minutes. . . .The pioneering work of Lovaas and the other behaviorists is no more than the first tentative step toward turning psychology and psychiatry into scientific disciplines.

A type of therapy directly related to behavioral therapy is reality therapy. Dr. William Glasser[38] discusses reality therapy as a set of procedures for establishing responsibility in the patient for his behavior. The patient must realize the consequences of his behavior, and he must realize that there are alternative behaviors he can engage in which will result in different consequences. The important thing is to attach punishment to the undesirable behaviors and rewards to the desirable behaviors. Reality therapy is based on the proposition the subject must face the real consequences or outcome of his behavior.

The major difference between clinical and behavior therapy is that the clinical therapist regards behavior as a *symptom* of an underlying problem, whereas the behavior therapist regards the *behavior* as the problem with which he must deal. The clinician wishes to reach the motives behind the behavior through insight into feelings of anger, frustration, and guilt, and therapy is based on self-control through expanded understanding, through verbal behavior. Behavior therapy, on the other hand, through counter-conditioning, conditioned avoidance, extinction, and behavior shaping deals directly with behavior.[39] Self-control for the clinician is replaced by environmental control for the behaviorist. "The therapist does not have direct control over the important rewards and punishments in the patient's environment."[40] The clinician does not deal with criminal behavior; he deals with psychic conflict and motives. The sociologist does not deal with criminal behavior; he deals with poverty, racial discrimination, unemployment, and delinquent associations. The behaviorist regards criminal behavior as the problem with which he must deal.

### Behavioral Engineering for the Future

The progress now starting in the science of human behavior, as witnessed in physiological and psychopharmacological studies of behavior, as well as the development of learning theories, may have a major impact in the world of tomorrow. The science and technology of behavior will be developed to the point where the major behavioral disorders can be brought under control.

The real value of such science is that it will be possible to design an environment in which children are reared in such a way that behavioral disorders are not produced (reinforced). We should be able to train parents to control their children without resort to either punishment (withdrawal of love or physical attacks) or to improper reinforcement (giving the child his own way or giving love and physical objects when the child misbehaves). A child who throws a temper tantrum and then gets his way with his parents and a teenager who lives away from home in Greenwich Village smoking pot in his pad with his girlfriend while his parents supply him with money are examples of situations where the environment (parents in these cases) reinforce undesirable behaviors. We know our youths are not educated because they lack motivation (reinforcement). We know our social welfare services are a failure because they perpetuate dependency and poverty (they reinforce people for not working). What is suggested here is that we completely overhaul the environments in which behavior occurs in order to prevent in the future the types of behavior we wish to control (poverty, crime, alcoholism, mental illness, and the like).

*Summary*

A new approach to human behavior is emerging in the form of behaviorism and environmentalism in place of the introspective, mentalistic clincial approach of former years. Behavior is studied within the framework of science, is regarded as a biophysical phenomenon explainable in the same terms as other natural events, and is regarded as an adaptive process to environmental conditions.

Behavior is future-oriented, not past-oriented. A man steals because by so behaving he can have a car or money in the future, not because in the past he experienced psychic trauma or a broken home or poverty or delinquent associates. Criminal behavior can be explained directly in terms of the consequences of the behavior, and not indirectly in terms of noncriminal variables such as poverty, race, or social class. Criminal behavior is therefore viewed as the problem to be dealt with, and not symptomatic of other problems—i.e., poverty, inner mental conflict, class conflict, unemployment, or undereducation. To change criminal behavior we must deal directly with criminal behavior by removing the environmental reinforcement which maintains the behavior.

## NOTES

[1.] Rollo Handy and Paul Kurtz, *A Current Appraisal of the Behavioral Sciences,* Great Barrington: Behavioral Research Council, 1964; Alfred de Grazia, Rollo Handy, E.C. Harwood, and Paul Kurtz, *The Behavioral Sciences: Essays in Honor of George A. Lundberg,* Great Barrington: Behavioral Research Council, 1968: James C. Charlesworth, ed., *Contemporary Political Analysis,* New York: Free Press, 1968; Van Court Hare, Jr., Systems Analysis: *A Diagnostic Approach,* New York: Harcourt, Brace and World, 1967; David W. Miller and Martin K. Starr, *Executive Decisions and Operations Research,* Englewood Cliffs: Prentice Hall, 1960; Ralph Deutsch, *Systems Analysis Techniques,* Englewood Cliffs: Prentice Hall, 1969; George R. Cooper and Clare D. McGillem, *Methods of Signal and System Analysis,* New York: Holt, Rinehart and Winston, 1967; Guillermo Owen, *Game Theory,* Philadelphia: W.B. Saunders Co., 1968; Morton D. Davis, *Game Theory,* New York: Basic Books, 1970; A.M. Slickman, *An Introduction to Linerar Programming and the Theory of Games,* New York: John Wiley and Sons, 1963; Henri Theil *Operations Research and Quantitative Economics,* New York: McGraw-Hill Book Co., 1965.

[2.] Don Martindale, *The Nature and Types of Sociological Theory,* Boston: Houghton Mifflin Co., 1960, p. 377 ff.; George Simpson, *Man in Society,* Garden City: Doubleday and Co., 1955, p. 49 ff.; Roscoe C. and Gisela J. Hinkle, *The Development of Modern Sociology,* New York: Random House, 1954, p. 52 ff.

[3.] Ernest R. Hilgard, *Introduction to Psychology,* 3rd ed., New York: Harcourt, Brace, and World, 1962, pp. 14-18.

[4.] Handy and Kurtz, op. cit., p. 6; de Grazia, Handy, Harwood, and Kurtz, op. cit., pp. 63-85.

[5.] B.F. Skinner, *Science and Human Behavior,* New York: Macmillan Co., 1953; Arthur and Carolyn Staats, *Complex Human Behavior,* New York: Holt, Rinehart and Winston, 1963; Werner K. Honig, *Operant Behavior,* New York: Appleton-Century-Crofts, 1966; George C. Homans, *Social Behavior,* New York: Harcourt, Brace, and World, 1961.

[6.] Thomas Szasz, *The Myth of Mental Illness,* New York: Hoeber-Harper, 1961.

[7.] Walter Buckley, ed., *Modern Systems Research for the Behavioral Scientist,* Chicago: Aldine Publishing Co., 1968 p. 96.

[8.] James V. McConnell, "Psychoanalysis Must Go," *Esquire,* October 1968, p. 176 ff.

[9.] Buckley, op. cit., p. 55.

[10.] David Kretch, Richard S. Crutchfield, and Norman Livson, *Elements of Psychology,* New York: Alfred A. Knopf, 1969, p. 471.

[11.] Lloyd Woodbourne, *The Neural Basis of Behavior,* Columbus: Charles E. Merrill, 1967; Philip Teitelbaum, *Physiological Psychology,* Englewood Cliffs: Prentice Hall, 1967; David Peskman, "The Search for the Memory Molecule," *New York Times Magazine,* July 7, 1968; *Time Magazine,* May 17, 1968.

[12.] Roger G. Barker, *Ecological Psychology,* Stanford: Stanford University Press, 1968, pp. 137-138.

[13.] De Grazia, Handy, Harwood, and Kurtz, op. cit., p. 110, pp. 64-65.

[14.] Buckley, op. cit., pp. 287-289.

[15.] Kretch, Crutchfield, and Livson, op. cit., p. 44.

[16.] For discussions of operant conditioning, see the following: B.F. Skinner and James Holland, *The Analysis of Behavior,* New York: McGraw-Hill Book Co., 1961; John Nurnberger et al., *An Introduction to the Science of Human Behavior,* New York: Appleton-Century-Crofts, 1963; Thom Verhave, *The Experimental Analysis of Behavior,* New York: Appleton-Century-Crofts, 1966; Roger Ulrich et al., *Control of Human Behavior,* New York: Scott, Foresman and Co., 1966; Honig, op. cit., Staats, op. cit.

[17.] Kretch, Crutchfield, and Livson, op. cit., p. 302.

[18.] Verhave, op. cit., pp. 20-21.

[19.] Ibid., pp. 447-449.

[20.] Menachem Amir, "Forcible Rape," *Federal Probation,* Volume 31, No. 1 (March 1967), p. 51 ff.

[21.] N.H. Azrin and W.C. Holz, "Punishment," in *Operant Behavior* by Honig, op. cit., pp. 440-441.

[22.] Marshall B. Clinard, *Sociology of Deviant Behavior,* 3rd ed., New York; Holt, Rinehart, and Winston, 1968, p. 262.

[23.] Azrin and Holz, op. cit., p. 380 ff.

[24.] Leonard Krasner and Leonard P. Ullman, *Research in Behavior Modification.* New York: Holt, Rinehart, and Winston, 1966, p. 3.

[25.] George C. Homans, "Human Behavior as Exchange," *American Journal of Sociology*, May, 1958, pp. 597-606.

[26.] Amitai Etzioni, *Modern Organization*, Englewood Cliffs: Prentice-Hall, Inc., 1964, p. 20 ff.

[27.] Ibid., pp. 34-35.

[28.] Ibid., p. 48.

[29.] Ibid., pp. 59-60.

[30.] Elizabeth Douban, "Social Status and Success Strivings," *Journal of Abnormal and Social Psychology*, Volume 52 (1956) pp. 219-223.

[31.] Alex Carey, "The Hawthrone Studies: A Radical Criticism," *American Sociological Review*, June 1967, p. 403.

[32.] McConnell, op. cit., pp. 280-281.

[33.] Cyril M. Franks, *Behavior Therapy: Appraisal and Status*, New York: McGraw-Hill Book Co., 1969, pp. 192-194.

[34.] Roger Ulrich et al., op. cit., pp. 170-186.

[35.] H.J. Eysenck, ed., *Behavioral Therapy and the Neuroses*, New York: Pergamon Press, 1960.

[36.] Joseph Wolpe, Andrew Salter, and L.J. Reyna, *The Conditioning Therapies*, New York: Holt, Rinehart, and Winston, 1964.

[37.] McConnell, op. cit., p. 286.

[38.] William Glasser, *Reality Therapy*, New York: Harper and Row, 1965.

[39.] Perry London, *Behavior Control*, New York: Harper and Row, 1969, pp. 39-70; see also Albert Bandura, *Principles of Behavior Modification*, New York: Holt, Rinehart and Winston, 1969. Cyril M. Franks, ed., *Behavior Therapy: Appraisal and Status*, New York: McGraw-Hill Book Co., 1969.

[40.] London, op. cit., p. 40.

# Chapter 12

# Science, Research Methodology, and the Causes of Crime

*Nature of Science*

Since the eighteenth century, there has been a growing concern for environmental adaptation through sensory observations and empirically verifiable knowledge. The growth of the physical and biological sciences, along with the applied fields of medicine, engineering, and technology, has been the major development in modern Western civilization. Urbanization and industrialization cannot be separated from science and technology.

The advances in scientific knowledge have been marked by carefully controlled laboratory experiments and the use of instruments to extend man's sensory capacity. As has been argued in an earlier chapter in this book, man's behavior is dependent upon his sensory system, and man as a scientist has extended his abilities to see and hear by means of the telescope, microscope, electrocardiograph, stethoscope, X-ray, microphone, radar scope, oscilloscope, and other such devices.

Though the physical and biological sciences have made great advances, the social and behavioral sciences are just now starting to use scientific procedures. There exists in the social sciences the division discussed earlier between the Verstehen, or humanistic, school and the behaviorist, or scientific, school. The humanistic school denies that a science of human behavior is possible (see Chapters 7 and 11). The position taken in this book is that the natural science methodology can be applied to the study of human behavior.

Research methodology can be classified as (1) naturalistic observation, (2) systematic assessment or surveys, and (3) experimental analysis.[1]

Naturalistic observation depends upon the observation of events in a natural setting without controls over the variables. We can watch pigeons in the park or we can use the official records of a police department via naturalistic observation.

Survey techniques—tests, interviews, questionnaires—use a stimulus situation to elicit a preexisting response rather than studying the conditions which caused the response. Since neither naturalistic observation nor systematic assessment controls the independent or extraneous variables, no convincing conclusions concerning causal relations can be made.[2]

The only model by which causal relations can be determined is through experimental analysis. Experimental models are based upon (1) manipulation of the independent variable by the experimenter, (2) control over extraneous variables, and (3) measurement of change in the dependent variable. The classic model for experimental analysis is a before-after model wherein changes in the dependent variable are measured after the introduction of an independent variable.

X = independent variable

Y = dependent variable

| Before X | After X |
|----------|---------|
| value of Y | value of Y |

If we want to know if a given drug (X) cures cancer (Y), we measure the incidence of cancer before and after the drug is administered to determine if a change has occurred in Y because of X. Only by controlling the conditions under which X influences Y can we determine the influence of X upon Y. One must control all extraneous variables before one can infer a causal relationship between X and Y. The reason the laboratory is the scientific method par excellence is that in the laboratory one is able to control the influence of extraneous variables. The object of science is prediction and control of events under controlled conditions. The less control the experimenter has over his variables, the less scientific he must be. The ideal experimental situation is one wherein all variables are held constant except for the independent and dependent variables. The experimenter systematically alters the value of X while observing changes in the value of Y. The relationship between X and Y can thereby be determined. If an increase in X results in a decrease or increase in Y, we can assume a relationship between X and Y. If change in X does not result in a change in Y, we can assume no relationship exists between X and Y. The formula is $Y = f(X)$ under k, or Y is a function of X under constant condition k.[3]

*Research in Criminology*

Criminological research has centered about the study of individual criminals or about the study of statistical patterns of criminal traits. The individual case study versus statistical approach controversy has been carried on in the behavioral sciences for years. Mueller and Ohlin have classified criminological research as inventory research, scholarly analysis, hypothesis-forming research, hypothesis-testing research, demonstration projects, and action projects.[4]

The case study method, favored by the psychiatrist, looks at the life history of the individual criminal. Such case histories are gathered by verbal interviews, questionnaires, and personal records. The psychiatric interview is one major method used to collect such data. The therapist looks for early sex experiences, feelings of rejection by parents, and other early childhood events. This method depends almost entirely on intro-spection as expressed in verbal behavior.

Statistical studies have correlated the incidence of crimes or criminals with some other variable such as age, sex, race, broken homes, urban areas, working mothers, personality types, gang memebership, poverty, housing, unemployment, and education. Correlations are found between such factors and crime, but these correlations are not causal relationships. As a Congressional Report in 1960 states, "many factors frequently cited as causes of delinquency are really only concomitants. They are not causes in the sense that if they were removed delinquency would decline."[5]

Experimental research in criminology is rare. Examples of experiments usually cited in the literature are the Cambridge-Somerville study, the Highfields study, and the study of girls at a vocational high school.[6] Such studies assign subjects to an experimental group which receives treatment, and the results are then compared to those of a control group which has not received the treatment. Such projects are often criticized because of poor control over the selection of control groups or because of a lack of control over the independent variable (treatment given) or over other extraneous variables. Most criminological studies must be regarded as indecisive because the investigator did not exercise sufficient control over the variables with which he dealt.

*Problems in Criminological Research*

*(1) Most criminological studies are ex post facto;* that is, after a person is a delinquent, an attempt is made to go back in time to discover the cause of delinquency. This can be done by means of a psychiatric interview

of an offender or a statistical study of many offenders. A clinician will look for crucial events in the life history; a statistical survey will correlate several variables with crime or criminals. The Gluecks found over 400 correlations from the studies they made of 500 delinquents.

The problem with such an approach is that the investigator does not control the variables which influenced the behavior of the criminal. If we study a criminal at the age of twenty-three, we do not know if he is a criminal because of family background, sex, urban residence, psychological makeup, ethnic background, education, poverty, or unemployment. These variables were not properly controlled so as to allow us to relate any combination of variables to crime.

The scientific method manipulates variables in the *present* and observes results in the *future*; statistical and clinical studies observe the end product and go back in time for the causes. Science goes from *cause* to *effect*; clinical and statistical studies go from *effect* to *cause*.

*(2) In much criminological research,* even when variables selected are from the present and not the past, the investigator observes and describes the rate of crime, but he does not control the variables he is describing. Stating that criminals are young adult males from minority groups living in slum areas does not allow one to control the influence of age, sex, race, or urban areas on crime rates. This is the difference between description and explanation. Science does more than describe. A scientific study of crime would manipulate the value of age, sex, or urban residence and then measure the influence of each variable on the crime rate.

(2a) Most criminological studies do not give the investigator control over the independent variables he is studying. If lack of education causes delinquency, then we must first be able to control education before we can control delinquency. A statistical study may reveal a relationship between education and delinquency, and yet it is of no help to know this if one is unable to change the educational system of urban slum areas.

Science implies control and prediction. Control implies prediction; prediction does not imply control. We can predict the weather; we do not control it. We can predict death rates through actuarial tables; we do not control the death rate through actuarial rates. We control polio through the control of relevant variables, as is possible by the use of vaccines.

(2b) In most criminological research, there are inadequate controls over extraneous variables. Any observed relationship between A and B is subject to several different interpretations. The influence of other variables on A or B must be known before we can conclude that A influences B or B influences A. If criminals have low intelligence scores, we must know (1) noncriminals do not exhibit the same characteristics to the same degree, and (2) some factor other than intelligence did not influence the crime rate. Control groups are often used to determine both of these issues, but the use of control groups in criminology has not been very fruitful, either because the control group has not been adequately matched with the experimental group or because extraneous factors have affected the control group so that it is no longer an adequate measure of change in the experimental group.

*(3) Many criminological studies are based on indirect*, rather than on direct, observations of behavior. Interviews, questionnaires, test scores, and official records are used as sources of information on crimes and criminals. Such studies tell us how people respond to interviews or how official records on crimes are kept, but they do not give us first hand information about behavior. Criminologists must develop better techniques for studying crimes and criminals.

*(4) Mentalistic concepts are used to explain criminal behavior.* Terms such as ego, self, need, motive, and personality are based on a belief in the dualism of mind and body. Such concepts are inferred from behavior and then are used to explain behavior. There is no way to prove the existence of such concepts independent of the behavior they purport to explain. Scientific concepts must be subject to operational definition.

*(5) Criminologists study criminals who have been caught.* Although a few studies, such as Sutherland's *The Professional Thief,* have been made of nonincarcerated criminals, most studies are based on those criminals in prisons. Since the hidden rate of crime figure is high, it is impossible to know to what extent the apprehended criminal represents the general criminal population. The fact that few criminals are caught may be more important from a theoretical point of view than the study of those few criminals who are in our prisons.

*(6) In summary,* and related to all of the points made above, the sociologist studies the individual criminal rather than the environmental conditions which produce the crime. This is in agreement with the general orientation of sociologists that the study of behavior focus upon the individual, not upon the environment. Hinkle and Hinkle have labeled this orientation "voluntaristic nominalism," or individuals who know, feel, and will. Cognition, affect, and volition are still the major topics of concern in such an analysis of behavior.[7]

*Causation and Criminal Behavior*

Sociologists and criminologists have been divided as to the number of factors needed to explain criminal behavior. Some prefer a single-factor theory, such as the one Sutherland and his followers have used. Leslie Wilkins argues that only through a single-factor approach can a solution to crime be found.[8] Cohen has argued that a single *theory* of crime is not the same as a single-*factor* approach to crime.[9]

The critics of the single-factor approach argue that crime is too complex to be analyzed in terms of any one factor. The multiple-factor advocates point out that crime is a product of many factors: race, age, sex, broken homes, poverty, urbanization, unemployment, and so on. Hirschi and Selvin argue that one must view crime in terms of many factors, not just one.

The crucial point is not the number of variables one takes into account, but the manner in which such variables are related to criminal behavior. The fact that a variable is statistically correlated with crime means no more than that two variables coexist in the universe. A relationship between A and B can mean (1) A causes B; (2) B causes A; (3) both A and B are influenced by a third variable C; or (4) A and B are related by chance. Correlation is not causation. The fact that criminals come from backgrounds of poverty does not prove that poverty causes crime. The analysis of causation is perhaps the weakest link in the total discussion of crime prevention and control.

As Hirschi and Selvin have indicated, causal inferences require the prior satisfaction of three conditions:

(1) association between variables;

(2) time sequence, and;

(3) lack of spuriousness—that is, knowledge that a third variable is not influencing the original relationship.[11]

By association is meant that a change in the value of X will result in a change in the value of Y, or Y is a function of X under condition k. If X increases, Y increases or decreases.

By time sequence is meant that X comes before Y, not after. Historical studies, such as surveys and case studies, often do not tell us the time sequence. The Gluecks found a relationship between lack of affection of father for son and delinquency of son. Which caused (influenced) which? Did, as the Gluecks assume, the father contribute to the son's delinquency, or did the delinquency of the son cause the father to lack affection for the son? Severe parental discipline also was found by the Gluecks to be associated with delinquency. Does severe parental discipline cause delinquency, or does delinquency cause a parent to be severe with his son? It is obvious that the Gluecks' study did not yield causal relationships, although they claim to have discovered facts which could lead to causal inference.

The third condition for causal inferences states that all extraneous variables must be controlled before a relationship between X and Y can be discovered. As Selvin noted in a 1957 article, a statistical test of significance is of no value unless extraneous variables have been controlled or randomized. "The basic difficulty in design is that sociologists are unable to randomize their uncontrolled variables, so that the differences between experimental and control groups are a mixture of the effects of the variable being studied and the uncontrolled variables or correlated biases."[12] If we know that poverty is correlated with crime, then we must know the relationship between poverty, crime, and other potential variables. It may be that crime is also influenced by lack of education, or that lack of education influences poverty, which influences crime.

According to Blalock,[13] there are ten possible relationships between X (independent variable), Y (dependent variable), and Z (extraneous variable). If we look for the possible relationships between poverty (X), education (Z), and criminal behavior (Y) we have the following:

[1]      education influences poverty
education influences criminal behavior
poverty does not influence education
poverty does not influence criminal behavior, i.e., the relationship is spurious

[2]      education influences criminal behavior
poverty influences education
education does not influence poverty
poverty does not influence criminal behavior directly, but does so via education, i.e., education is an interpretive link between poverty and criminal behavior

[3]      poverty influences criminal behavior
poverty does not influence education
education does not influence criminal behavior directly, but does so via poverty, i.e., education is an explanatory (antecedent) link in explaining the relationship between poverty and criminal behavior

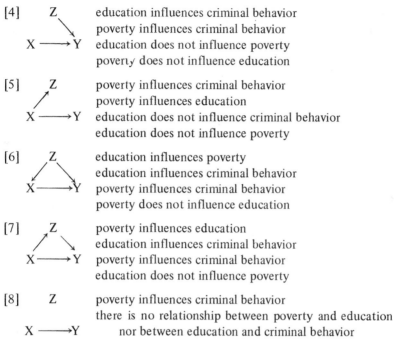

[4] Z
X ⟶ Y

education influences criminal behavior
poverty influences criminal behavior
education does not influence poverty
poverty does not influence education

[5] Z
X ⟶ Y

poverty influences criminal behavior
poverty influences education
education does not influence criminal behavior
education does not influence poverty

[6] Z
X ⟶ Y

education influences poverty
education influences criminal behavior
poverty influences criminal behavior
poverty does not influence education

[7] Z
X ⟶ Y

poverty influences education
education influences criminal behavior
poverty influences criminal behavior
education does not influence poverty

[8] Z
X ⟶ Y

poverty influences criminal behavior
there is no relationship between poverty and education
nor between education and criminal behavior

[9] Z
X    Y

education influences criminal behavior
there is no relationship between poverty and education
nor between poverty and criminal behavior

[10] Z
X    Y

there is no relationship between poverty, education, and
criminal behavior

Blalock made three assumptions in his statement, following Simon's model: (1) there is no two-way causation; (2) Y is a dependent, never an independent variable; and (3) all other variables influencing X, Y, and Z are randomized.

If we dispense with these assumptions, our diagram looks like this:

Z
X ⟷ Y

poverty influences education
education influences poverty
education influences criminal behavior
criminal behavior influences education
poverty influences criminal behavior
criminal behavior influences poverty

Such a model is much more cumbersome, but it is more representative of reality than are the other models. There is a two-way influence between education and poverty, and criminal behavior influences poverty and education as well as being influenced by them.

If we take education, poverty, and criminal behavior as our three variables, we find several interrelationships among them. Education is influenced by poverty; social class studies have indicated that the higher one's class standing, the greater the education received, quantitatively and qualitatively. Education also influences poverty, since the greater the amount of education, the higher the average life earnings. Education and poverty are interrelated, since education determines income to a considerable degree, and income determines education.

Criminal behavior is influenced by education, since high school dropouts have a much greater delinquency rate than do high school or college graduates. A criminal career influences education, since, if a student is arrested, he is taken out of the school system and often does not complete high school. A delinquent record may interfere with education. Delinquency is influenced by poverty, but delinquency also influences poverty since a police record makes one unemployable, thus lowering one's income, which leads to poverty.

According to the aforementioned methodological statements, one cannot state the causal relationship between two variables without knowing the influence of extraneous variables. If we state that poverty causes delinquency, we must know that other variables are not influencing poverty or delinquency. If we add one variable, education, we find that education also influences and is influenced by poverty. If we view criminal behavior as an independent as well as a dependent variable, we find criminality influencing education and poverty. The influence of poverty on delinquency can be analyzed only in terms of the interaction of poverty, education, and crime.

Crime is not a product of two variables, however, but of many. Hirschi and Selvin note this fact when they argue for a multiple-factor theory, but they do not analyze these several variables within an experimental model. It is not adequate merely to state that multiple factors cause crime; the interaction of these variables must be spelled out through experimental analysis. As Blalock and Simon note, the influence of extraneous variables must be randomized; otherwise the relationship between X, Y, and Z is unknown. The influence of other variables on crime is not randomized, however, and thus we must add other variables to our model.

What variables do we alter or control in order to reduce crime and delinquency? Do we alter unemployment, undereducation, poverty, family stability, personality development, discrimination and segregation, urban slum conditions, neurotic behavior patterns, or what? Can we alter the employment rate for Negro youths without first altering the urban educational system? Are sixteen-year-old youths with a fourth-grade education employable? Can we work with a welfare family composed of a twenty-one-year-old Negro girl, three illegitimate children, and a father figure who is unable to support his family because he is uneducated and unemployable? Do we (a) work with the children in Headstart Projects; (b) make the mother employable and self-supporting; (c) require the father to support the family though he is not employed; (d) foster better use of birth control techniques and reduce the rate of illegitimacy; or (e) support father, mother, and children on welfare programs paid for by other working men and women who are trying to support themselves? It is obvious from these examples that we must know the influence of one variable on another before we can start to plan an effective program for social rehabilitation. If we pass social welfare regulations which force men out of the homes, do we solve the problem or contribute to its further growth? If we place children in Headstart projects, do we know enough about learning theory and education to educate them? If we pay mothers for illegitimate children, do we increase or decrease the illegitimacy rate? If we start job training programs, do we know enough about behavioral psychology to motivate our ghetto youth to complete the programs?

One of the major causes for the failure of our welfare programs is that we do not know what variables to deal with in order to produce the changes desired. Nowhere is this more evident than in the fight against crime. We can list the many factors associated with crime, but we cannot spell out the relationship among the variables. A list of the variables involved in crime and their interaction is depicted in Table 2.

The cycle of interaction between crime and other variables is as such:

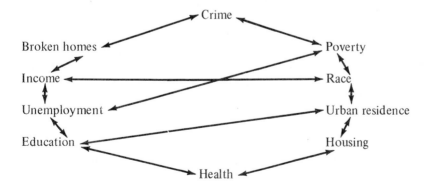

Table 2

**CORRELATES OF CRIME**

| | Age Role | Sex Role | Broken Homes | Poverty | Race | Education | Urban Residence | Housing | Poor Health | Employment | Income | Criminal Behavior |
|---|---|---|---|---|---|---|---|---|---|---|---|---|
| Age Role | | X | X | X | X | X | X | X | X | X | X | X |
| Sex Role | X | | X | X | X | X | X | X | X | X | X | X |
| Broken Homes | X | X | | X | X | X | X | X | X | X | X | X |
| Poverty | X | X | X | | X | X | X | X | X | X | X | X |
| Race | X | X | X | X | | X | X | X | X | X | X | X |
| Education | X | X | X | X | X | | X | X | X | X | X | X |
| Urban Residence | X | X | X | X | X | X | | X | X | X | X | X |
| Housing | X | X | X | X | X | X | X | | X | X | X | X |
| Poor Health | X | X | X | X | X | X | X | X | | X | X | X |
| Employment | X | X | X | X | X | X | X | X | X | | X | X |
| Income | X | X | X | X | X | X | X | X | X | X | | X |
| Criminal Behavior | X | X | X | X | X | X | X | X | X | X | X | |

This chart depicts correlational relationships between variables, from which causal inferences are NOT to be inferred.

The two variables in each of the following relationships are interactive; that is each influences the other: poverty and race, race and urban residence, urban residence and housing, housing and health, education and health, education and unemployment, unemployment and income, income and broken homes, broken homes and crime.

Crime influences and is influenced by poverty, race, urban residence, housing, health, education, unemployment, income, and broken homes. Education may influence income which influences crime, or income may influence education which influences residential area which influences crime. Race may be related to crime because of a lack of education among Negroes, or because of a lack of employment among Negroes, or because of the urban residence or income of Negroes, or some combination of influences. If race influences education which influences employment which influences income which influences residence and housing and health and family stability, then which of these variables is responsible for crime?

The only way to determine the influence of any one variable on crime is to (a) hold all other variables constant, and (b) to change the value of the variable under investigation. It is not enough to state that statistically delinquents are high school dropouts; we must increase the educational level of the delinquent and then measure any changes that may occur in the delinquency rate.

## Conclusions

A science of human behavior is beginning to emerge, but at this point in history nominative and descriptive studies dominate the field of criminology. Some quasi-experimental studies on the effectiveness of treatment have been made, but we do not know the relationship of variables to crime since proper controls over extraneous variables have never been achieved.

Action programs based on humanistic values and a service orientation are used in lieu of research programs to prevent and control crime. Antiscientific feelings are found not only among politicians, but among professional social scientists who want results without telling us how to achieve these results. The goals of human behavior are a result of environmental conditioning and experiences and are subject to the same analysis as behavior in general. We cannot indicate a crime control program until (1) we know what variables must be controlled, and (2) we know how to control the relevant variables.

The most basic need today is for a scientific approach to human behavior, including criminal behavior. Policy decisions must be based upon scientific evidence rather than scientific efforts being limited by policy decisions. We do not know the causes of or cures for crime because we have not done the basic research needed to determine the causes. We try to prevent and control crime through political decisions before we have adequate knowledge needed to control crime. The prevention and control of crime is predicated upon the prior discovery of scientific relationships between crime and environmental variables. As the President's Crime Commission concluded:

> Approximately 15 percent of the Defense Department's annual budget is allocated to research. While different fields call for different levels of research, it is worth noting that research commands only a small fraction of 1 percent of the total expenditure for crime control. There is probably no subject of comparable concern to which the nation is devoting so many resources and so much effort with so little knowledge of what it is doing. It is true, of course, that many kinds of knowledge about crime must await better understanding of social behavior.[14]

## NOTES

[1.] William A. Scott and Michael Wertheimer, *Introduction to Psychological Research,* New York: John Wiley and Sons, 1967, p. 69.

[2.] Ibid., p. 69 ff.

[3.] Leon Festinger and Daniel Katz, *Research Methods in the Behavioral Sciences.* New York: Dryden Press, 1953; Claire Selltiz, et al. *Research Methods in Social Relations.* New York: Henry Holt and Co., 1960; Travis Hirschi and Hanan C. Selvin. *Delinquency Research.* New York: Free Press, 1967.

[4.] Gerhard O.W. Mueller, "The Function of Criminology in Criminal Justice Administration," *Criminological Abstracts,* January, 1970, pp. 583-584.

[5.] U.S. Department of Health, Education, and Welfare, *Report to The Congress on Juvenile Delinquency.* U.S. Government Printing Office, 1960. p. 21.

[6.] Hermann Mannheim, *Comparative Criminology.* Boston: Houghton Mifflin Co., 1965, p. 174 ff.

[7.] Roscoe C. and Gisela J. Hinkle, *The Development of Modern Sociology.* New York: Random House, 1954, p. v.

[8.] Mannheim, op. cit., pp. 10-11.

[9.] Edwin H. Sutherland and Donald R. Cressey, *Principles of Criminology.*

[10.] Hirschi and Selvin, op. cit., p. 114 ff.

[11.] Ibid., p. 37 ff.

[12.] Hanan C. Selvin, "A Critique of Tests of Significance in Survey Research," *American Sociological Review,* Vol. 22, No. 5 (October 1957), pp. 519-527.

[13.] Hubert M. Blalock, *Social Statistics.* New York: McGraw-Hill Book Co., 1960, p. 339; Ina A. Jeffery, "Behavioral Experimentation in the Control of Academic and Criminal Behaviors of Ghetto Youths," Ph.D. dissertation. The American University, 1968.

[14.] President's Commission on Law Enforcement and Administration of Justice. *The Challenge of Crime in a Free Society,* 1967, p. 273.

Chapter 13

## Science and Technology

### Present Strategies

The strategy to apply science and technology to the criminal justice area was designed by the Institute of Defense Analysis[1] and is currently being implemented by the Office of Law Enforcement Assistance Administration. The model used, as was discussed in Chapter 1, is as follows:

Crime → Police → Prosecution → Courts → Corrections

This strategy is based on the positive school of criminology with emphasis on the *individual offender after* the crime has been committed. The failure of deterrence and rehabilitation has led to increased efforts to apply the old model rather than to any search for a new approach to the crime problem. This chapter will review the current effort and will suggest some different ways in which science and technology might be used.

### THE POLICE

The Law Enforcement Assistance Administration has concentrated on "action grants" to police departments, with seventy to eighty percent of the total budget being used to upgrade police personnel and equipment.[2] Such grants have focused heavily on salaries and equipment, not on research and experimentation.

Training programs for police officers have been established, with little knowledge as to what curriculum to develop. As a result, a collection of materials from police manuals, criminology, criminal law, race relations, urban sociology, and abnormal psychology have been pulled together. No one has ever bothered to ask if these materials have any bearing on the way the police perform their job, or even if such materials are relevant to police performance. Police-community relations courses are especially popular today due to the assumption that if people talk about the bad image of the police in the ghetto, the problem will improve or disappear.

Attempts at improving the equipment used by the police have taken several forms—better communication systems, including small portable walkie-talkies to be carried by individual police officers; improved car radio systems; and improved central communications systems are examples. The Task Force report emphasized that unless a criminal was named or arrested at the scene of the crime, the chances of arrest were slim. The shorter the response time, the higher the apprehension rate.[3] This finding has led to concentration on a response system capable of handling calls for help made to the police within two or three minutes, because a delay of six minutes or more reduces the arrest rate to an insignificant figure. The use of special police emergency numbers, such as 911 in New York City, is an example of this use of communication by police departments.

Computerized information systems, whereby criminal histories, fingerprints, name identification files, wanted persons files, gun registration, modus operandi, and statistical information are stored for further use are now being widely recommended. The National Crime Information Center and the New York State Intelligence and Identification System are examples of criminal justice information systems.[4] Such computerized systems allow the police to keep track of wanted persons or stolen vehicles, and thus to increase the rate of apprehension. Computerized systems are also used to deploy squad cars into high crime rate areas.

Efforts also are being made to redesign police vehicles, to create nonlethal weapons, and to improve the analysis of physical evidence in crime laboratories.[5]


## THE COURTS

OLEA appropriations to the courts have amounted to about six percent of the total budget,[6] which means the Court system is being neglected while the police phase of criminal justice is being supported and implemented.

The Task Force report focused on reducing the delay in the processing of felony cases in our court system and on computer simulation of the criminal justice process.[7] Other uses of computers that have been suggested or are in use are for arranging court calendars, issuing warrants, scheduling cases, notification of parties (lawyers, witnesses), gaining of presentence information on defendants, and monitoring of bail, warrants, and summons. It is obvious that the computer can handle the paper work of the court much more effectively than it is now being handled.

Some attention is also being paid to the design of courtrooms and the use of architectural skills to solve some of the problems now facing the court. Our example is a plastic booth for defendants who are disruptive of trial procedures (as in the trials of protesters in Chicago and New York), being designed by the American Institute of Architects and the American Bar Association.[8]

Such changes in court procedures are necessary, but in the long run such measures will only enable the criminal courts to process more cases more effectively; these measures will not reduce the crime rate and, in fact, will lead to an overall increase in the crime rate.

## THE CORRECTIONAL SYSTEM

The OLEA appropriations for corrections amounts to about fourteen percent of the total budget. No new ideas have been initiated under these grants, and the programs undertaken are discussed above in Chapters 6, 8, 9, and 10. Programs undertaken include improvement of correctional centers for juveniles, halfway houses, work-release programs, programmed instructional education, and statistical studies to aid in treatment and probation decisions.[9]

## SCIENCE AND THE CONTROL OF CRIME

The use of science and technology as outlined above is not adequate as a crime control model; it seeks to make the handling of criminals and criminal cases more efficient rather than preventing or controlling the incidence of criminal acts. Any application of science must be designed to reduce crime, not to keep better records on its incidence. Such a system must have the following capabilities:

(1) It must be based on a science of behavior, yet to be developed but now in its childhood, as seen in experimental psychology, environmental ecology, behavioral biology, biochemistry, and systems analysis.

(2) It must be designed to control *criminal behavior,* not welfare, poverty, education, guided group interaction, or therapeutic verbal behavior. The system must be one of direct, not indirect, controls over behavior.

(3) It must be capable of preventing crimes before they occur, not dealing with them after they occur. Prevention must replace detection, prosecution, and imprisonment of criminals after they have become criminals.

(4) It must alter the environment in which crimes are committed, since criminal behavior will occur so long as the environment producing the behavior is allowed to exist. Altering the family system, school system, court system, or correctional system will not influence criminal behavior in such a way as to control it.

(5) It must be designed so as to minimize the unanticipated future consequences that now accompany many of our social action programs.

## REWARDS AND PUNISHMENT

To control criminal behavior we must remove the rewards from criminality while at the same time reinforcing lawful behavior. Criminal behavior is maintained by the material and social rewards which come from it, and if such behavior is no longer rewarded, it will cease.

Removing the reward for a given response is called negative punishment, as was discussed above. We can extinguish a response by punishing the person after he has behaved in an illegal manner. However, such use of punishment is most ineffective, as has been pointed out by the positivists who wish to rehabilitate criminals rather than punish them (see Chapters 2 and 3). Positive punishment must be certain, immediate, unavoidable, and the total threat of punishment must be greater than the gain or reward possible from the criminal act. The manner in which punishment is administered by our legal system is sloppy and ineffective; we must therefore conclude that the ineffective use of punishment leads to ineffective results. Also to be considered is the fact that punishment creates in both the punisher and the punished undesirable avoidance and anxiety responses which often interfere with the development of other, desirable responses.

Two different but related approaches to criminal behavior can be derived from what we now know about punishment.

First, the most efficient way to eliminate a criminal act is to remove the possibility of reward by means of environmental engineering. If the gain from criminal behavior is reduced to a point below the effort needed, then the individual will no longer behave in that manner.

Second, the next best way to eliminate a criminal act is to increase the threat of punishment. Thus, while decreasing the reward available, we are increasing the punishment available. If we increase the punishment while at the same time we do not eliminate the reward, the possibility is high that the response will continue (see Chapter 3). A rewarded response will continue even in the face of punishment.

The punishment used must be negative—i.e., the removal of a stimulus desired by the punished person. Imprisonment must be replaced with loss of monetary or social rewards. Money is a powerful reinforcer, and our total economy is based on it; yet we ignore this principle when we resort to prisons for the control and rehabilitation of our criminals. The obvious problem is that many of our criminals are too poor to pay reparations, but there is no reason why public works programs cannot be substituted for idle imprisonment.

It is probably true that we do not have the behavioral technology to do what has been outlined above, but we do have the means to do research along these lines if we ask the right sorts of questions. At this point in our history, we are trapped in a deterrence-rehabilitation argument which does not allow us to solve the crime problem. We must move beyond deterrence or rehabilitation before we are going to solve the crime problem.

## Crimes Against Property

The President's Commission on Crime for the District of Columbia discovered that in the case of commercial burglaries the following means of entering existed[10]:

    7%—unlocked doors
    22%—unlocked windows
    35%—broken windows
    30%—locks forced

Of these establishments surveyed, only thirty-three percent had burglary-proof locks installed.

In the case of residential burglaries, the following means of entry were used:

    9%—unlocked door
    10%—unlocked window
    11%—broken window
    52%—locks forced
    45%—located on first floor

A survey revealed that forty-two percent of car thefts involved unlocked ignitions.[11] The National Auto Theft Bureau reports that eighty percent of those cars stolen were unlocked.

These figures indicated that a vast majority of property offenses are committed because security measures are lax or nonexistent. Buildings that are easy prey to criminals make criminal opportunities possible. The crime rate is a direct result of the number of opportunities for crimes existing in the community. Several professional burglars have recently published articles concerning the ease with which burglaries are committed, and they have offered practical suggestions as to how the potential victim can protect himself.[12]

The protection of private property by locks, alarms, and surveillance systems is possibly the easiest system available for crime control. The above figures indicate that even though such devices are currently available, they either are not used or are used improperly. Like birth control devices, crime control devices which are not used are not effective. New technology must be created, based on research as to the conditions under which the commission of a crime occurs. New and better means of making property secure are not beyond the means of our science and technology, and since ninety percent of the crimes committed involve property in one way or another, a great deal can be done in this area of crime control.

## Crime Control by the Police

The police spend a great deal of time in preventive patrol, cruising the streets looking for crimes in progress. However, the President's Commission found that only twelve percent of the burglaries and two percent of the robberies can be detected via police patrol. An individual police officer can be expected to detect a burglary no more than once every three months, and a robbery no more than once every 14 years.[13] Added to this is the fact that very few police are in the field at one time, given all the things police do besides law enforcement.

A new concept of prevention must be used by our police department wherein the emphasis is on prevention methods, rather than law enforcement after the fact. A division of the police department would be trained in crime prevention, and it would be responsible for potential opportunities for crime. A block-by-block survey of the precinct could determine danger spots and remedial measures taken before a crime is committed. We now do something of this sort in fire prevention inspections, except that such inspections are not enforced to the extent that they should be. Buildings that are unsafe as potential health or fire hazards are (or should be) condemned; likewise, buildings that are unsafe as far as criminal activity is concerned should be condemned until corrected.

A few moves in this direction are now being undertaken. The New York City Police Department has undertaken a campaign to publicize ways in which the citizen can protect himself from residential burglary, and there is now in existence a nationwide campaign appealing to drivers to protect themselves from auto theft. The Detroit Police Department recently established a Counter Crime Clinic, which has organized crime-prevention campaigns in the areas of:

(1)  residential burglaries;

(2)  newsboy robberies;

(3)  driver-salesman robberies;

(4)  cab driver robberies;

(5)  financial institution robberies;

(6)  protection for women and children; and

(7)  street and park lighting.

These beginnings at crime control should be encouraged and expanded in a major effort to involve our police departments in crime prevention measures rather than in detection and apprehension measures.

### Crime Control and the Citizen

The citizen is involved in crime as the victim or the witness to crimes. As buildings are targets of crime, so are individuals. As Von Hentig pointed out years ago in his *The Criminal and his Victim*, [14] many crimes are victim-precipitated. Victims cause crime in the sense that they set up the opportunity for the crime to be committed. By changing the behavior of the potential victim, we can reduce the crime rate.

Potential victims can be educated (in cooperation with the police department) in how to protect one's property as well as one's person. Secretaries who leave their purses on their desks or who walk down deserted streets late at night are only asking to become victims of a criminal. Men who leave the car unlocked or load the back seat with expensive luggage or clothing are also inviting criminal activity. Every criminal act involves a victim, and so far, in our positivistic approach to crime, we have only concerned ourselves with changing the criminal. Changing the behavior of the victim would be much easier and would be much more effective.

Citizens can also act as a potential force for law enforcement through involvement in and support of the law enforcement process. Apathy on the part of citizens, as illustrated by the Kitty Genovese case in New York City—wherein more than forty people did nothing while a woman was murdered—must be overcome. Citizens' groups can act as educational agents in law enforcement needs and prevention techniques. They can encourage citizens to report crimes and to act as witnesses in court, something most citizens are reluctant to do.

Such organizations need political and financial support, since they contain within them meaningful means for crime control. Government policy should be changed so as to reward citizens, both financially and in terms of social recognition, who aid in the prevention of crime. The system now operates as to discourage anyone from reporting a crime to the police or from acting as a witness in court. These negative results must be changed if we expect our citizens to become involved in crime prevention and law enforcement.

Before citizens can be encouraged to take crime prevention measures, there must be some reward given for doing so. Theft insurance is one way to encourage both private citizens and businessmen to be less careless with their property, if we require as a part of every policy that certain inspection standards be met. We now require holders of fire insurance to meet fire safety standards, so why not require holders of theft insurance to do the same? Periodic inspections of a premise, as suggested above under preventive police patrol, could be used to ensure that the building was secure and theft-proof. Anyone not complying would be ineligible for theft coverage. For example, any car left unlocked and without a locking mechanism on the steering column would not be covered by car theft insurance if the car were stolen. We only encourage car thefts if we insure the owners against loss without requiring that they protect themselves.

Compulsory theft insurance should be required by the federal government, with some provisions for helping low-income people in high crime rate areas to secure such insurance.[15] It is obvious as things now stand that those in greatest need of such insurance are not covered. We must cover our citizens for thefts, but at the same time require that they protect themselves from such crimes.

The idea of victim compensation for crimes has gained support in recent years.[16] Victim compensation plans will only encourage crimes, as the victim can gain redress from the government, *unless* the victim is required to demonstrate that he did not contribute through negligence to the crime.

*Crimes Against the Person*

So far we have discussed crimes against property, since these are the most frequent crimes, and since property offenses are the easiest to handle via surveillance systems.

Crimes against the person (robbery, rape, murder, assault) are more difficult to prevent, since they often involve a different pattern of interaction between t'e criminal and his victim. Murders, assaults, and rapes are usually committed, not by strangers, but by friends and relatives, and they occur in privacy, without a prior break-in or illegal entry. The victim and aggressor in most murder or rape cases are members of the same racial group, social class, and residential area. Such crimes almost always involve arguments or social interaction between criminal and victim, and the victim often precipitates the act through insults, drinking, or sexual overtures.[17]

Environmental changes that might apply to controlling crimes against property can be classified as (1) alarm and surveillance systems, (2) urban design, (3) environment and behavior, and (4) citizen participation.

Crimes against the person cannot be prevented by the usual alarm systems to any great extent, since many such acts occur in homes, stairwells, elevators, and other private, secluded areas, and in situations in which the criminal is not an illegal intruder. An electronic system for signaling an alarm for help could be installed in homes and business establishments, provided it could be activated in time of emergency without too much difficulty. The design of such a system would be difficult since people being assaulted do not have the time or presence of mind to make use of the system.

Some crimes of violence occur in deserted, isolated spots such as parks, lonely streets, and vacant buildings. A recent account of the murder of a University of Louisville coed described the scene as "a hazardous area, poorly lighted and isolated from the main portion of the campus." Urban design could do a great deal to eliminate such potential danger spots, a topic we will discuss in the next chapter.

Human aggression is a response to environmental conditions, usually ones containing elements of punishment and frustration for the aggressor. A better scientific understanding of aggression must be forthcoming before we can design an environment which will control aggressive behavior. A distinction must be made between positive reinforcement and negative reinforcement, or the removal of an aversive stimulus (see Chapter 11). A crime of robbery for money (positive reinforcement) must be distinguished from an act of murder (negative reinforcement) where the gain is the removal of an aversive stimulus—the person murdered. Rape probably contains elements of both sexual gratification and aggression. In our discussion of property offenses, we emphasized the removal of the positive reinforcement. How to accomplish this with the negative reinforcement from crimes against the person is more difficult to achieve. The role of the victim in cases of murder, rape, and assault must again be recognized, and attempts must be made to change the behavior of the victims in order to make them less vulnerable to such attacks. The victim often precipitates the crime, and he must be made aware of the ways in which he encourages or makes possible the commission of criminal acts.

One of the best pr ective devices for personal security is neighbors who are aware of what is going on and are willing "to become involved." We mentioned the Genovese case, above, and could cite many other such cases where people have stood aside and allowed a murder or assault to occur. Protection through community effort applies here, as in the case of property offenses. The use of a reward system for those going to the aid of a citizen in distress might be a major step in the right direction, since the risk (punitive) of involvement would be offset by the reward, both monetary and social, for such acts of law enforcement.

The police could establish special patrols to escort people home late at night from subway or bus stations. Similarly, citizen patrols could be established. Citizens can be trained in crime prevention measures, which would include measures to be taken to ensure personal safety as well as the safety of property.

*Research*

The effort to control crime must start with well-designed experimental research. An experimental district or precinct should be selected for a total analysis of every crime committed in the area, including an attempt to gain information on those crimes not officially reported. Such a project would determine the type of crime, the manner in which the crime was committed (means of entry or access to the victim), the object of the crime, the role of the victim in the crime, the contribution of urban design to the crime, and the police response to the crime. From such information, an experiment in environmental/behavioral engineering would be undertaken to prevent the same type of offense in the future. These changes would be introduced into the experimental district for every situation (human or physical) which might present an opportunity for a crime in the future.

A follow-up study would be made after the recommended changes had been made, in order to determine the effectiveness of the measures taken. Where new crimes are committed, the analysis will continue as outlined until such time as the area has been made as crime-proof as possible. Those criminal acts still not under control would become the concern of the second phase of the research project.

In this way a model for crime control could be developed, and once the defects are worked out, it could be offered as a model for nationwide adoption. Rather than having thousands of projects involved in disconnected but duplicated efforts, without any direction by a top flight research team, the project outlined above would lead to systematic verified results. To those who say communities need help now and such research will take five years to complete, the answer is they needed help five years ago, and they will need help five years from now unless systematic research in the environmental control of crime is undertaken.

Research on the influence of the environment on behavior, especially as to the conditions responsible for aggressive assaultive behavior, must also be pursued beyond its current modest beginnings.

*Summary*

Science and technology can be applied to the prevention and control of crime, but they must go beyond the computerization of police records and court procedures. A technology must be designed that will prevent crime before it occurs, which will act as a direct control over criminal behavior, and which will alter the environment in which crimes are committed.

# NOTES

[1.] President's Commission on Law Enforcement and Administration of Justice, *Science and Technology* (Washington, D.C.: Government Printing Office, 1967).

[2.] Wall Street Journal, February 4, 1970.

[3.] *Science and Technology,* op. cit., pp. 8-9.

[4.] Ibid., p. 69.

[5.] Ibid., p. 14 ff.; James H. Scheuer, *To Walk the Streets Safely,* Garden City: Doubleday and Company, 1969.

[6.] Wall Street Journal, February 4, 1970.

[7.] *Science and Technology,* op. cit., pp. 37-39.

[8.] New York Times, February 13, 1970.

[9.] Wall Street Journal, February 4, 1970; *Science and Technology* pp.44-46.

[10.] President's Commission on Law Enforcement on Crime in the District of Columbia, *Report* (Washington, D.C.: Government Printing Office, 1967), p. 86 ff.

[11.] President's Commission on Law Enforcement and Administration of Justice, *The Police* (Washington, D.C.: Government Printing Office, 1967), p. 221.

[12.] Robert Earl Barnes, "Advice from a Master Burglar," *U.S. News and World Report* (September 9, 1968, p. 96 ff. Nicholas Pileggi, "1968 Has Been the Year of the Burglar," *New York Times Magazine* (November 17, 1968), p. 54 ff.

[13.] *Science and Technology,* op. cit., p. 12.

[14.] Hans von Hentig, *The Criminal and His Victim* (New Haven: Yale University Press, 1949).

[15.] Select Committee on Small Business, United States Senate, Report: Contributions of Science and Technology to Federal Crime Insurance (Washington, D.C.: Government Printing Office, 1967).

[16.] Stephen Schafer, *The Victim and His Criminal* (New York: Random House, 1968).

[17.] Marshall B. Clinard, *Sociology of Deviant Behavior* (New York: Holt, Rinehart, and Winston, Inc., 1968), p. 25 ff.

*Chapter 14*

## Crime Control Through
## Urban Planning and Design

*The Urban Environment*

That man is a product of his environment there can be no doubt. The biologist has conclusively proven that the physical makeup of man is an adaptation to environmental influences; even the genetic structure of inheritance is dependent upon environmental stimulation. The development of the brain depends upon protein intake and early environmental conditioning. The psychologist has shown the importance of environmental conditioning, and many psychologists today regard behavior as man's adaptation to environmental conditions.[1] The sociologist and the anthropologist have referred to culture and society as adaptive responses to environmental situations. Regardless of whether we use as a unit of analysis the cell, the individual organism (a collectivity of cells) or the group (a collectivity of individuals), we have come to regard adaptation to the environment as the crucial process.

Throughout this book we have interpreted behavior within this framework—behavior as an adaptation to environmental situations. Criminal behavior thus is behavior adapted to or produced by given environmental conditions.

The National Commission on the Causes and Prevention of Violence concluded that violent crime was primarily a phenomenon of large cities.[2] The Commission painted the following picture of the city of the future unless drastic public action is taken:

> Central business districts in the heart of the city surrounded by mixed areas of accelerating deterioration, will be partially protected by large numbers of people shopping or working in commercial buildings during the daytime hours, plus a substantial police presence and will be largely deserted except for police patrols during nighttime hours.

214

High rise apartment buildings and residential compounds protected by private guards and security devices will be fortified cells for upper-middle and high-income populations living at prime locations in the city.

Suburban neighborhoods, geographically far removed from the central city, will be protected mainly by economic homogeneity and by distance from population groups with the highest propensities to commit crimes.

Homes will be fortified by an array of devices, from window grilles to electronic surveillance equipment, armed citizens in cars will supplement inadequate police patrols in neighborhoods closer to the central city, and extreme left-wing and right-wing groups will have tremendous armories of weapons which could be brought into play.

High speed patrolled expressways will be sanitized corridors connecting safe areas, and private automobiles, taxicabs, and commercial vehicles will be routinely equipped with unbreakable glass, light armor and other security features. Inside garage or valet parking will be available at safe buildings in or near the central city. Armed guards will ride shotgun on all forms of public transportation.

Streets and residential neighborhoods in the central city will be unsafe in different degrees and the ghetto slum neighborhoods will be places of terror with widespread crime perhaps entirely out of police control during nighttime hours. Armed guards will protect all public facilities such as schools, libraries and playgrounds in these areas.

The above statement from the Commission was quoted in some detail because it points to the place of the urban environment and its design—streets, expressways, apartment buildings, schools, playgrounds, parks, and commercial buildings—in the incidence of crime.

The purpose of this chapter is to examine the ways in which the structure of the urban environment can be used to control and prevent crime. Since it is well known that urban environments produce high crime rates, it is only logical that environmental engineering can be used to reduce those urban crime rates.

Urban environments can influence criminal behavior in particular and behavior in general in two ways—physically, by providing the physical surroundings to which individuals respond; and socially, by providing the social relationships to which individuals respond.

The physical characteristics of the urban environment are noise, pollution, overcrowding, and refuge. The social characteristics are alienation, loneliness, anxiety, and dehumanization.[3]

*Urban Planning for Safety*

The way we design our urban environment determines the crime rate and type of crime to a great extent, and yet to my knowledge we have never considered crime prevention an integral part of urban planning. We have finally gotten around to considering education, transportation, recreation, pollution, and shopping as variables with which any city planner must cope, but security of person and property is not yet an item taken into consideration when we design and build cities.

Though little has been written on the subject, we do have some preliminary knowledge about urban design and crime control. Jane Jacobs has given us some good ideas from which we can start our analysis.[4] She notes that streets which are isolated, unused, and nonfunctional are unsafe streets, whereas streets that have both residential and commercial use twenty-four hours a day are safe streets. Streets which have pedestrian and vehicular traffic, which have small shops and cafes open late at night, and which have residents living in apartments overlooking the street level are safe streets. Because they have multiple purposes, such streets have eyes. People must have some reason for using the sidewalks; otherwise they stay indoors. The author lived on Bleecker Street in the heart of Greenwich Village, and this street is packed at night by people walking up and down as tourists or as customers of a variety of shops. Though drug use and homosexuality are widespread in the Village, the streets themselves are relatively safe compared to the quiet, unused suburban streets of other areas.

If people are afraid, they remain inside behind locked doors, and such withdrawal increases the isolation of the streets and thus increases the crime rate. A vicious cycle is created whereby crime forces people off the streets and out of the parks, and nonuse of streets and parks results in a further increase in crime.

What we have said about streets also applies to parks.[5] Parks with multiple uses—restaurants, theatres, zoos, movie houses, art galleries—are safe because they are used. As Jacobs points out, a park must be a part of its surrounding environment and must be used by the people in the area. A park in an office building district will be used during the day for passage of noontime strolling, but after 5 p.m. the office workers leave and the park is left to the perverts or skid row derelicts. Parks must be located where people live so they can be used during leisure time for ball games, concerts, boating, and bicycling.

It is well known that parks in most cities are often very dangerous pieces of land. Many parks have developed reputations for homosexuality and muggings. Today in New York City, Central Park is regarded as a very dangerous place to be after dark, and for that reason people have deserted the park as they have deserted the streets, thus increasing the potential of the park as a dangerous place.

Buildings can be constructed so as to be dangerous, with corridors and passageways hidden from public view. Elevators are another source of danger, as are basements used for storage or washing. Slum clearance has not reduced the crime rate, since modern housing projects are so designed as to be very dangerous places to live. Such developments are often isolated from the main flow of traffic, both human and automobile, and, as such, they are closed to public use and public view.

Interstitial areas have always been high crime rate areas.[6] Shaw and McKay found in the 1920s in Chicago that the area of transition between business and residential areas was a high crime rate area. Lander found in Baltimore that the high crime rate area was the mixed Negro-white area, not the homogeneous ethnic area.[7] Homogeneous ethnic areas (called culture islands) often have a very low crime rate because of their community organization and informal social controls. Jane Jacobs points out that in New York City the Cross-Bronx Expressway created a vacuum area, which is dangerous.[8] Likewise, universities such as Columbia University and City College of New York are now high crime rate areas, because they are isolated from the rest of the environment. We have reference here to physical isolation, not social isolation of the university from the urban community, which is another problem and another story. (Jacobs argues that universities, like parks, should have a public use at night so as to maintain a flow of traffic which will act as a deterrent to criminals.) It is no coincidence that in *West Side Story* the setting for the "rumble" was under an expressway, or that the hero (Tony) was killed in a playground.

Subways are another source of danger because of their isolation from view. In New York City, the police now patrol the cars at night, which has reduced the amount of crime in subways considerably, but the platforms and exits are still not designed for personal security.

A major research project should be undertaken to determine the ways in which urban design contributes to crime, and criminologists should work with urban designers in the planning of cities, in the same way in which medical experts, transportation experts, lighting and heating experts, and pollution experts are involved in city planning.

### Ports and Terminals

Throughout history, ports and terminals have been high crime rate areas. Eighteenth- and nineteenth-century London had such a crime problem on the Thames River that the Thames River Police Act was passed in 1800.[9] In more recent years we have witnessed a high crime rate on the New York-New Jersey waterfront, as well as at John F. Kennedy Airport in New York City. Why should terminals, like parks, produce crime, and what can be done in terms of urban planning and design to reduce the crime rate in these national crime areas?

One interesting little quasi-experiment in crime control was undertaken recently at the New York City Bus Terminal under the direction of Mr. Jack Rosen, Director, Terminal Department, Port of New York Authority, and Mr. Marvin Weiss, Manager, Bus Terminal.[10]

Bus terminals, in general, are collecting spots for derelicts and petty criminals, and the New York City terminal is no exception. Indigents use the waiting room of the terminal for its benches, restrooms, heating, and air conditioning. Elderly Greek men (there is a Greek settlement in the neighborhood) use the terminal as a place for meeting and conversation. Homosexuals and alcoholics also use the facilities of the terminal, as well as using the terminal as a place to meet prospective victims or colleagues. Some men live out of lockers, so to speak, at the terminal for weeks at a time, paying twenty-five cents a day rent on a locker.

Because derelicts and alcoholics are nuisances and interfere with the overall operation of the terminal, some measures were taken to cut down on antisocial behavior in the terminal. The center well of the terminal was a favorite spot for homosexuals and hustlers, who could view the flow of traffic from there. This area was cordoned off so that the problem people could not lean on the railing. Bench seats were replaced with bucket seats so that people could not sleep on the seats. Seats were also removed from the phone booths. The women's section of the waiting room was redecorated in light blue and pink, with more feminine accessories, and this kept the men out of the section. The level of lighting was increased in certain crucial areas, certain loading areas and exits of the building were closed at night, and the flow of traffic was contained in one controlled area. Corridors were sealed off and mirrors were placed at blind corners so as to eliminate surprise attacks in isolated sections of the terminal.

These changes, though minor in nature, indicate the direction in which we can move to control behavior via environmental engineering. It is obvious that the environment of a bus terminal creates certain behaviors, so the remedy is to redesign the environment so as to eliminate the behavior. Future terminal construction should be carried out with security as one of the major considerations.

*Urban Planning for Social Cohesion*

The impact of urbanization and industrialization upon group structure and individual behavior has been a topic of concern to social scientists for many years, as seen in the writings of Weber, Redfield, Tönnies, Park, Main, Becker, and others (see Chapter 3). The movement has been from homogeneous to heterogeneous, from sacred to secular, from primary to secondary groups, from folk to urban, and from mechanical to organic.

Throughout the history of sociology, emphasis has been placed on social cohesion or the lack of it as a factor in group and individual behavior. Durkheim used the term "anomie" to explain the breakdown in the cohesiveness of group structure, resulting in the absence of strong normative standards for governing behavior. Cooley used the term "primary group" to refer to the close, informal, personal relationship which characterizes some social groups. The anomic concept has been used by contemporary sociologists such as Merton, Ohlin, and Cloward to explain deviant behavior (see chapters 7 and 8).

Many studies have shown that deviant behavior is correlated with isolation. Calhoun has shown that a colony of rats living under conditions of overcrowding develop major social pathologies.[11] Sociologists and psychologists have placed emphasis on the role of isolation, depersonalization, and the breakdown of primary group relationships in social pathologies (see chapters 8 and 9). As a result, attention has been given in recent years to the use of groups to change the behavior of criminals and delinquents, such as T-group training, encounter groups, and guided group interaction. Through such groups, it is expected that the behavior of criminals can be changed (see Chapter 8).

Thus far we have discussed two basic, but contradictory developments: (1) the influence of primary group norms over group members, and (2) the decline and dissolution of primary groups in modern industrial society. The issue, then, is to what extent informal group relationships can control human behavior in today's society. Christopher Alexander has written that the current attempts to re-create strong primary groups, as seen in T-group training, in sensitivity training, or in group therapy and guided group interaction, is doomed to failure. "So far none of these methods has met with any great success. So far the forces which are breaking primary groups apart have been stronger than the efforts to construct artificial primary groups."[12]

Alexander suggests using urban design to reestablish human contact in the city. Specifically, he outlines an urban plan whereby houses are on streets with a communal room visible from the street, thus allowing passersby to see if the inhabitants are available for visiting. He also states that houses must have private rooms as well as public ones, must be on short streets, must be on common land which several households share and use, and must be located at a density rate high enough to allow people to have intimate contact with at least four other households in the neighborhood.

Alexander argues that the decline of primary groups in industrial cities has created social pathologies and an autonomy/withdrawal syndrome which must be countered by the way in which we design our urban areas. He is resorting to the type of environmental engineering which is so essential if we are to control and prevent crimes in the future.

In what ways will social cohesion aid in crime control? As Jacobs and others have argued, in a city we lack the sense of personal identification and trust in others so necessary for controlling deviant behavior. Peace is kept by voluntary controls enforced by the citizenry.[13] Mutual aid can be a great deterrent to crime, providing individuals accept the responsibility to protect each other. A house or street or car watched by several concerned neighbors is a safe house or street or car. Citizens who do not "get involved" are not preventing crime.

Artificially created groups are effective only so long as the offender is a member of the group. The environment-controlling behavior is limited to the group. When the offender leaves the group, as when he leaves prison, he is under the influence of a much stronger and wider environment than that provided by the therapeutic group, and his behavior will be adapted to his new environment. As Alexander points out, artificial primary groups are not strong enough to counter other environmental influences. Group interaction operates on the model of the individual offender after the offense; the model herein discussed is based on changing the environment to which the individual responds, not changing the individual through group processes (which can be done only within the limits of the influence of the group.)

### Urban Renewal and Social Welfare

Two major sources of expenditures now plague our economic policy—military and welfare. There is no return to the society in terms of improved social or economic conditions; once the money is spent, it is lost to the community. The war in Vietnam is beyond the scope of this book, so we will concentrate on the millions of dollars spent each year directly and indirectly on welfare cases.

The welfare system is set up on a subsistence model; it allows the person to live from month to month without providing any way in which the person will in the future become productive or in which society will benefit from the activities of the welfare recipient. The only return society now receives is the alleviation of guilt feelings which would result if welfare recipients were allowed to starve to death.

The welfare system not only does not rehabilitate people, but it destroys the incentives to become productive. If a man is paid for not working, why should he work? We noted in Chapter 10 that many young delinquents refused jobs because they either could hustle or could receive welfare payments. We must establish a policy of full employment, and with it we must control the nonproductive means to income—crime and welfare.

The inner city is in great need of rebuilding, and yet we spend millions a year to keep people alive and nonproductive. We need new housing, hospitals, highways, schools, recreation centers, and so forth. The task of rebuilding vast aspects of our urban communities could involve thousands of people for years to come. Although politicians have talked about getting people off welfare roles and into productive jobs, this has never been accomplished because we continue to operate the welfare system in the same old way.

Mayor John Lindsay of New York recently stated that the welfare system was a total failure, and he called for a system which will reward working families and will encourage them to work and stay together.[14] He also called for taking the tax load on income off the backs of middle-income taxpayers in the city. Though Lindsay advocates such a policy, his administration has resulted in the largest welfare load and highest tax burden in the history of New York City. The failure of city administrations to solve the city's welfare problems clearly calls for a dramatic new approach to city planning. The Nixon Administration has also proposed a program wherein the emphasis is on employment, rather than on welfare (see Chapter 10).

What is suggested here is a new approach to employment, wherein all unemployed persons sixteen years of age or older would be drawn into public works projects. Such employment would not be voluntary, since the financial support of the individual would be dependent upon his employment. If we argue that the dignity of work is a right of every citizen, then it follows that a corresponding duty exists on the part of the citizen to society. No one should be unemployed, either because no jobs are available or because individuals refuse to work.

A program should be established whereby unemployed men, derelicts, alcoholics, and dropouts are placed in work details. Such details would start at a very menial level, such as cleaning the streets, planting shrubbery, and painting old buildings. Those interested in learning a skilled trade would be placed in a job training program which was part of an ongoing urban renewal project. Rather than training these individuals in job corps centers at a cost of millions a year, these individuals would be trained in local community projects so that at the end of a year there would exist a new school or hospital, a refurbished neighborhood, a new highway or recreation center. Very careful behavioral controls must be applied so that a high level of productivity and behavioral change is achieved. In many job corps situations trainees either leave the program or put a minimum effort into the program. Many remedial education programs tolerate students who show a high rate of absenteeism, lack of concern, or in other ways fail to benefit from the program. We can no longer tolerate a system which pays people for substandard performance.

Prison programs must likewise be changed in order that inmates are productive and self-sufficient. Federal and state laws which limit prison employment must be changed, in order that prison-made goods may circulate and compete in the general economy. There is no reason why men who are able-bodied must be supported by the state just because they have committed a criminal offense. Rather than cost the state $12,000 or more a year to support the inmate and his family, the prisoner ought to be able to earn a decent salary which would support him and his family while he is in prison.

The human services field is another area where great use of unskilled people could be made. The new careers program is developing guidelines and procedures for training subprofessional aides in human services, but again the impact on our hospitals and schools has not yet been realized.

The educational system must likewise be revised and interfaced with a public works program. It should be possible for a person desiring more education to attend classes simultaneously with a job training program. Those students who wish to attend college should be encouraged to do so, providing they have the capabilities and motivation. Students who fail to perform adequately should not be allowed to take up space in our college system, and such students should be placed in jobs with some provision for night school or weekend classes.

The idea that everyone must possess a college degree must be realistically reappraised, and the needs of the economy must be tied to the educational system. It might even be suggested as a way-out idea that all young people be trained in a job category which can be used at any time as a means of making a living while attending college or as a supplement to income from other sources later in life. In this connection, we might consider making use of volunteers who would work ten to twelve hours a week on urban renewal projects on a nonpay basis as a contribution to the community. We have our youth throwing bricks through college windows; perhaps we should ask them to lay bricks on the weekend to build a new college or pediatrics clinic. Again, this idea of a domestic peace corps has been discussed, but has never been implemented. Perhaps a banker or school teacher would enjoy an opportunity to help rebuild a part of his community on a volunteer basis during his spare or leisure time. Rewards such as special recognition for public service or tax rebatement could be used in connection with such a service program.

The usual complaint raised by social welfare administrators is that most of the people on welfare are not able to work. This is only true because of our definition of work. A young child of five years of age can "work" if we mean by that participating in an education program which will develop his potentialities during the next ten or twelve years. Unless we want the current group of kindergarten students to be dropouts in ten years, we had better prepare them to function as productive citizens. Youngsters can earn their way via education programs. Why cannot we pay students for achievement, providing we see to it that only those who achieve are paid? Why keep a child on AFDC payments for ten years if by the age of sixteen he or she is a high school dropout, unemployed, delinquent, and the father or mother of illegitimate children?

The only two categories of individuals not included in this plan for full employment are the sick and the elderly, and if our economy does away with its wasteful usage of human resources, and requires or provides that every citizen be completely productive and self-sufficient, then we can easily afford to pay the sick and elderly, when they are unable to work, through insurance and pension programs.

To implement such a plan would require that we reject the welfare morality wherein we degrade people through charity, and realize that everyone can and must work, not only for the support of the economic system, but for his own personal dignity. Anyone who says jobs are not available has not walked the streets of New York City recently to observe the tremendous need for human labor in reconstituting the urban condition.

The above plan, though not developed here in any great detail, could reduce the cost of running our cities while at the same time adding individuals to taxable payrolls. Taxes on middle-class incomes are now so high as to pose a serious threat to our tax system. Joseph Barr, Secretary of the Treasury, recently warned that a taxpayers' revolt could occur if taxes were not reduced considerably in the near future,[14] and yet cities such as New York, although operating on a multimillion-dollar budget, are unable to meet existing expenses or to expand on needed services and programs.

The present strategy of mayors and governors is to call for more tax money from the federal government, which means the suburban areas will be taxed to pay for the high cost of crime and welfare in the major urban centers. What is called for is not a heavy tax burden on our taxpayers, but a reduction in the crime rate and the welfare rolls, which would then allow for an overall reduction in the tax rate for all citizens. The urban areas have a high cost of operation because they are supporting nonproductive activities. If we break the crime/welfare cycle, not only would the cost of running our cities decrease considerably, but the inhabitants would be tax-paying citizens rather than tax burdens.

The welfare model now followed provides materials and services to the poor—clothing, food, rent, medical care, dental care, and so forth. The model herein advocated would not provide such services, but would allow the individual to purchase his own housing, clothing, or medical care. One of the reasons the poor are powerless and unable to control their own destiny is that they lack the means to reward others—e.g., to pay for goods and services. Slum areas exist only because people cannot afford to live in areas where rents are higher. If people now living in substandard housing could afford to move into better housing, the demand for housing would result in a supply of housing without any official government programs for urban renewal or low-cost housing projects. If people can afford to hire personal physicians, rather than waiting all day at a public welfare clinic for medical services, the people will receive better medical service without cost to the taxpayer. The way to provide better housing, clothing, education, and medical services to the poor is to give the poor economic power so that they can demand a better grade of housing, education, or medical care. So long as the public taxpayer is providing and paying for the services which welfare recipients receive, these services, for economic and social reasons, must be and will remain inferior and degrading.

### Summary

Crime can be controlled through urban design, wherein safety and security are designed into streets, buildings, and parks. Our cities are unsafe because they present opportunities for the commission of crimes.

Cities can also be designed so as to increase human contact of an intimate nature. Anomie, loneliness, and alienation need not characterize our urban life.

Urban renewal can be substituted for the welfare system, and people can be put to work building an environment supportive of the biological and social development of its inhabitants.

## NOTES

[1.] David Krech, Richard S. Crutchfield, and Norman Livson, *Elements of Psychology* (New York: Alfred Knopf, 1969, 2nd ed.); Norman L. Munn, L. Dodge Fernald, and Peter S. Fernald, *Introduction to Psychology* (New York: Houghton Mifflin Co., 1969, 2nd ed.).

[2.] New York Times, November 24, 1969.

[3.] Rene Dubos, *So Human an Animal* (New York: Charles Scribner's Sons, 1968).

[4.] Jane Jacobs, *The Death and Life of Great American Cities* (New York: Random House, 1961), p. 29 ff.

[5.] Ibid., p. 89. ff.

[6.] Ibid., p. 258 ff.

[7.] Clifford Shaw, *Delinquent Areas* (Chicago: University of Chicago Press, 1929).

[8.] Jacobs, op. cit., p. 258 ff.

[9.] Leon Radzinowicz, *A History of English Criminal Law and its Administration from 1750,* London: Stevens and Sores, 1956, Vol. 2, p. 349 ff.

[10.] Personal conversations with Mr. Rosen and Mr. Weiss.

[11.] William R. Ewald, ed., *Environment for Man,* Bloomington: Indiana University Press, 1966, p. 44.

[12.] Ibid., p. 87.

[13.] Jacobs, op. cit., p. 32 ff.

[14.] New York Daily News, May 27, 1969.

[15.] New York Times, January 18, 1969.

*Chapter 15*

## Control of Morality, Trust,
## and Organized Crime

*Introduction*

So far we have limited our discussion to crimes against individuals—
personal or property. It has been noted in the literature that though crimes
against the person strike fear into the citizens, and thus safety in the
streets is the theme of political campaigns, other types of criminal activity
are more costly in dollars.

Three types of criminal activity do not involve crimes against the
individual:

(1) Crimes against morality, such as crimes involving alcohol,
narcotics, gambling, sexual behavior, and vagrancy. Such crimes do
not involve a victim; the victim is the criminal, and there is no
complaining witnesses to prosecute the case.

(2) Crimes involving a violation of financial trust or of laws
regulating business activity. Such crimes are committed by middle-
or upper-class people, not lower-class ghetto dwellers, and they do
not involve the use of force or violence.

(3) Crimes by organized syndicates engaged in illegal, semilegal, and
legal business activities. Such crimes involve the basic political and
economic organization of the social system, as well as the cooperation of that portion of the public which wants the illegal services
provided by the syndicate.

The control of crimes in these categories is not possible through the
traditional techniques discussed herein, or by the new methods suggested
herein through science, technology, and urban design.

(1) Deterrence through punishment—i.e., imprisonment—does not
work, since few white-collar or syndicate criminals are in prison. The
alcoholics, drug addicts, prostitutes and homosexuals who are in
prison are not thereby reformed.

(2) Rehabilitative measures, such as therapy, counseling, and probation are not useful with white-collar and syndicate criminals, since these individuals are not poverty-stricken, unemployed, psychotic, neurotic, or in need of job training. These rehabilitative measures have not demonstrated any effectiveness in the treatment of alcoholism, drug addiction, or sexual deviance.

(3) The usual theories of criminal behavior—poverty, blocked opportunities, mental illness, and differential association—do not explain organized crime, white-collar crime, or crimes involving morality.

The positivist's attempt to explain crime in terms of the characteristics of criminals has not come close to explaining the sorts of crime discussed in this chapter. An environmental analysis of such behavior could contribute to both the understanding and the control of nonstreet offenses.

## Crime and Morality

As was discussed in Chapter 3, the extension of the criminal process into the area of private morality has been challenged in recent years. Overcriminalization of the judicial process has brought cries that we should remove the criminal sanction from alcoholism, drug addiction, gambling, and consensual sexual offenses. The Supreme Court has already declared alcoholism and drug addiction to be illnesses, not crimes. The "labeling school" of criminology contends that a deviant is one who is labeled as such by his social group (which is obvious), and therefore the label "deviant" should be removed from many acts now labeled criminal (which is not so obvious).

Professors Norval Morris and Gordon Hawkins[1] take the position that the criminal sanction should be removed from morality offenses, since the criminal law only drives up the price of the illegal activity, creates large-scale organized crime, creates property offenses by addicts who must pay for illegal drugs, removes the police from felony cases, and creates crimes which result in political corruption of the legal process.

Professor Edwin Schur[2] also regards overlegislation as a cause of many of the problems we have with our criminal justice system. He joins the overcriminalization argument and the labeling argument in his discussion of the difficulty of handling alcoholics, sex offenders, drug addicts, and juvenile delinquents as criminals.

On the other hand, Professor Donald Cressey[3], has noted that legalized gambling in Nevada, England, and the Bahamas has led to further syndicate control of gambling, and thus legalized gambling could not decrease the profits of organized crime syndicates. Fred J. Cook, in a review of the Morris-Hawkins book[4] states that their example of legalized gambling in Nevada is completely in error.

> The principal lesson of Nevada is virtually the opposite. It was Bugsy Siegal who opened up Nevada as a big-time gambling oasis for the national crime syndicate, and throughout the decades since, czars of the American underworld have maintained a tight grip on many of the casinos in Las Vegas. . .what legalization of gambling did was to provide the mob with a legal facade behind which to operate; millions of dollars were skimmed off the top before tax officials got their bite.

The British plan for legalized narcotics distribution has come under heavy attack in recent months due to a dramatic increase in drug addiction in England.[5] Prostitutes and drug pushers have indicated to the author that they would prefer to have such an act outlawed, since it adds to the profits available from such crimes. Thus, the argument is most inconclusive as to whether legalizing certain behaviors would alleviate the problem or merely shift its character of operation.

One can accept the fact that the criminal sanction is not the proper one for dealing with this class of offenses without assuming, as the Morris-Schur argument does, that decriminalization of the system is an answer. Such behaviors will still be of concern and will be regarded by a large segment of the population as social problems. Such legal doctrine is potentially very dangerous, for it leaves the community unprotected, leaves the "ill" person without treatment, and leaves these problems in the realm of mental illness and psychiatry rather than of behavioral/environmental problems.

One solution to the problem is to legalize behavior that is private, consensual, and does not interfere with the rights of others. Sex offenses, abortion, and gambling can be legalized, so long as the ramifications for others are defined specifically. Drug addiction and alcoholism are more difficult problem areas, since the alcoholic who panhandles or appears in public in an intoxicated state is a nuisance and a possible threat to others. The drug addict who is committing other criminal acts or who is not self-sufficient may also represent a threat to the community. One way of redefining alcoholism and addiction would be to regard as criminal those acts which interfere with the general public. A drunk who is in a public place, is driving a car, or is assaultive can legitimately be subject to public sanction. The concepts of private and consensual are the crucial ones in defining behavior as noncriminal.

Even legalization of private acts plus stiff legal penalties for the public consequences of private acts is by no means an adequate answer to the problems involved in addiction and alcoholism. The harmful effects of drugs and alcohol are such as to require a more scientific approach to these behavioral problems, and a behavioral approach must replace a medical or social work approach to such problems. The use of drugs and alcohol represents a response to a given environmental situation, and the best hope for control lies in (1) knowing the environmental conditions that produce alcoholism and addiction, and (2) making the necessary changes in the environment so as to reduce the severity of such behavior. Such a research program would involve biochemistry, psychopharmacology, experimental psychology, and sociology. One possibility is the treatment of addiction and alcoholism biochemically; another is to develop behavioral control techniques whereby the stimulus situation is so engineered as to enable the individual user to better control his behavior. Individual conditioning therapy or reality therapy can make a contribution in this regard. Without basic behavioral research, we will only perpetuate these problems for years to come.

## Organized Crime

Both professional criminologists and the lay public have shown a keen interest in organized crime, by which is meant (1) a complex organized group united by family ties and background, (2) a political/business system involving graft and corruption, and (3) organized control of illegal activities—gambling, rackets, prostitution, drugs, and alcohol, as well as semilegal and legal activities involving labor unions, hotels and restaurants, warehousing, loan sharking, coin-operated businesses, construction work, and dry cleaning.[6]

Several problems exist for anyone wishing to discuss the control of organized crime: (1) Does the Mafia or Cosa Nostra exist? (2) How does one separate the legal and illegal business operations of the organization? (3) How does one discuss criminal activities involving the basic political/economic organization of the society?

Although skeptics have existed for years as to the true nature of the Mafia, the recent publication of the Valachi Papers,[7] the Task Force Report on Organized Crime,[8] and a book by Donald Cressey[9] has again raised the fundamental question of the existence of the Mafia. Cressey uses the Oyster Bay Conference on Organized Crime definition of a "single, loosely knit conspiracy, Italian dominated, operated on a nation-wide basis, and representing a powerful group in organized crime."

Cressey found twenty-four families that form the Cosa Nostra, or crime confederation, in the United States.[10] Morris, in his recent book on crime control, denies the existence of a Mafia and regards it as a myth to be studied by anthropologists.[11]

Whether or not the Mafia exists depends on the way in which one defines the concept. To idealize it, as is so often done in the literature, as a criminal superagency with clear lines of authority, membership, and activity is probably a gross error, as Morris has documented in his discussion. A similar mistake is made by criminologists who regard juvenile groups as well-organized, formal systems.[12] On the other hand, to state that there is a close relationship between illegal business activities and urban politics, that corruption and bribery occur in this setting, and that control by Italians (and others) over certain shady political and business activities does exist is obvious and beyond debate. Stripped of its glamor and appeal, organized crime refers to political corruption and illicit activities occurring in any major urban setting where a profit is to be had from such activities. Where political corruption ends and crime begins, or where legal business activity ends and crime begins, has never been spelled out, and thus the definition of organized crime remains unsettled.

Cressey advocates making organized crime illegal, thus moving from the individual to the organization.[13] Such a move would be difficult in light of the difficulty involved in defining organized crime. But even more burdensome is the fact that such a law would have to be enforced, and there is no reason for assuming that this would be the case. The system for administration of justice now operates at a very low efficiency level, and adding to it the burden of organized crime is not very helpful. The American belief that to pass a law is to control a problem is fallacious and must be firmly recognized as so.

A view opposite to Cressey's is put forth by Morris, who advocates the control of organized crime by the removal of criminal sanctions from areas discussed above, such as gambling, addiction, and prostitution.[14] He quotes an economist who finds that profit motivates and perpetuates such crime (an argument we have presented through this book for crime in general) and thus, by legalizing such acts, the profits would be diminished or eliminated. As was pointed out above, the legalization of gambling and drug addiction has not reduced the profits in those instances where it has been tried. If we legalize gambling, it is still profitable, but now the profits are legal.

Two crucial distinctions must be made in order to define and control organized crime: (1) a distinction must be made between violent and nonviolent acts by the syndicate; (2) a distinction must be made between legal and illegal acts by the syndicate. It is almost impossible to control illegal acts involving the consent of the victim, especially if they involve corruption on the part of the local political officials. One can state that it is more crucial to protect the rights of a citizen who is threatened by the mob with physical violence than it is to use official action where the public is consuming syndicate services because it demands such services. We can strengthen and make operative legal sanctions against intimidation, assault, murder, and arson, and thus protect any citizen who does not want to be bothered by the syndicate. On the other hand, people who wish to stay in a syndicate-owned resort motel, use syndicate-distributed drugs or alcohol, and gamble at a syndicate casino should be allowed to do so within the limits of legalization of such activities as discussed above.

In summary, acts of a *criminal* nature, as opposed to acts of a moral or business nature, should be outlawed for the syndicate as they now are for all citizens. The problem is not that such acts are not criminal, but that the legal code is not enforced effectively in any area, including organized crime.

The problem of police/political corruption which surrounds urban politics and organized crime is not new, nor does it lend itself to traditional methods of crime control. To say behavior is controlled by the environment is one thing; to change that environment is another. We can resort to behavioral engineering and urban planning to control street crimes, but such crimes assume a victim who wishes to be protected. The victim of corruption is the general public, not one individual, and this public is often either uninformed about or uninterested in political corruption. The first step in control is detection, and, until we can detect corruption, we cannot control it. One approach would be to devise new methods for such detection; another would be to work through the political institutions so as to lessen corruption.

The only point the author would make is that we must change the environment within which such behavior occurs if we wish to alter the behavior; we will not do it by punitive or therapeutic procedures applied to the individual offender. The positivistic orientation of criminologists and criminal law makes it difficult to handle such concepts as organized crime and corruption, since individual crimes and treatment measures are the major concern of our legal system. Perhaps organized and white-collar crime should be regarded not as problems in criminology but as problems of politics and economics. If it is true that the criminal sanction cannot successfully be extended to all social problems, such as illegitimacy, poverty, delinquency, alcoholism, and addiction, then it might also be true that the criminal sanction is not the proper one for organized and white-collar crime. Nonlegal measures which will remove the profit from illegal behavior and regulate the legal use of gambling, drugs, alcohol, and business need to be developed and implemented.

## White-Collar Crime

White-collar crime refers to business or occupation crime, either violations of financial trust (embezzlement, fraud, bribery) or violations of laws regulating business, such as antitrust, pure food and drug, or labor relations regulations.[15] Most of what was stated above concerning organized crime applies to white-collar crime:

(1) The definition of white-collar crime is a subject of controversy.

(2) The prosecution of white-collar crime is weak, though the financial loss to the community is great.

(3) The usual theories of criminal behavior do not explain white-collar crime. Though Sutherland attempted to apply differential association to white-collar crime, there is no more evidence to support the theory in this area than for other types of crime. Cressey did not find support for the theory in his study of embezzlement (see chapter 7).

(4) The usual deterrence/treatment procedures do not apply or have not been applied to white-collar criminals.

Professor Gilbert Geis[16] has suggested that white-collar crime be limited to the behavior of individuals within the corporate structure rather than to the artificial construct of corporate crime. Geis accuses Sutherland of confusing corporate entities with the executives who engage in the white-collar offenses, and he notes that the law requires that corporate officials shall authorize, order, or do a positive act which is in violation of the law. He is here drawing a distinction between crimes requiring criminal intent or mens rea and strict liability offenses for which no mens rea or individual culpability is needed.

It is of academic interest whether we hold corporations per se or individuals per se responsible for the criminal activities of corporations. However, from a behavioral point of view, it makes a great deal of difference if we hold the corporation liable, since then we can fine the corporation; but the usual situation is such that the gain from the illegal activities outweighs the fine, and it is to the advantage of the corporation to pay the fine. If the corporate official is imprisoned, the deterrent impact on him is such as to control his behavior, probably to a much greater extent than is the case of the lower-class criminal. Geis suggests that executives are aware of the negative consequences of corrections and imprisonment. The basic thesis of this book is that environmental design must take place prior to the commission of a crime in order to eliminate the opportunity for a crime to be committed. This means detection of criminal acts as well as the correction of those situations which make profitable illegal behavior. In the case of white-collar crime, urban design will not be of any real value. Surveillance devices, including new and effective accounting and monitoring procedures for people involved in positions of financial trust, are needed. As in the case of organized crime, many of the basic issues raised by white-collar crime are of a political and economic nature—e.g., political corruption, urban politics, corporate management and organization, legal controls of business activities, and economic competition. To deal with such problems within the confines of traditional criminology is a mistake. Probation, prisons, group therapy, and sentencing procedures are not the answers to white-collar crime. The restructuring of the environment which we have discussed herein in terms of its physical and social aspects must be expanded to include the political and economic structure of our system. Given the thrust of this book, which is the control of the criminal acts of individual offenders, it is difficult to discuss the criminal activities occurring within our political-economic system in the same terms. The scope of criminology is extended to legal control of the economic system in general. At this point in history, criminologists are not prepared to make meaningful statements about the prevention and control of white-collar crime. Criminology does not have either the theoretical or research base needed for the analysis of such problems and rethinking these issues within the structure of a major research project is called for at this time. Rather than looking at the characteristics of individual offenders, we must look at the basic characteristics of the political environment within which such crimes occur.

Edwin Costikyan has suggested[17] that urban politics has failed because of: (1) the destruction of the political machine in the cities, and (2) the shortage of a supply of cheap labor. The political machine, which was destroyed by liberal reformers who wanted to eliminate corruption, was able to provide services for the local community and thus give the citizen immediate access to his government. In its place, a civil service bureaucracy now stands between the mayor and the public and makes ineffective any attempt to reform the government. As an example, the police department has higher salaries, more men, and more equipment, and yet fewer policemen than ever are on the streets. John Lindsay has not been able to change the character of the police department. The civil service is immune from discipline by elected officials and thus it can be as inefficient as it wishes. The cost of providing essential services has increased by fifteen percent in New York City, while the revenues have increased by five percent.

The second problem, a shortage of cheap labor to rebuild the city, Costikyan regards as a major factor in the decay of the urban environment and urban services. He suggests an emergency urban work force made up of young volunteers who would devote several years of life to urban development. This corps would be along the lines of the Peace Corps and is essentially what was discussed above in Chapter 14. The author would add to the domestic urban corps the employable people now on public welfare (one in eight in the case of New York City). Political and environmental engineering, as suggested by Costikyan, is crucial in any solution to organized and white-collar crime.

### Summary

Crimes involving morality, political corruption, and financial violations do not fall within the structure of conventional criminology, either in terms of theories of criminal behavior or of means used to deal with individual offenders. The usual suggestions for controlling such crimes fall into two general categories: (1) legalize such acts, or (2) pass new, more restrictive laws suppressing such acts. The overcriminalization/labeling approach must be regarded as impractical. New controls over deviant behavior must be found if legal controls are removed, a better distinction must be drawn between lawful behavior and the unlawful consequences of behavior, or between strictly private acts and private acts with public consequences, and between violent acts against the public as opposed to illegal services demanded by the public.

The argument that we need new laws to control crime assumes that if we pass a law, we handle a problem. The history of criminal law reveals the fallacies of this approach, and it would be futile to overlegislate in an area which is now regarded by many professionals as already overcriminalized.

The answer may lie in new nonlegal controls over many areas now regarded as criminal. Criminology is equipped neither by research nor theory to handle issues involving major political and economic factors. The overextension of criminal law into areas of morality, financial trust, and political corruption has led to a corresponding overextension of criminology into these areas. Political and economic solutions which change the environment within which such behavior occurs must be found, in cooperation with criminology but outside the scope of criminology, unless criminology includes the solution of all social problems.

## NOTES

[1.] Norval Morris and Gordon Hawkins, *The Honest Politician's Guide to Crime Control,* Chicago: The University of Chicago Press, 1970, pp. 1-28.

[2.] Edwin M. Schur, *Our Criminal Society,* Englewood Cliffs: Prentice-Hall, 1969, pp. 115-118, pp. 191-228.

[3.] Donald R. Cressey, *Theft of a Nation,* New York: Harper and Row, 1969, pp. 293-296.

[4.] *Saturday Review,* April 4, 1970, p. 36.

[5.] New York Times, March 30, 1970, p. 1; Morris and Hawkins, op. cit., pp. 9-10.

[6.] Walter C. Reckless, *The Crime Problem* (ed.), New York: Appleton-Century-Crofts, 1967, pp. 319-343. Also J. Smith, *Syndicate City,* Chicago: Henry Regency Company, 1954.

[7.] Peter Maas, *The Valachi Papers,* New York: G.P. Putman's Sons, 1968.

[8.] The President's Commission on Law Enforcement and Administration of Justice, *Organized Crime,* Washington, D.C.: U.S. Government Printing Office, 1967.

[9.] Cressey, op. cit.

[10.] Cressey, op. cit., p. 20.

[11.] Morris and Hawkins, op. cit., p. 204 ff.

[12.] Lewis Yablonsky, *The Violent Gang,* New York: Macmillan Company, 1962.

[13.] Cressey, op. cit., p. 299 ff.

[14.] Morris and Hawkins, op. cit., pp. 234-235.

[15.] Edwin H. Sutherland and Donald R. Cressey, *Principles of Criminology,* 7th ed., Philadelphia: J.B. Lippincott Company, 1966, pp. 43-45; Reckless, op. cit., pp. 344-359.

[16.] Reckless, op. cit., pp. 359-365.

[17.] Edwin Costikyan, "Cities Can Work," *Saturday Review,* April 4, 1970, p. 19.

Part V

**POLICY FOR CRIME CONTROL**

# Systems, Analysis, Decision Theory, and Crime Control

## Systems Analysis

The newer fields of the behavioral sciences have been associated with systems analysis and decision theory. This movement has borrowed liberally from biology and computer engineering and is found in psychology, sociology, anthropology, public administration, business administration, and political science.[1]

Though there is no one approach to a theory of systems, certain basic assumptions run throughout the literature.

(1) The approach is behavioral; it deals with what is, rather than with what ought to be. A separation of facts and values is made, and values are handled as part of a factual situation.

(2) The approach is environmental; it places great emphasis upon the environment in which a system—be it a cell, an organism, or a factory—exists and functions. Adaptation is an important concept.

(3) Communication, feedback of results, and self-correcting or -controlling devices are emphasized. Cybernetics is concerned with the principles of feedback systems.

(4) Emphasis is placed on interrelationships not only of the parts of the system, but of the system to larger systems.

(5) A system has structure and function. Structure-functionalism is a critical and important aspect of current thinking about systems.

(6) Systems analysis looks to the future outcome or consequences of present decisions. It is scientific in its view of human behavior, has a scientific methodology, and is interested in what will occur if I do so and so, rather than showing an interest in what has already occurred.

A system has been defined as a whole by virtue of the interdependence of its parts.[2] Another definition of a system given by Kaplan is a set of interrelated variables maintained under the impact of environmental influences.[3] Van Court Hare has defined systems analysis as "the formulation and evaluation of precise alternatives, with the selection of activities and their level, with the integration of short and long range plans, with the specification of values and objectives, and with the implementation of strategies of diagnosis, trouble-shooting, repair, and control."[4]

A system can be a closed system—one that does not interact with the environment—or it can be an open system, capable of receiving messages from and responding to environmental conditions. The system we are most interested in is an open system or input-output system, since human biological and psychological processes are of this nature. A cell responds to changes in the environment surrounding it. A human being responds to signals he receives from the environment. As was noted in Chapter 11, the human organism is made up of receptors, connectors, and effectors, and open systems have receptors, connectors (or detectors), and effectors.[5] A system can also be classified as instantaneous or dynamic. An instantaneous system responds to a signal at that point in time; a dynamic system has a memory which can store past experiences or signals for future action.[6]

The usual analysis of a system is $X \rightarrow \square \rightarrow Y$, where X is input, Y is output, and the black box represents the organism or organization receiving the message and responding to it. Whatever transformation of information received, occurs in the so-called "black box."[7] Feedback loops can be added.

$$X \rightarrow \square \rightarrow \square \rightarrow \square$$

The decision process can also be added in the form of a diagram of a decision tree.

$$X \rightarrow \square$$

## Decision Theory

Decision theory concerns itself with the process by which choices of alternative actions concerning means and ends are selected, including the allocation of materials and manpower.

Lasswell has identified several stages of decision-making: identification of the problem, information search, formulation of alternatives, selection of alternatives, enforcement, implementation, monitoring and review, and termination.[8] March and Simon identify four decision-making processes: problem-solving, persuasion, bargaining, and politics.[9]

Drucker has defined decision-making processes as identification of problems, classification of problems, specification of problems, decision, action for solution of problems, and feedback of results of action.[10]

Decision theory involves communications networks, information theory, input and output analysis, feedback channels, utility or payoff tables, and prediction and control of the outcome of human action. Linear programming, operations research, and probability theory are used to determine the outcome of a given decision, given a set of facts and values. Decision theory has been useful in organizing strategies for the actualization of given objectives.[11]

Related to decision theory is game theory,[12] a model of the decision process designed to maximize gain and minimize loss, where strategy depends upon the reaction of one or more opponents, as in a football or a card game. Probability statistics play a crucial role in the formulation of mathematical models of gaming strategies. To the extent that decisions are based on unknown or uncontrolled variables, the decision maker must decide on the basis of the probability of an event. A decision to go to a movie is based on a high probability the movie house will be open; a decision to remain home to await a possible phone call is based on a much different probability figure.

Game theory can involve a zero-sum game, where the gain for one player equals the loss for another.[13] Most card games and athletic games are of this sort. A strategy game or non-zero-sum game differs in that the players stand to gain or lose depending on what each player does under all conceivable circumstances.[14] All players can win or lose depending on the strategy. Military and political strategy is much better characterized by this model, since certain strategies will produce a gain for all parties (an agreement between a union and management or between the President and a governor may produce a gain for both, or it could produce a loss for both). The model used in a strategy game depends on a number of variables, two of which are crucial:

(1) The players may or may not know the payoffs or consequences of different strategies. The value of each decision may be fixed at any degree of certainty or uncertainty.

(2) The players may or may not be in communication with each other, or the communication may be unilateral or bilateral. Coalitions can be formed whereby the players agree to a strategy which maximizes the gain for all.

The Prisoner's Dilemma[15] exists only because each player is ignorant of the decision of the other players; the strategy changes depending on the knowledge each player possesses of the other player's decisions.

*Systems Analysis and Criminal Justice*

As has been pointed out above (Chapters 1 and 13) the present use of systems analysis as applied to the administration of justice is:

Crime committee → Police → Courts → Corrections

Table 3 diagrams the process in operation. The new model advocated in this book is:

Before Crime Committed → Prevention Measures →
Reduced Crime Rate → Prevention and Control of Crime

The old model, based on deterrence and rehabilitation of individual offenders, has been a failure. That much we know and to continue to work within this model in an attempt to repair it will not result in any substantial gain in the prevention and control of crime. The new model, based on prevention before the crime has been committed through environmental and behavioral engineering, has never been put into practice to any great extent, and the results of such a model must be subject to future implementation and evaluation. However, from a theoretical point of view the model should prove to be highly effective.

One major difference between the two models, besides the obvious fact that the two stand diametrically opposed to one another in terms of assumptions and procedures, is that the old model channels new criminals and recidivists back into the system, whereas the new model channels new criminals and recidivists out of the old system and into a new prevention system. Any model of crime control must reduce the number of cases entering the system, otherwise the loop from police → courts → corrections → police continues indefinitely.

Systems analysis can help us see the interrelatedness of the parts to the whole system, or the consequences of action in one part of the system on the system as a whole. For example, increasing the efficiency of the police with OLEA funds without also increasing the capabilities of the courts and correctional parts of the justice system not only will not aid in the fight against crime but will further burden the courts and corrections beyond the point to which they are now overburdened. Another example which might be cited is plea bargaining. It has been said that, if guilty pleas were reduced by as much as twenty-five percent, the court system would stop functioning altogether.

The critical aspect of any system is the input-output relationship, or the payoff for human action. In the case of crime control models, the present input (over $50 million a year) has no measurable output of a positive nature (reduction in crime rate), and it produces many negative outputs. The inputs must change from deterrence and rehabilitation of individual offenders to inputs of environmental design. A new input system will then result in a new output, an output which might be a reduced crime rate and a new crime control system.

One critical element in the present crime control model is the correctional system. Any changes in the police and court system will in themselves be futile if they result in more offenders being placed in the correctional system, since the correctional system has failed to deter or rehabilitate. The logic of systems analysis would force one to develop a correctional system first, before any changes in the police-court system are undertaken, and since changes of any consequence are neither now in operation nor are promised for the future, any effort expended in the police-court system is bound to fail.

Systems analysis makes one aware of the following issues, which are often ignored in social planning:

*(1) Planning must be based on future possibilities, not past events.* Social planning, as now carried out, is based on the past history of discrimination, segregation, poor housing, and inferior education for a segment of the citizenry. It is often said today that we have had a four-hundred-year history of social injustice which justifies current radicalism and unrest. The history of a problem is not the solution, and to use history as a justification for social action is to ignore the fact that the action taken may not alleviate the condition and, in fact, may only intensify and irritate it. A popular argument today is that riots and social protests are a reaction to past conditions of poverty and racism. Riots involve present conditions, but the reaction to these conditions is based on the anticipated consequences of the riots for the future. A rioter is interested in producing changes in military, university, or community policy in the future. To the extent he is correct in his anticipation of the consequences of his action, he is successful. To the extent that he misjudges the consequences of social action, he fails to achieve his goals. A major defect of social action policy is that the consequences are usually not those desired or anticipated.

*(2) Decisions are often made on the basis of philosophical and ideological issues,* rather than on the basis of empirical evidence. If a program is justified as satisfying an ideological position, such as fighting crime, discrimination, poverty, poor housing, or inadequate education, the fact that the measures taken do not help or may even make matters worse is ignored. Justice and social equality are used to justify political programs.

Table 3.  OLD MODEL

| Crime Committed | Police | Courts | Corrections | Outcome | Future |
|---|---|---|---|---|---|
| Action taken for deterrence of individual offender | Investigations Arrests Identify criminals so they can be punished | Determination of guilt via prosecution, sentence for punishment deterrence Imprisonment | Custodial case of inmates, use of prisons, to deter individual criminal | Low success rate Low rate of arrest and police efficiency High rate of civil liberties violations Low conviction rate – high rate plea bargaining Failure of prison systems to deter; overcrowding of criminal justice system | Failure of deterrence model High crime rate, high recidivism rate, continued overcrowding of facilities; inadequate facilities for police, courts, corrections; continued pressure for more repressive measures against criminals |
| Action taken for rehabilitation of individual offender | Investigations Arrests Identify criminals so they can be rehabilitated | Determination of need of treatment Define behavior as illness to be treated Indeterminate sentence, probation, parole, juvenile court, mandatory treatment of sex/narcotics offenders | Rehabilitate individual offender via therapy, group interaction, job training, education; parole with case work supervision | Low rate of success of therapy, job training welfare programs, prison programs, probation, parole casework; Failure of rehabilitative model plus serious violations of civil liberties of accused | Failure of treatment, rehabilitation model High crime rate, high recidivism rate, High rate of unemployment, delinquency, school dropouts; inadequate parole/probation facilities; continued pressure for more treatment programs; new criminals enter justice system at police phase; recidivists enter justice system at police phase |

Table 4.  NEW MODEL

| | Prevention Through Environmental Engineering | Prevention Through Behavioral Engineering | Outcome | Future |
|---|---|---|---|---|
| Before crime is committed | Surveillance systems Urban Planning and Design Removal of opportunities to commit criminal acts | Reward lawful behavior Remove rewards from criminal behavior Preventive police patrols Citizen involvement Education of potential victims Insurance Programs Social cohesiveness of urban neighborhoods | Reduced crime rate; Reduced pressure on citizens, police, courts, corrections; low rate of civil liberties violations; less money spent on criminal activities; more money spent on urban developments, environmental improvement, education, employment | Reduced crime rate; improved environmental conditions; lower cost of crime; lower cost of welfare; rebuilding of urban environment; reduced behavioral disorders |
| After crime is committed | Development of rapid response system; scientific evidence for conviction; computerized data system; modern communication system; better detection/apprehension system | Environment/behavior research on control of criminal behavior for those cases not under control at this time; use crimes committed as basis for further research | Channel criminals into urban work force; development of behavioral controls over criminal behavior | Recycle new crimes into prevention system, not into courts or correctional system |

whereas the justification of such programs must lie in the behavioral knowledge needed to structure the means and ends of human activity. *Brown v. Board of Education* did not desegregate the school system, and it contributed to a further political and racial division of the country. The *Gault* decision has not reformed a single juvenile delinquent. The late Arnold Rose has argued that legal rules often have unanticipated consequences, including the creation of new social problems, as well as the nonalleviation of social problems which the law is designed to eliminate. He uses for examples laws dealing with homosexuality, drugs, alcoholism, mental illness, juvenile delinquency, and poverty. Rose notes that civil rights legislation, including the desegregation cases, played a central role in creating social problems. As he states, the law cements or stabilizes certain social problems that would otherwise wither away and disappear, and it expands and systematizes certain minor social problems into major and comprehensive ones.[16]

No one can argue that recent legislation and judicial decisions have eliminated poverty, segregation, discrimination, or crime. Recent civil rights legislation has created *legal equality* but without *social and economic equality*. The black citizen is not interested in Supreme Court decisions, but in employment, education, and housing. The U.S. Commission on Civil Rights found in 1967 that ninety percent of the black elementary school students attend majority-black schools, racial isolation in public schools in the North has increased rapidly since the *Brown* decision in 1954, and in schools in the South only a slight amount of desegregation can be found, along with a substantial increase in the number of blacks attending all-black schools.[17] Such findings ten years after the *Brown* decision raise crucial issues concerning the role of law in social change.

*(3) Social policy often involves a confusion of means and ends.* Violence has been used to try to achieve racial integration, to try to change college policies and practices, to try to end the war in Vietnam, and to attempt to achieve other ends in addition. We thus find bombs planted in buildings and property destroyed because the protesters object to bombings in Vietnam. Universities are shut down by demonstrations in the name of free speech and freedom.

The high rates of crime and violence have brought more popular and political support for the police and suppressive measures, as seen in the recent legislation in New York State, which allows preventive detention, uncorroborated testimony of accomplices, and arrests without a warrant on the basis of suspicion rather than on that of first-hand knowledge.[18] It is a paradox that violence stems from the belief that the police are too suppressive, and yet the violence of the protesters has brought about more public indignation and a call for more suppressive penal measures. A recent CBS news poll revealed that the American public is more willing now than it was years ago to sacrifice liberty to maintain order. "The use of physical violence against the people, property and institutions of the United States in deviance of the law have created a climate of fear in the country, and under the dominion of fear, a great many people now seem willing to choose sides at the expense of some of their liberties."[19] A recent survey by the Carnegie Commission on Higher Education found that eighty percent of the university faculty members interviewed found protesters to be a threat to the freedom of the university community, and the liberally oriented faculty members were assuming a much more conservative attitude toward issues of violence and order.[20] A recent Gallup Poll found the public taking a hard "law and order" stand on bombings, hijackings, and riots.[21] The use of force in the name of freedom from aggression is producing the greater use of force by the police and public, and, rather than achieving the stated goals of peace and love, these protest movements have accomplished exactly the opposite, which makes the attainment of the original goal even more difficult and remote.

*(4) The ends or goals of a system must be behaviorally defined, not logically or ethically defined.* It may be the goal of a system to achieve racial integration or a reduction in the crime rate; however, the crucial variable is the impact of the program on human behavior in the future. A desegregation order may stiffen opposition to integration and may drive a larger percentage of the population into a more conservative type of politics. Mayor John Lindsay recently announced a budget deficit and recommended a stiff increase in taxes for the taxpayers of New York City. The taxes will undoubtedly drive many businesses and middle-income families out of the city, thereby reducing the overall tax base and increasing further the tax burden for the future. Rather than increasing taxes, a plan to reduce welfare and crime costs, plus a more effective educational system, would be a more systematic way to control the variables involved in financing a large urban center.

In summary, decisions made on the basis of past events and philosophical beliefs, decisions which confuse means and ends, and decisions which ignore the behavioral reaction of the population to the policy lead to unanticipated consequences.

Writers on organizational theory have written about the conversion of ends into means and the latent or unanticipated function of human behavior.[22] The unanticipated consequences of social policy are legendary, because the behavioral consequences of policy are ignored or unknown.

*Decision Theory and Crime Control*

Decision theory obviously has implications for crime control, since crime control involves strategy for maximizing gain and minimizing loss. Decision theory can be applied at two levels in the criminal justice system: (1) the strategy used by the criminal justice system in the fight against crime; and (2) the development of a career line for individual criminals.

Decision theory assumes that (1) goals must be identified and conflicts in goals resolved; (2) alternative means must be identified and evaluated; and (3) choice of alternative means of strategies to attain the goal must be based on allocation of resources and personnel, knowledge of the facts, cost effectiveness analysis, and probability of outcome. Such a decision process assumes knowledge of the facts and rationality as to the selection of an alternative course of action. To the extent that either is lacking, the social policy established will fail to reach its stated goal, and will result in unanticipated consequences.

In the criminal justice system, two goals are identifiable—the minimization of the crime rate and the maximization of individual freedom, liberty, and security. Any policy selected must satisfy both of these requirements or else it will fail to meet the needs of the system.

The alternative means to control crime have been spelled out in our discussion as (1) police, courts, and corrections, or (2) urban planning and design, science and technology, and environmental behavioral control. We have limited ourselves to two models, though a third or fourth could be added. The selection of an alternative policy would depend on the cost of the program plus its efficiency in reaching the goals. A decision process based on this model would reject the present criminal justice system as too costly and too inefficient to be worthy of consideration. The decision process involves selection of alternatives, implementation, and feedback of results, and, by these standards, the present model is a failure. A new model is suggested which is more in line with the requirements of a decision process, since the probability of outcome is in the direction of lower costs and greater efficiency. The new model introduces a high degree of control over the outcome of the measures taken to control crime, and thus it increases the probability of maximization of gain and minimization of loss. The key to the process is the relatedness of means and ends, or the feasibility of policy to reach stated social goals.

Game theory can be used in the construction of a crime control model. The commission of a crime can be viewed as a game among the criminal, the police/courts/correctional system, and the victim. Any strategy of crime control selected must take into account the possible response of the criminal and the other alternative strategies available. The assignment of more police to the robbery detail, rather than to the narcotics detail, must be viewed in terms of the impact of each strategy on the total crime picture. An alarm system must be designed with the possible reaction of the intruder in mind. If an alarm system can be disarmed or in some way made ineffective, or if it can be activated by mice or street noise so as to show a high false alarm rate, then the system will not produce the desired consequences. The commission of a crime can be viewed as a zero-sum game, since the gain for one party is a loss for the other, although it may not be a perfect zero-sum if partial gains or losses occur. A non-zero-sum game is also possible, where both parties gain—e.g., an agreement between political figures and organized crime for the control of narcotics or gambling. The critical element is the degree of control law enforcement officials have over the outcome of the game. The more certain the probability of outcome, the greater the degree of precision in program planning and execution.

A decision model can also be used to explain several aspects of the development of a criminal career line. Certain key decisions occur at crucial times in the life history of a delinquent, such as the decision to drop out of school, to seek employment without skills, to commit a criminal act, and so forth. Each step in the decision process limits the future potential alternatives available to the individual. If he drops out of school, he has limited his choice of a college education, most occupational positions, income, place of residence, and other related consequences (see Figure 1). Figure 1 uses only one decision process—that involving the decision to drop out of high school—as a decision which influences possible future decisions the individual may make. The decision to drop out of high school could in itself be analyzed in terms of the possible variables involved such as (a) boredom or failure of school situations; (b) need to support a family; (c) desire for a car; and (d) desire to be with friends who have dropped out of school; as balanced by (a) future employment and income if one completes high school; (b) the effort and money needed to continue in the school system; and (c) the desire of the family or counselors that the individual remain in school. The former factors are short-term gains for dropping out, the latter are long-term gains for remaining in school. Since many decisions are made on the basis of short-term gains, the long-range consequences of the decision are ignored or unknown. It is not herein suggested that all the variables present in such a decision are presented in the example given, nor is it suggested that we know how the decision to drop out of school is reached, only that a decision model could be constituted for which further empirical verification would be needed.

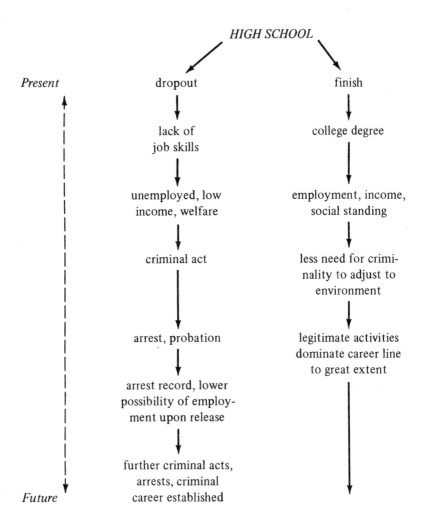

Figure 1

DELINQUENT CAREER LINE AND DECISION PROCESS

A decision model could be constructed for the actual commission of a criminal act. The decision to commit a crime involves the past experience of the subject, the immediate opportunity (presence of victim, open door, cash available in liquor store) for a crime, plus the chances of apprehension or injury. The decision is made in terms of the potential payoff versus potential loss. If the person decides the odds favor the payoff, he will commit the crime. If he is aware of some potential danger, he will decide in favor of temporarily bypassing the opportunity. This does not mean, of course, that he is aware of all potential dangers; for example, the owner of a liquor store may have a gun which he is willing to use. (A few crimes are so ridiculous as to make apprehension almost a certainty, and some critics of decision theory will state that people are not rational when they commit crimes. Since we do not know all the factors that go into a decision process, it appears to us that it is an irrational act. Perhaps when we know more about human behavior we will understand the responses which are now classified as irrational.)

A test of the above model could be set up in a laboratory under controlled conditions, and an experiment could be designed in such a way that the following payoffs were available:

| Crime | Gain | Loss | Probability of Apprehension |
|---|---|---|---|
| A | $.05 | Life in prison | 100% |
| B | $10.00 | 1 year in prison | 90% |
| C | $1,000.00 | $2,000.00 fine | 80% |
| D | $1,000.00 | $2,000.00 fine | 50% |
| E | $100,000.00 | 1 year in prison | 20% |
| F | $1,000,000.00 | $5.00 fine | 1% |

By systematically controlling the gain, loss, and probability of loss (apprehension), we can establish a decision model of this type. The situations are so structured that crimes A, B, and C would never occur, since the loss is always greater than the gain. Crime D would not occur in most cases, since the gain equals the loss. Crimes E and F would always occur since the potential gain is much greater than the potential loss. Obviously, the criminal does not know the potential gain or loss to the exactness we have postulated, but he must, in his decision process, substitute arbitrary estimates of values for the fixed values we have used. He may err in his estimation, which means the outcome may differ from what was the anticipated consequence. No robber enters a liquor store with the intent of being killed. We must also consider the relative value of gains other than money. We used money as our measure of value, but we could have substituted cars, sexual gratification, murder, or assault as the gain, which again would change the values of the payoff.

This model is one which has been emphasized throughout the book. In Chapters 4 and 5, we stated that the low rate of detection, apprehension, and conviction was a factor in the crime rate (the potential loss); we stated in Chapter 2 that the future consequence of the behavior controlled the response (the payoff, gain, or reward) and noted that criminal behavior could be represented by an equation of potential loss as *estimated* by the criminal actor. And, through the book, we have argued that the most feasible way to control crime is (1) to decrease the opportunities for crime (gain) while (2) increasing the probability of apprehension (loss).

### Summary

The use of systems analysis and decision theory forces one to see the inconsistencies of the system and the interrelatedness of parts to whole or of decisions to outcome. The major defects in present social policy involve the use of the past to justify policy, the use of philosophical ideals to justify policy, the confusion of means and ends, and the failure to define the goals of social policy in behavioral terms.

The most crucial element in the process is the future outcome of present behavior. The failure of our social policy to end war, poverty, discrimination, and crime is due to the fact that means used are not necessarily those which result in the achievement of the desired ends or goals, and, as a result, the unanticipated consequences of social policy are legendary.

Public policy must be based on a decision model, which will ensure that the objectives of the policy are attained through the proper allocation of research, resources, and probability of outcome. The critical element is knowledge as to the impact of policy on the behavior of those it touches.

## NOTES

[1.] James C. Charlesworth, ed., *Contemporary Political Analysis,* New York: Free Press, 1967; Walter Buckley, ed., *Modern Systems Research for the Behavioral Scientist,* Chicago: Aldine Publishing Company, 1968.

[2.] Buckley, op. cit., p. xvii.

[3.] Charlesworth, op. cit., p. 150.

[4.] Van Court Hare, Jr., *Systems Analysis: A Diagnostic Approach,* New York: Harcourt, Brace, and World, 1967, p. 9.

[5.] Ibid., p. 112.

[6.] Ibid, p. 112 ff.; George R. Cooper and Clare D. McGillem, *Methods of Signal and System Analysis;* New York: Holt, Rinehart, and Winston, 1967, p. 14.

[7.] Ibid, p. 27 ff.

[8.] Charlesworth, op. cit., p. 180.

[9.] Ibid., p. 180.

[10.] Marshall E. Dimock and Gladys O. Dimock, *Public Administration,* 4th ed., New York: Holt, Rinehart and Winston, Inc., 1969, p. 58.

[11.] Henri Theil et al., *Operations Research and Quantitative Economics,* New York: McGraw-Hill Book Co., 1965; David W. Miller and Martin K. Starr, *Executive Decisions and Operations Research,* Englewood Cliffs: Prentice Hall, Inc., 1960.

[12.] Buckley, op. cit., p. 474 ff.; John Von Newmann and Oskar Morgenstern, *Theory of Games and Economic Behavior,* Princeton: Princeton University Press, 1953; Ewald Burger *Introduction to the Theory of Games,* Englewood Cliffs; Prentice Hall Co., 1963; R. Duncan Lurce and Howard Raiffa, *Games and Decisions; Introduction and Critical Survey,* New York: John Wiley and Sons, 1957; Anatol Rapoport, *Fights, Games and Debates,* Ann Arbor: University of Michigan Press, 1960; Guillenno Owen, *Game Theory,* Philadelphia: W.B. Saunders Co., 1968; A.M. Glickman, *An Introduction to Linear Programming and The Theory of Games,* New York: John Wiley and Sons, 1963; Morton D. Davis, *Game Theory,* New York: Basic Books, 1970.

[13.] Buckley, op. cit., p. 480; Davis, op. cit.

[14.] Buckley, op. cit., p. 480-481; Davis, op. cit.

[15.] Buckley, op. cit., p. 481.

[16.] Arnold Rose, *Social Problems,* Volume 16, No. 1 (Summer, 1968), pp. 33-43.

[17.] U.S. Commission on Civil Rights, *Racial Isolation in the Public Schools,* Washington, D.C.: U.S. Government Printing Office, 1967, p. 199.

[18.] New York Times, April 14, 1970.

[19.] New York Times, April 19, 1970.

[20.] New York Times, April 23, 1970.

[21.] New York Times, April 23, 1970.

[22.] Amitai Etzioni, *Modern Organizations,* Englewood Cliffs: Prentice Hall, Inc., 1964, p. 10 ff.; Robert K. Menton, *Social Theory and Social Structure,* Glencoe: Free Press, 1957, pp. 61-62.

# Chapter 17

# Training in Criminology, Criminal Justice, and Corrections

### Who is the Criminologist?

The term "criminologist" can apply to a variety of people with wide differences in training and skills. This is so because of the nature of the field, which includes chemists, ballistics experts, anthropologists, economists, sociologists, educators, lawyers, psychiatrists, psychologists, police administrators, systems analysts, social workers, and computer engineers.

The field can be divided basically into:

(1) *Detection and Law Enforcement*
Police
Engineers
Criminalistics Experts

(2) *Administration of Justice*
Lawyers
Social Workers
Psychologists

(3) *Corrections*
Social Workers
Sociologists
Psychologists
Psychiatrists
Educators

(4) *Research into Criminal Behavior*
Anthropologists
Psychologists
Psychiatrists
Sociologists

Individuals are not trained as criminologists, but as lawyers, psychiatrists, sociologists, or social workers. There exists in the field a major disagreement as to whether criminology is a discipline, and whether certain professional activities qualify one as a criminologist. Sellin and Wolfgang make a distinction between pure and applied criminology, and they define criminology in terms of science and research. Wolfgang excludes penology from criminology except for research activities associated with the effectiveness of penal measures.[1]

The European view of criminology is much broader, including the practical work associated with probation, parole, and prison management. Szabo regards criminology as a separate discipline which engages both in research and in the application of knowledge to practical problems.[2] Hermann Mannheim states that it is "difficult and invidious to distinguish between the scientific and technical side of criminology," and Radzinowicz adds that "to rob criminology of its practical function is to divorce criminology from reality and to render it sterile." "There remains the vitally important problem of combating crime. The systematic study of all the measures to be taken in the spheres of prevention of legislation, of the enforcement of the criminal law of punishment and other methods of treatment constitutes an indisputable and integral part of criminology."[3]

The President's Commission on Law Enforcement and Administration of Justice found that "sociology, psychology, social work and other fields relevant to corrections have tended to ignore the potential of corrections, both as a career for graduates and as a source of example and experience for the enrichment of classroom discussion."[4]

Polk regards the antivocationalism and departmental specialization of universities as primary factors in the rejection by universities of criminology and corrections as academic fields.[5] The professional identification of "criminologists" is not with criminology but with other disciplines in which they were trained, such as law, medicine, sociology, or psychology, and the American view of criminology as expressed by Sellin and Wolfgang has dominated American criminology. As Reckless notes, few sociologists identify with criminology, and even fewer belong to the American Society of Criminology.[6]

### Training in Criminology

In Europe, training in criminology has usually been associated with schools of law. In England, criminology is associated with the social sciences, though the connection between law and criminology has remained strong in England. In the United States, training in criminology, penology, corrections, and law enforcement has been scattered throughout several departments or schools, including sociology, psychology, law, social work, public administration, and police science. [7]

A survey of manpower needs in criminal justice by Piven and Alcabes[8] showed that the preferred academic field for probation and parole is social work; for work in corrections, the preferred academic field is corrections; and for diagnosis and treatment, the preferred fields are social work, clinical psychology, and psychiatry. They found that few social workers, clinical psychologists, or psychiatrists go into the criminal justice field. Furthermore, this survey showed that only law schools train their students for practice in the field of criminal justice. Psychiatric residential centers offer limited introductory coursework to criminal justice, and social work schools and clinical psychology programs offer no formal coursework in criminal justice and corrections. "Analysis of professional school programs, except for those of the law schools, raises serious questions about whether qualified graduates are being provided for criminal justice." [9]

Two conclusions can be made from the Piven-Alcabes survey: (1) Individuals are not trained in criminology or criminal justice. (2) The individuals involved in the applied aspects of criminal justice are from clinical and service disciplines, such as law, social work, clinical psychology, and psychiatry, and not from research disciplines. "The three professions to which they generally refer are clinical psychology, psychiatry, and social work. . .no identifiable education in sociology, general psychology, or criminology is advocated as a preferable alternative by any substantial number of professional organizations or academic executives." [10] The lack of training in general psychology, sociology, and criminology is unbelievable in itself, but when one adds behavioral psychology (including behavior change techniques and behavioral therapy), urban planning and design, systems analysis, biopsychology, and other of the newer behavioral science disciplines, one can only conclude that criminological training is poor and neglected.

### Sociology and Criminology

In the United States, criminology has traditionally been taught in departments of sociology. [11] During its early period of development, sociology was most concerned with social problems, such as race, poverty, crime, and divorce. This was the "sex, sin, and sewage" period of American sociology, according to Howard P. Becker. In the 1920-1940 era, criminology was a strong part of general sociology; today, however, criminology is often not regarded as a part of sociology. Most departments will offer only one or two courses in criminology; thus the student taking a Ph.D. in sociology will have very little training in criminology or corrections.

A sociology course in criminology typically deals with (a) the sociological theories of criminal behavior, and (b) a criticism of biological, psychological, and psychiatric theories of criminal behavior.

A student who has a Ph.D. in sociology is not trained in criminology, corrections, or criminal justice. A few programs exist which offer specialized training, such as the M.A. program in sociology with criminology as a speciality at the University of Pennsylvania.

### Law Schools and Criminology

Law schools typically teach a course in criminal law and one in criminal procedure. Beyond that, there is little attention paid to the area of criminal justice at the undergraduate (LL.B.) level. In recent years, foundations—notably Ford and Russell Sage—have supported law and social science programs at Chicago, Wisconsin, Northwestern, California (Berkeley), Denver, and Pennsylvania. More and more law schools have been offering seminars in juvenile delinquency and criminology at the graduate level. New York University Law School offers an LL.M. degree in criminal justice, the program for which includes criminology, delinquency, social deviance, criminal law, and law and psychiatry. These courses are taught by a combination of lawyers, sociologists, and psychiatrists. The usual law school does not offer courses in behavioral or social sciences; New York University is an exception in this respect. The Harvard University Law School has had Sheldon and Eleanor Glueck on the faculty for years doing research in delinquency. Yale Law School has pursued a law-social science program with McDougal, Lasswell, and others. The Yale program is highly psychoanalytic in orientation, though sociologists such as Jerome Skolnick, Richard Schwartz, and others have been associated with the Yale Law School. Jay Katz, a psychiatrist, is on the staff and has been writing in cooperation with lawyers on the Yale faculty.[12]

The University of Chicago had a Law and Behavior Science Program for a number of years under a Ford Foundation grant. A number of sociologists were fellows at the Law School under this program, and the jury trial studies were undertaken at the same time.[13] A seminar in law and criminology has been offered for several years in the law school.

The University of Michigan Law School has had Andrew Watson, a psychiatrist, as a member of the faculty for several years. The University of Wisconsin Law School conducted the survey on the Administration of Criminal Justice in the United States under the direction of Frank J. Remington, a law professor. The staff included several sociologists, including, at one time or another, Lloyd Ohlin, Harry Ball, and Donald J. Newman.[14]

The University of California at Berkeley has a Center for the Study of Law and Society, which includes such sociologists as Jerome Skolnick, Philip Selznick, Sheldon Messinger, David Matza, and others. The University of Denver has a joint law-sociology program in which a student receives training in both fields. Several sociologists teach in the law school program, including Gresham Sykes and Laurence Ross.

The above discussion indicates that law schools are becoming aware of the role of behavioral sciences in the training of lawyers. It also indicates that "law and psychiatry" is a popular combination, as illustrated by the law and psychiatry class description in the bulletin of the Harvard University Law School. The course is designed to "familiarize the law student with theories of behavior," especially "a detailed and critical survey of one particular theory of behavior: psychoanalytic" (Harvard University Law School Catalogue). At New York University, a research project, financed by funds from the Ford Foundation, supports a law and psychiatry project wherein students work in a psychiatric clinic in order to familiarize themselves with psychiatric concepts. The presence of sociologists on the staff of law schools does not change the fact that psychiatry is still regarded by most lawyers as the supreme interpretation of human behavior. Though sociology has managed to make some inroads into the legal profession, psychiatric thinking still dominates law school training. Though the effects of psychoanalysis upon social work have been written about, the first major critique of the influence of psychoanalysis upon law has yet to be written.

Law school training follows a historical, humanistic, case study approach. Lawyers are trained on appellate court cases wherein past decisions are analyzed and used as guidelines for current legal issues. The lawyer is trained in a logic quite foreign to the scientist, in that he is trained to look backward to learn what people have said, rather than to look forward to the future consequences of his research. One of the major shortcomings of the legal process is that the profession does not pay enough attention to the consequences of legal decisions—i.e., what happens after a delinquent is placed in an institution or placed on probation, or what happens when a man is given a twenty-year sentence, compared to a one-year sentence.

*Social Work and Criminology*

Social work training is important for criminology because of the role of the caseworker in probation and parole. The basis of social work training is the casework method, premised upon worker-client interaction modeled on the therapist-client relationship of medicine. Klein has noted that the "surrender of social work to psychiatry" has resulted in a slighting of the social sciences.[15] Because of this middle-class clinical orientation of social work, social workers have emphasized adaptation of the individual to the environment, rather than changing the environment to the internal psychic makeup of the client.[16]

Social work training does not involve course work in criminology and penology, though field placement in a correctional setting is routine in most social work schools. The lack of training in behavioral science and in law is a major handicap to the social worker who must work with delinquent children; the social worker is an agent in the administration of justice, since he or she is in charge of reviewing case histories and recommending disposition of cases to the judge, or of recommending probation or parole for inmates.

*Medicine and Criminology*

Physicians receive very little training in the social sciences; what little training they do receive draws upon a psychoanalytic theory of behavior. Training in psychiatry is not broad enough to include experimental psychology and sociology. The physician works within a very narrow conception of human behavior, based on his biological training, plus some knowledge of the effects of drugs on behavior, plus his training in psychoanalytic theories of behavior.[17] The physician occupies a very powerful position in the administration of justice because of the prominence given by the lawyer to concepts of responsibility and mental illness, and some physicians are exposed to a general law and psychiatry seminar in which the meaning of legal rules of responsibility are explained to them. The physician does not possess the training in behavioral science, sociology, and law needed to participate as he does in the judicial process wherein issues of the causes of criminal behavior are raised. In contrast, in the area of pathology the physician is well trained to determine the causes of death and to give testimony in court where the cause of death is at issue.

*Education and Criminology*

Most educators are not trained in sociology or criminology. Behavioral psychology has had a great impact on education because of teaching machines and programmed instructional materials, and educational sociology is now a major division in many educational programs, involving the impact of social class, race, and community structure upon the educational system. The Center for Urban Education has several sociologists on its staff, including its Director, Robert Dentler. It is impossible to look at education in an urban environment without also looking at the problems of black-white relations, poverty, black family structure, urban politics, public administration of urban centers, unemployment, job training, and other related problem areas. Today we talk about the urban expert or urbanologist, such as Daniel P. Moynihan, who must be an educator, sociologist, and criminologist all at the same time. Frank Riessman, S.M. Miller, and Patricia Sexton are sociologists or psychologists working in the area of poverty, education, and urban sociology. The influence of education on delinquency is well known, since most delinquents are high school dropouts; thus, the educator must know something about criminology, and the criminologist must know something about urban education.

*Training in Police Science*

During the past thirty years, many junior colleges have established departments of police science. Most of these programs are prebaccalaureate in scope, though some colleges do offer an A.B. degree in police science.[18] A few universities offer an M.A. degree in public administration or law enforcement administration with emphasis on police science: California State College at Los Angeles, Fresno State College, Sacramento State College, University of Georgia, Michigan State University, John Jay College of Criminal Justice, Washington State University, University of Arizona, University of Iowa, Sam Houston College, and the University of Maryland.

Police science curricula are usually a combination of basic sociology, psychology, criminal law, and criminology, with a major emphasis on vocational courses rather than on more academic courses. Most of the instructors in police science schools are former police officers who have retired and taken positions with a school of police science. It might be healthier if there were less inbreeding by police science faculties and more reliance upon faculties from academic departments, as a sociologist, psychologist, or urban planning expert would be a great asset to a police science department. Police science training has been much too narrow and divorced from general academic and professional achievement.

A problem yet unsolved is the nature and type of training needed by police officers. A man does not need a Ph.D. degree to be a patrolman. On the other hand, a man with a Ph.D. degree enters the police department at the lowest rank of patrolman. What is needed is an organizational system wherein lawyers, sociologists, psychologists, urban designers, and administration experts have positions in the police department without the need to be patrolmen. There is no reason why the head of community relations, budgeting, or research should be a patrolman with twenty years on the force. Top-echelon jobs must be given to civilians with training in fields other than police science, and a major reorganization of police administration must occur before the base of policing can be extended beyond its current narrow range. However, police departments are opposed to outside interference, including that of civilians working in the department.


### Criminology and the Future

If criminology is going to emerge as a separate discipline, it must have a respectable academic standing, separate from but related to the traditional disciplines found in a large university. The precedent for this has been established in such interdisciplinary fields as public administration, urban affairs, meteorology, biochemistry, chemical physics, and biophysics. Criminology and criminal justice are crucial enough to the society to warrant professional status and academic standing comparable to allied disciplines.

The involvement of many disciplines in corrections and criminal justice—social work, clinical psychology, psychiatry, law, and education—without a meaningful relationship to criminology and criminal justice is a most undesirable situation. As was pointed out above, these disciplines have little or no contact with criminology, behavioral psychology, and sociology. An interdisciplinary program in criminology is needed at this time if we are to make any progress in the control of the crime problem.

Such a program should be both undergraduate and graduate. The undergraduate training should be of a liberal arts nature, with a concentration in criminology, corrections, and criminal justice. Such programs now exist in one form or another, and the crucial need is at the graduate level. Graduate training should be in a professional school which is independent of other disciplines, for only then will criminology enjoy a professional growth based on its own needs, rather than on the interests of social work, sociology, psychiatry, clinical psychology, or law. The faculty must be interdisciplinary—from law, sociology, and psychology, as well as from newer disciplines such as urban planning, public administration, statistics, systems analysis, computer engineering and biopsychology. The major input that the author would encourage above the usual programs in criminology is the use of urban planning, public administration, statistics, systems analysis, and computer engineering in the analysis of crime. An ideal graduate program would have available persons trained in these areas either on the faculty or affiliated with it from another part of the university.

Several schools now offer graduate work in criminology and criminal justice. They include the State University of New York at Albany, the University of California at Berkeley, the University of Southern California, and Florida State University. (These schools offer a doctorate in criminal justice or criminology. Programs in law enforcement and police science are not included in our concept of a school of criminology.) The major need today is not to train police or probation officers—though a shortage of personnel in these areas exists, and training programs are needed—but to train top-level researchers, social planners, and administrators to work in the criminal justice area. Federal and state programs must be established, as must major research centers, and teachers for the undergraduate programs in law enforcement, police administration, and corrections must be trained. A new breed of Ph.D. must be trained who can relate criminal justice to urban planning, systems analysis, computer technology, and the newer developments in human biology, environmental biology, and experimental psychology. We cannot train police and correctional officers without a body of knowledge and procedures appropriate to the task. Try to imagine training a surgical nurse, X-ray technician, or medical technician without a body of physicians capable of doing surgery or diagnosis. As things now stand, we train police and probation people without any procedures or framework within which they can operate. As Korn and McCorkle phrase it, "In effect, our treatment personnel are often told little more than go out and rehabilitate somehow—precisely how is not indicated."[19]

## Summary

Criminology has never been made a major part of the training of sociologists, psychologists, lawyers, psychiatrists, or social workers. People are trained in service disciplines to deliver services to individual criminals. These services follow the positivist's scheme of post-offense rehabilitation of the offender via social casework or clinical psychiatry, with the added measure of legal services for the accused and the accuser during this period of trial and incarceration. Lawyers and psychiatrists are called in *after* the crime has been committed. Social workers are called in *after* the juvenile is a delinquent. Sociologists and psychologists study criminal behavior *after* the individual is a criminal. No training is currently given in the prevention and control of crime *before* it occurs.

The training now given is in services, not in research, planning, or administration. A new concept of the training of criminologists must emerge which is free of the service orientation of law, social work, and psychiatry, as well as of the provincial boundaries of sociology and psychology. The major changes in the graduate-level training will come from the infusion of administration, urban planning, systems analysis, computer engineering and the behavioral/environmental sciences with criminology and criminal justice.

## NOTES

[1.] Walter C. Reckless, *The Crime Problem,* 4th ed., New York: Appleton-Century-Crofts, 1961, pp. 2-3; Norval Morris and Gordon Hawkins, *The Honest Politician's Guide to Crime Control,* Chicago: University of Chicago Press, 1970, pp. 241-242.

[2.] Denis Szabo, "The Teaching of Criminology in Universities," *International Review of Criminal Policy,* No. 22 (1964), New York: United Nations, Department of Economic and Social Affairs.

[3.] Leon Radzinowicz, *In Search of Criminology,* Cambridge: Harvard University Press, 1962, p. 168; Morris and Hawkins, op. cit., p. 242.

[4.] *Corrections,* President's Commission on Law Enforcement and Administration of Justice, U.S. Government Printing Office, Washington, D.C., 1967, p. 100.

[5.] Kenneth Polk, *The University and Corrections,* Washington, D.C., Joint Commission on Correctional Manpower and Training, 1969, p. 4 ff.

[6.] Reckless, op. cit., p. 7.

[7.] Denis Szabo, "The Teaching of Criminology in Universities," *International Review of Criminal Policy,* No. 22; Elmer Johnson, "Personnel Problems of Corrections and the Potential Contribution of Universities," *Federal Probation,* December, 1967, p. 57 ff.; *Joint Commission on Manpower and Training for Corrections,* edited by Charles Prigmore, New York Council on Social Work Education, 1966; *Education, Training, and Manpower in Corrections and Law Enforcement,* Herman Piven and Abraham Alcabes, U.S. Department of Health, Education and Welfare, 1967.

[8.] Herman Piven and Abraham Alcabes, *The Crisis of Qualified Manpower for Criminal Justice: An Analytic Assessment with Guidelines for New Policy,* Volume I, Probation and Parole, Volume II, Correctional Institutions, Washington, D.C.: Office of Juvenile Delinquency, 1969.

[9.] Piven and Alcabes, op. cit., Vol. I, p. 42.

[10.] Piven and Alcabes, op. cit., Vol. II, p. 35.

[11.] Szabo, op. cit., p. 18.

[12.] See for examples of such interdisciplinary writing, Richard C. Donnelley, et al., Criminal Law, New York: Free Press of Glencoe, 1962; Abraham S. Goldstein, *The Insanity Defense,* New Haven: Yale University, 1967; Jay Katz, Joseph Goldstein, and Alan Dershowitz, *Psychology, Psychiatry, and Law,* New York: Free Press, 1967; Joseph Goldstein and Jay Katz, *The Family and the Law,* New York: Free Press, 1965.

[13.] Rita James Simon, *The Sociology of Law,* San Francisco: Chandler Publishing Company, 1968.

[14.] Wayne R. LaFave, *Arrest,* Boston: Little Brown and Company, 1966; Lawrence P. Tiffany et al, *Detection of Crime,* Boston: Little, Brown and Company, 1967; Donald J. Newman, *Conviction,* Boston: Little, Brown and Company, 1966.

[15.] Philip Klein, *From Philanthropy to Social Welfare,* San Francisco: Jossey-Bass, Inc., 1968, p. 147 ff., p. 233 ff.

[16.] Klein, op. cit., pp. 164-165.

[17.] Paul Halmos, *The Faith of the Counsellors,* New York: Schocken Books, 1966, pp. 34-35.

[18.] Charles L. Newman and Dorothy S. Hunter, "Education for Careers in Law Enforcement: An Analysis on Student Output, 1964-1967," *Journal of Criminal Law, Criminology, and Police Science,* Vol. 59, No. 1 (March, 1968), pp. 138-143.

[19.] Richard R. Korn and Lloyd W. McCorkle, *Criminology and Penology,* New York: Henry Holt and Company, 1959, p. 593.

Chapter 18

# The Politics and Economics
# of Crime Control

*The Politics of Crime*

### PRESENT GOVERNMENTAL POLICY

The policy followed by the federal government has been outlined in the book. A recap of the major features incorporated in governmental policy includes the following assumptions:

(1) The individual offender, not the environment, must be the focus of concern.

(2) Deterrence and rehabilitation after the crime, rather than prevention and control before the crime, are the means used to control criminals.

(3) The criminal justice system is retained in its present form rather than changed in any drastic way.

(4) Indirect means of controlling crime are used, such as poverty programs, educational programs, and therapy programs.

As a consequence of this policy, the federal government has poured millions of dollars into poverty projects, job training, remedial education, law enforcement technology and training, and the court and correctional system. Little research is carried on, and no feedback of the effectiveness of the expenditures is attempted. Though one cannot argue from hard data that the programs are a failure, the very fact that no successful programs have been announced, plus the fact that there is no evidence the crime rate has been reduced, leads to the conclusion that the impact of these programs has been minimal. The author would be happy to argue from hard data if the various agencies spending money to combat crime would furnish us with such data. One of the secrets of governmental policy is to avoid exposure of the "success" of what one is doing.

## GOVERNMENTAL POLICY AND RESEARCH

The governmental view of the value of a science of human behavior is seen in several recent Congressional hearings. At a Senate hearing on subsidizing research in social problems, a group of senators concluded that we did not need research on them. As George Lundberg commented on this Senate performance, the Senate assumed "we know the solutions of our social problems already. If we would but listen to the philosophers, the seers, and the writers of great books down the ages and search our souls, we would find the answers. What we really need to do is to educate people so they will read and listen, not research, not new knowledge, but education in old knowledge is the key."[1] Another Congressional investigation led to the statement that "it is a pitiful assumption that the springs of human behavior can be reduced to formulae (science). Human beings are motivated by goals, by ethical and moral concepts, by exercises of free will."[2]

As a result of this notion of science and research as seen in our Congress, the following issues occur:

(1) Research is regarded as unnecessary and is not supported to any great extent. As was pointed out in Chapter 12 on research methods and Chapter 13 on science and technology, little or no money goes to the support of basic behavioral research.

(2) What research is supported is not of an experimental nature, but is descriptive or evaluative. Data are collected on the criminal justice system, or existing programs are evaluated for effectiveness. Such research is not experimental in the sense that it leads to causal inferences or hypothesis testing, and though it is necessary, it does not furnish a base for social policy or decision-making.

(3) Demonstration and action programs are supported, rather than research efforts. This is in keeping with the assumption that, since we know the answers, the only thing left to do is to begin a program. Such a political policy is not only popular with the electorate (it gets votes if you tell a community you are establishing a poverty program or drug addiction program in their community), but it also is a good cover-up for a lack of knowledge as to how to solve a problem.

(4) The people attracted to governmental positions are trained in law, social work, or education. The use of top-flight scientists in the formulation and implementation of social programs is limited, and when such a man is involved in government work he is crushed by the bureaucratic structure of Washington, D.C. The author has known several capable men in Washington who were made ineffective by their superiors, and who either left government service or resigned themselves to a life of mediocrity.

The men hired to run our criminal justice programs are the same men who have failed in the past to control crime. The same judges and lawyers who have failed to make operative the court system are hired to improve the courts. Retired police officers are hired to improve a police system they failed to change while serving in it for twenty or thirty years. Sociologists, psychologists, and social workers are hired to set up rehabilitiation programs for offenders although these same individuals have failed to rehabilitate or reform offenders in the past.

Merton,[3] in an article on bureaucracy and the intellectual, has stated that the social scientist is not highly regarded by Washington bureaucrats, because the bureaucrats are convinced that they have the knowledge needed for social policy. Policy makers will listen to social scientists, but in the end it is the policy maker who decides what social policy is to be followed. Intellectuals (scientists) who enter public service as government employees are corrupted and frustrated by the bureaucracy. "The state bureaucracy exerts a pressure upon the alienated intellectual to accommodate himself to the policies of those who make the strategic decisions with the result that in time the role of the intellectual may become indistinguishable from that of the technician." The unattached intellectual (university professor) is unable to influence policy because he is not in the bureaucracy (does not have the ear of the governor or President, as we say). If he moves to Albany or Washington, he is no longer an independent scientist, but a captive of the political bureaucracy. A scientist working for the government loses his scientific independence and must think in terms of the goals and desires of his employer.

(5) Related to (4) above is the fact that independent scientists (from universities or private research foundations) must tailor grant applications to fit the preexisting concepts of granting agencies, especially if the agency is a governmental agency. The scientific community is thus involved in doing research which others think ought to be done, rather than basic research based on the instinct of the scientist for what is important. (The physical and biological sciences are faced with the same problem.)

Very often behavioral scientists are asked to evaluate existing governmental programs. Evaluation, demonstration, and action do not constitute research as herein defined. "Another danger arises when carefully planned and extensive research is undertaken solely to provide scientific justification for an action program already selected. This represents a misuse of research sources."[4]

Two recent statements fairly well summarize the condition existing in Washington, D.C., as it applies to crime research and prevention programs. Daniel P. Moynihan, in a memorandum to the White House, stated:

> we really ought to be getting on with research on crime. We just don't know enough. . . .Lawyers are not professionally equipped to do much to prevent crime. Lawyers are not managers, and they are not researchers. The logistics, the ecology, the strategy and tactics of reducing the incidence of certain types of behavior in large urban populations simply are not things lawyers think about often.[5]

The conference of the National League of Cities and the United States Conference of Mayors concluded that the Law Enforcement Assistance Administration program "as presently administered by most states, will not have the necessary impact vitally needed to secure improvements in the criminal justice system. The states in distributing funds entrusted to them under the block grant formula of the Safe Streets Act have failed to focus these vital resources on the most critical urban crime problems. Instead, funds are being dissipated broadly across the states in many grants too small to have any significant impact to improve the criminal justice system and are being used in disproportionate amounts to support marginal improvements in low crime areas."[6]

## SCIENCE, HUMANISTIC SERVICE, AND SOCIAL ACTION

The word "science" is a dirty word in many parts of the intellectual community, and the approach to human behavior herein advocated is not a popular one today and will not find acceptance by many academicians. Behavioral scientists can be divided by orientation into (1) scientific, (2) social action, and (3) humanistic.[7] The action-oriented intellectual looks to involvement, relevance, and service as the solutions to social problems. The humanist looks to history, ethics, logic, and philosophical traditions for the answers. In both cases, the person assumes that the answers to social problems are known, and all we must do is to read the right philosophies or participate in a social revolution and take action in order to solve such problems. Only the scientist states that we do not know the answers, and only by looking to future research can we hope to solve our major social problems.

The present mood of the country is humanistic action. The solution to racial, educational, welfare, and crime problems is sought in protests, demonstrations, and riots. Even the academic community is a part of this movement, with many of the younger men in political science, sociology, psychology, law, and public administration asking for more relevant courses, more social involvement by professionals, and action in place of research. The proposal has even been made that "action Ph.D.'s" be granted to those who participate in community reform projects.[8] The recent annual meeting of the American Association for the Advancement of Science dwelt on this issue of research versus immediate solutions.[9]

Sociological texts are now advocating a commitment to a particular value system, denying ethical neutrality, espousing liberatarian values under the label of "building the good society with a liberal bias," and stating that "sociologists should be social agitators."[10] Gouldner has noted that the action framework of sociology has led the sociologist as a partisan into market research for the welfare state and liberalism.[11] Rather than being a neutral influence in the analysis of social problems, the social scientist of an action bent is a committed partisan to one particular political ideology.

Irving Kristol,[12] Professor of Urban Values at New York University, has recently argued that the university is best served by a community of individual scholars each involved in his own search for truth and knowledge. The current emphasis on action, involvement, and relevance has led to the involvement of academic departments and schools in collective and institutional action to solve social problems, which move has forced the university to become a political community. Universities are being forced to take a political stand on the Vietnam War, on social injustice, and other pressing social issues, with the result that individual faculty members are intimidated through fear, shame, and violence to subscribing to official political views. Kristol is critical of the view that universities ought to be responsible for building model neighborhoods, model school systems, or model business ventures. His conclusion is that "the collective responsibility of the university is education. That is its original mission, that is its original purpose, that is the only thing it can claim expertise or authority for. To return to his original purpose, with renewed seriousness, would be an action at once radical and constructive."

A sociologist, Robert Nisbet,[13] has recently summarized the move to subjectivity and action which characterizes much of contemporary social science:

One is obliged by the evidence to conclude that the most unbelievable thing is the astonishing reversal of belief in the scientific, that is, the objective, the detached, the dispassionate character of the social sciences. What makes it unbelievable is that this reversal is to be found. . .in the social sciences themselves; more precisely, in the minds of a constantly increasing number of younger social scientists and among these most crucially of students in the social sciences. . . .First, the declaration by self-styled radical social scientists that objectivity of inquiry is not even a proper end of the social sciences. . . .The point is to destroy and then remake society.

Nisbet goes on to note that "what the disciples of social-science-as-action can never seem to understand is that if action is the magic word, there are always others, less burdened by the trained incapacities of scholarship, who can act more swiftly and ruthlessly. What the man of action looks to the scholar and scientist for is knowledge, not barricade gymnastics."

The recent violence and deaths on American university campuses, including Yale and Kent State Universities, bears out the theme presented by Kristol and Nisbet. The movement of social science from objectivity to subjectivity and social action is more than evident in our federal poverty programs, and, as Moynihan has written in that respect, the social scientist did the country a disservice by becoming an advocate of policy instead of being an impartial evaluator of the consequences of social policy (see Chapter 9).

## SCIENCE AND VALUES

Throughout recent history there has been a dichotomy between politics and administration, facts and values, and science and values (see Chapter 16).

Today, the critics of behaviorism are saying that attention must be paid to human values and social ethics rather than to science and behavior.[14]

The distinction is often made among prescriptive statements (how one ought to behave), descriptive statements (how one does behave), and explanatory statements (a scientific statement as to the conditions under which behavior occurs). It is assumed that statements about the way men *ought* to behave are of a different character than those concerned with how men *do* behave, and we even have different academic disciplines for the study of each—i.e., philosophy and ethics versus psychology, sociology, and human biology. As was noted above, the humanist derives his values from history and traditions, and he argues that certain values have a truthfulness and rightfulness not possessed by other values. Such an assumption is usually backed by an appeal to natural law, reason, or intellectual tradition.

Several problems exist as a result of this separation of *ought* and *is,* or of values and facts.

*(1) No means have been found to prove or disprove a value system.* An empirical statement can be proven or disproven; a value statement is taken as a given without the need for proof or disproof. Because of this, most crucial social issues involve conflicting opinions or assumptions as to how people ought to behave. Those who defend the war in Vietnam resort to a morality drawing on constitutionalism, legal obligations under international treaties, the immorality of communism and aggression in Southeast Asia, and on and on. The opponents of the war resort to a morality based on Christian ethics, brotherhood and love, the inhumanity of war, and the illegality of the war. Students who destroy a university campus by protest wrap themselves in the morality of their cause by stating that an immoral war justifies an immoral reaction to the war.

*(2) Values are not above and beyond behavior,* to be viewed as part of a different universe; they *are* behavior. Values grow out of the past experiences of a person or group and are subject to the same environmental determinants to which any behavior is subject. When the writer was in sociology classes, he was told that two people exposed to different experiences would behave differently; i.e., one would speak French, one English, or one would believe in monogamy, one in polygamy. Introductory sociology and anthropology were filled with such concepts as culture, ethical neutrality, cultural relativism, and ethnocentrism.[15] Quoted in every introductory text was the statement that "the mores make it right," which is to say, behavior is right depending on the social situation within which it occurs. Some people eat dogs, monkeys, lambs' testicles or other people. The test of any good anthropology student on a field trip is his ability to partake of his tribal host's offering of food (or of his wife, in the case of certain Eskimo tribes). Some tribes go around naked, which shocked students who watched films of primitive Australian tribes (my experience goes back twenty years, before *Oh, Calcutta* and *Hair,* I am afraid).

For some reason related, to be sure, to the move into a social action framework as discussed above by Nisbet—who also had his training in sociology when cultural relativism was a popular concept—these basic tenets of sociology and anthropology have been forgotten. In the case of poverty, racism, crime, and welfare, it is assumed one value system is superior to another. Those who state that racism is wrong ignore (a) the fact that they feel that way because of their past conditioning history, and (b) the fact that those who have racial beliefs do so because of their past conditioning history. If a child is taught racism, he will behave that way as an adult. Be it right or wrong, it is a fact. The only way to have complete uniformity of behavior is to subject all people to the same experiences.

*(3) The issue of how people ought to behave is a critical one in criminology* because of the impact of the labeling, or decriminalization, school on the field. This argument states that the only thing wrong is the law, not the behavior, and if we make crime (or some crimes) legal, we have disposed of the problem. Some criminologists go so far as to state that open rebellion against unjust laws is justified, but then who is to decide which laws are just and which unjust (see Chapters 3 and 15)? If people behave so as to oppose narcotics addiction or alcoholism, making such acts legal will not change their behavior.

Telling people how they ought to behave does not mean that they will behave as they are told. If people behaved as others think they should behave, we would have no social problems.

*(4) Social scientists, by taking sides on controversial issues,* lose their objectivity and thus their value as scientists to the community. Impartiality and ethical neutrality have been a cornerstone of academic pursuits and scientific endeavor. As Max Weber noted years ago, science as a vocation must remain ethically neutral if the objectivity of social science is to be maintained. Weber argued that science can study values as aspects of a factual objective situation, but science cannot provide values or norms by which men live, and he pleaded for a "value-free" science of sociology. This position has been all but ignored in the context of the contemporary urban crisis, as Nisbet has pointed out so succinctly. The social scientist who becomes an advocate of a given value position can do so only by stating the behavioral consequences of his position and by stating that his preference is based on his own experiences and developmental history.

Values are those behaviors people exhibit to bring about expectations as to the future. Earlier in the book, we discussed the $E - O - E$ arc (see Chapter 11) whereby past experiences are transformed into present behavior based on future expectations. Values are preferences for certain future contingencies, as compared with other possibilities, and as such cannot be separated from behavior and the decision process.

*Future Needs*

### ROLE OF SCIENCE IN SOCIAL POLICY

The above discussion underlines the need for an ethically neutral behavioral science which does not advocate political policy and involve itself as a committed party to social issues. The scientist is in no better or different position from that of any other citizen when it comes to stating his preferences for social policy. However, he is in a unique position to point out the possible behavioral consequences of social policy and to guide the democratic process in its arrival at a decision for such policy. The behavioral scientist should be in a position to make known the consequences of desegregation decisions, of new public school policy, new housing policy, or new crime control policy. If the decision to desegregate the schools will result in more divisiveness and racism, with schools under physical siege, with political counterforces being created, and with less, not more education taking place, then the future consequences of such policy should be made known to the public in order that they could be taken into account in the decision process. If riots and student demonstrations result in more, not less, police action and suppression, with the result that citizens are willing to sacrifice liberty for order and security, then such facts ought to be made available to all responsible parties. The best service the behavioral scientist can provide is to let it be known what the future will be like *if* certain policies are or are not pursued. The major defect in policy is not that individuals lack goals or values, but that they assume they are moving in the direction of reaching the goals, whereas, in fact, they are behaving so as to destroy the goals or to frustrate the chances of fulfilling such goals.

The scientist can, within the limits of his knowledge, specify the possible alternative courses of action available and the possible future consequences of alternative actions, which information can then be used by policy makers to make decisions. The scientist can also point out that different social groups have different value systems, the result of which is chaos for social planning unless we find the means to accommodate such conflicting value positions. And finally, the scientist is obligated to let it be known that there is a vast difference between telling people how they ought to behave and the way people actually behave. Policy must be based on what will happen, not on what we hope or wish will happen.


## *ROLE OF GOVERNMENT IN RESEARCH*

The government—state, federal, and local—must support significant research into the causes of behavioral problems, including crime. The present policy of supporting service and action programs must be replaced by one of basic research. Rather than granting money to hundreds of police departments for training and weaponry, we would do better granting the money to three or four research centers which would be responsible for a five- to ten-year research program in crime and criminal justice. The centers would be attached to universities, independent of any governmental agency, and the research emphasis would be determined by the scientists, not by the governmental bureaucracy. Each scientist involved would have the discretion to decide what he considered a significant research problem, and he would be accountable only to his peers, who would in time determine whether or not the research made a significant contribution to the knowledge available to policy makers. Uncommitted funds for behavioral research are absolutely essential if we are to find solutions to our behavioral problems.

Such research centers would be staffed with behavioral scientists of a research orientation, plus biologists, mathematicians, computer technologists, and systems analysts not now found in a research center devoted to crime and criminal justice. The research potential of the physical and biological sciences would be made a part of criminology to a much greater degree than is now the case.

The political argument against this is, of course, that it will take five to ten years to achieve, and we need the solutions today, not in ten years. Another counterargument is that politicans must give a little money to every city or state agency, and there is no political appeal to centering the funds in major research centers. Politicans use appropriations for political gains, and the problem of crime, as well as all the others confronting our major urban centers, must be removed from the political arena. After the solutions are found, the political process can take over, but not before. There is no reason to assume that our governors, mayors, and congressmen are going to find the solution to crime, and to allow politicians to act as the experts and spokesmen for the community on the crime problem is only to allow the crime issue to remain in the political arena rather than in the arena of science and technology.

Another argument against the proposals herein presented is that they would require a major change in our political and social system, such as a complete rebuilding of our urban environment and a complete overhaul of our welfare and educational systems. Rather, the politicians want to establish a new house for drug addicts, a new social service agency for delinquents, or a new procedure for handling delinquents in juvenile court. The economics of crime control is such that it will cost millions initially to do the research and programming for crime control but in the long run, the decrease in crime will more than cover the cost of the initial investment. To pour millions into ineffective programs, as we now do, not only is a costly waste of money, but we have no future gain to show for it in the way of a decreased crime problem. It is shortsighted economics to state we cannot budget for crime control today, knowing that we must continue in the future to pay the cost of a very high crime rate.

## GOVERNMENTAL POLICY AND SOCIAL DISORDERS

According to the analysis pursued in this book, behavior is determined by its future consequences. If this is true, the noticeable increase in violence in recent years by minority groups and students must be viewed in terms of a system of reward and punishment. The use of violence as a political weapon is related to its effectiveness in mobilizing support, in gaining publicity, and in creating a threat which must be met. The reinforcement present from violence is paired with a lack of punishment for a great many acts of violence. Dean Brustein[16] of Yale University has well summarized this when he notes that

> the spectacle of students holding university officials prisoners or of the Young Lords preventing church services from taking place or of the SDS running through high school corridors screaming "jailbreak" has little of the heroic about it. Even those recently discovered bomb factories which had such a dreadful toll on the very people preparing the destruction of official and commercial buildings suggests a serious dissociation on the part of the revolutionaries from the consequences of a murderous action. . . .The sentimental radicals on the other hand who are invariably more violent, enact their scenarios in a university or a church which they regard as sanctuaries from the civil authorities. . .thus an idealistic goal can be used to justify any behavior, no matter how fearsome, even though this is the same kind of hypocritical reasoning that justifies the conduct of the military in Vietnam. . .those of us dedicated to resisting illegitimate authority must continually remind ourselves that not all authority is illegitimate. To accept accountability for our actions, and to demand accountability of others—young and old, black and white, radical and reactionary—is to take the first step toward a genuine revelation of the spirit without which the body of this nation will not long survive.

The fact that the first demand of student protesters is amnesty, the second being nonnegotiation of the demands, bears evidence to the lack of accountability as Brustein discusses it. Throughout our discussion, emphasis has been placed on the need to make people responsible for the consequences of their actions, including those labeled mentally ill, juvenile delinquent, alcoholic, or drug addicted (see Chapters 5 and 11). By responsibility is meant acceptance of the consequences of one's actions. The basic tenet of reality, as well as of behavioral therapy, is that a person must be confronted with the consequences of his behavior. It is in this manner that behavior change and personality growth occur. The present policy of many government and community officials is to grant amnesty to juveniles or students, and by doing so, to reinforce the use of violence until the point at which counterviolence had to be used. Students would not have been killed or injured on college campuses had the administrators of our universities made the decision to expel students at the first sign of disorder (expulsion after a hearing with legal safeguards of due process). Student unrest assumed a more violent form only after students discovered that no one was willing to risk holding them responsible for their actions. A basic tenet of psychology must be made a point of our social policy unless we wish to allow protest to escalate to the point of open warfare.

We have also emphasized the same point in regard to how the welfare system reinforces dependency, not self-sufficiency; how the criminal justice system reinforces violations of the criminal law, not law-abiding behavior; and how the educational system reinforces dropping out, not studious behavior. Our policies need not punish as a means of behavioral control but they cannot reinforce the sorts of behaviors we are attempting to discourage or eliminate. A point constantly made in this book is that social policy must be based on a science of behavior, if it is to be effective.

### General Summary and Conclusions

#### CRIMINAL LAW

Law must be enforced to be effective.

Law must be related to a science of behavior, as a means of social control through the scientific application of rewards and punishment.

Law is a critical social control agent in an urban, industrial society, due to the absence of strong informal controls in such a society, but the effectiveness of legal controls over behavior is minimal due to the lack of enforcement and application.

The overdependence of society on legal controls had led to an overcriminalization of the criminal process. Morality and crime must be separated, and the criminal law must be used only to control those behaviors best handled by criminal sanctions. Crimes without victims, white-collar crimes, and organized crime must be dealt with by sanctions other than the criminal law.

#### BEHAVIOR

A science of behavior must be developed on the model of an input-output system, with adaptation to the environment as a key component.

The study of behavior as a response to the environment must replace the study of the inner psychic (mentalistic) concept of man.

The knowledge needed to reform criminals and prevent crime is not available at this time.

The causes of behavior are in the future consequences of the act, not the past experiences. Past experiences and present environmental conditions interact to create goal-oriented expectations as to what these future consequences of behavior will be.

Whereas the therapist directs his attention at the past experiences of the patient, the behaviorist directs his attention to the future experiences of the individual, and, through environmental design, he controls the flow of information (experiences) to the individual.

Behavior has to be treated directly as behavior, and not indirectly as a symptom of psychic conflict, interpersonal trauma, poverty, education, or urban living.

### CRIMINAL BEHAVIOR

Criminal behavior is a product of environmental conditions.

Criminal behavior is a product of a reward system wherein the gain from the crime outweighs the possibility of punishment.

The causes of criminal behavior lie in the future consequences of crime, not the past experiences of the actor. Crime is not caused by poverty, urban living, undereducation, psychopathology, or broken homes.

The analysis of criminal behavior must focus on the environment in which crimes occur and the targets of crime, not on the individual offender. People commit crimes not because of the nature of the individual but because of the nature of the environment.

The biological makeup of the criminal and the physical makeup of the environment may be more crucial than the social, and the reinforcing quality of material rewards versus social rewards must be reevaluated.

One must influence criminal behavior directly through environmental design and not indirectly through therapy, education, or job training. We must treat behavior as the problem and not as a symptom of an underlying cause.

### CRIME CONTROL MODELS

Punishment must be certain, not severe, to be effective.

The deterrence model has failed because of the lack of enforcement of the criminal law.

All phases of the criminal justice system—police, courts, corrections—contribute to the breakdown in law enforcement. At the end of the criminal justice system is a correctional system which neither deters or rehabilitates, and so long as prisons are failures, the rest of the system is a failure.

The rehabilitative model is now the reigning concept, with its focus on the individual offender.

The rehabilitative model ignores legal issues concerning definitions of crimes, due process, and civil liberties.

The rehabilitative model has failed through programs to implement it, such as poverty programs, therapy, guided group interaction, job training, and remedial education.

A successful crime control model must deal with behavior before the crime occurs, must deal directly with criminal behavior, and must deal with environmental design, rather than the individual offender.

Control over the environment necessary for crime control can come about through urban planning, science and technology, and behavioral therapy.

## SOCIAL POLICY AND PLANNING

Social planning must involve systems analysis and decision theory.

Planning must be scientific, not humanistic or action-oriented.

Support must be given for research on human problems, not services to the poor, the criminals, the addicts, and the alcoholics.

The present welfare system must be eliminated and a substitute for it found in work crews for urban renewal and the general improvement of the environment.

Policy and social planning must be based on the consequences of human action for the future, and not on past history, political idealism, or ethical statements as to how people ought to behave.

Policy must take account of the fact that human goals are behaviors which are subject to the same environmental determinants as any other behavior.

## THEORETICAL STRUCTURE OF CRIMINOLOGY

The classical school of criminology has some relevance for modern criminology. It sought clear definitions of crimes and punishments; it advocated limitations on criminal sanctions; it protected the rights of individuals accused of crimes; and it made clear in advance the consequences of behavior.

The classical school focused on the prevention of crime before it occurred. However, the classicists made a serious error in focusing attention on deterrence through *punishment of the individual offender.* Punishment is an effective deterrent only if certain, and the criminal justice system has never been able to use punishment in an effective manner.

The positive school of criminology has little relevance for the future of criminology, since it is based on a philosophy of rehabilitation of the offender after the offense has been committed. No means have been found to change individual behavior without first changing *the environment within which the behavior occurs.*

A new school of *environmental criminology* must emerge, based on scientific procedures, behaviorism, and environmentalism. The basic principles of the classical school—i.e., prevention of crime before it occurs and certainty of consequences for behavior—would be retained, but the emphasis would shift from punishment to reinforcement and from the individual offender to the environment. The major form of control would be reinforcement of lawful behavior and the removal of reinforcement for illegal behavior. The focus would be the environment in which crimes are committed, not the individual offender.

## NOTES

[1.] Sheldon Glueck, *The Problem of Delinquency.* Boston: Houghton Mifflin Co., 1959, p. 29.

[2.] Everett K. Wilson, *Sociology: Rules, Roles and Relationships.* Homewood: Dorsey Press, 1966, pp. 697-698.

[3.]. Robert K. Merton, *Social Theory and Social Structures.* Glencoe: Free Press, 1957, pp. 207-224.

[4.] Gerhard O.W. Mueller, "The Function of Criminology in Criminal Justice Administration," *Criminological Abstracts,* January, 1970, p. 585.

[5.] *Congressional Record,* March 4, 1970, E 1636-37.

[6.] *Congressional Record,* February 17, 1970, S 1789-96.

[7.] Wilson, op. cit., p. 693.

[8.] *New York Times Magazine,* December 7, 1969, p. 48 ff.

[9.] New York Times, January 4, 1970.

[10.] See, for example, Steven E. Deutsch and John Howard, ed., *Where It's At: Radical Perspectives in Sociology,* New York: Harper and Row, 1970.

[11.] Alvin Gouldner, "The Sociologist as Partisan: Sociology and the Welfare State," *The American Sociologist,* Vol. 3, No. 2 (May 1968) pp. 103-116; Alvin Gouldner, *The Coming Crisis in Western Sociology,* New York: Basic Books, 1970.

[12.] *New York Times Magazine,* March 22, 1970, p. 30 ff.

[13.] *New York Times Book Review,* April 5, 1970, p. 1 ff.

[14.] Mulford Q. Sibley, "The Limitations of Behavioralism," in *Contemporary Political Analysis,* James C. Charlesworth, ed., New York: Free Press, 1967, pp. 51-71.

[15.] See, for example, Leonard Broom and Philip Selznick, *Sociology,* 4th ed., New York: Harper and Row, 1968; Everett K. Wilson, *Sociology,* Homewood: Dorsey Press, 1966; John Cuber, *Sociology,* New York: Appleton-Century-Crofts, Inc., 1959.

[16.] New York Times, April 18, 1970.

# EPILOGUE

This work was done over a period of five years, and the completed version is by now almost two years old. A great many new footnotes would have to be added to bring the argument presented herein up to date. However, the crime control model which has been so severely attacked in this book—i.e., the deterrence-rehabilitation approach through individual offenders after they have become offenders—is still the only approach pursued by our governmental policy makers.

The criminal justice system has completely collapsed in our major urban centers. An article in *Life* magazine portrayed the justice system of New York City as one that was able to operate only by taking guilty pleas from those caught in the web of justice. One defendant was told bluntly by his attorney that if he pleaded guilty he would go free today, while if he asked for a trial he would be incarcerated for another lengthy period.[1]

The inability of the courts to handle the caseload resulted in major riots in the New York House of Detention in August and September of 1970. Up to seventy-five percent of the inmates were being held awaiting trial. As of today, the city of New York has been unable to find a solution to the problems of overcrowding of facilities, or of long delays before trials.[2]

*Time* magazine recently featured an article on "U.S. Prisons: Schools for Crime."[3] The failure of the correctional system and the national disgrace represented by our prison facilities was once again documented in great and lurid detail.

The state of Florida is now involved in a major controversy as to how to handle the overcrowding of the prison system which recently resulted in a major riot at the Raiford State Prison. The Director of Corrections for Florida is advocating the creation of two new prisons in Florida, whereas the Secretary of Health and Rehabilitation Services has opposed the use of more prisons as a way out of our crime control dilemma.[4]

President Richard Nixon has recently asked for a complete overhaul of the judicial system, which he characterized as "trying to push back a flood with a broom."[5]

Whereas the experts are all agreed that the criminal justice system is one monumental mess, the resolution of the mess is still far from clear. The same old theories and practices which resulted in the mess are being recommended as the new solutions.

▪ The President's Task Force on Prisoner Rehabilitation stated that "there was no need for us to search for new ideas about rehabilitating prisoners."[6] The Task Force recommended job training and employment programs, regional correctional facilities, and community-based correctional programs relying on probation, parole, counseling, and employment.[7]

▪ Former U.S. Attorney General Ramsey Clark, in his recent book *Crime in America*, stated that "in its most direct contacts with crime—prevention, detection, apprehension, conviction, and correction—the system of criminal justice fails miserably."[8] He went on to argue that "rehabilitation must be the goal of modern corrections," through counseling, guidance, parole supervision, indeterminate sentences, vocational trainng, work-release programs, halfway houses, and other community-centered projects.[9]

▪ Recently, in Congress, two bills were introduced to improve the correctional system. One bill provided for the construction of model correctional institutions which would make use of job training, conjugal visits, counseling, and new methods of treatment. The second bill dealt with court congestion by requiring speedy trials for those in custody.[10]

▪ The Youth Development and Delinquency Prevention Administration (formerly the Office of Juvenile Delinquency) has put forth a position paper which stated that "the development of a viable national strategy for the prevention and reduction of delinquency rests on the identification, assessment, and alteration of those features of institutional functioning that impede and obstruct a favorable course of youth development."[11] Delinquency is regarded as a product of the failure of our institutions to properly socialize our youths for a meaningful, law-abiding life. The YDDPA program is designed to provide access to desirable social roles for our youth, to avoid premature labeling as delinquent, and to reduce the alienation, rejection, and estrangement of our youth from society.

▪ The Ford Foundation recently announced support for a program to improve our prison system and another to cut down on crowded court calendars.[12] (At the same time, the Secretary of Health and Rehabilitative Services for Florida announced that speedy trials are filling the prisons of Florida faster than they can be built.[13])

From these measures, it is argued that the delinquency rate will be reduced. These projects are based on the myth of rehabilitation of individual offenders after the crime, or the reduction of the crime rate by building more prisons and courts and staffing such facilities with more people doing the same things our judicial and correctional people now do. For some strange reason, it is assumed that, if we build more facilities and train more people, we will reduce the crime problem, even though such measures have failed in the past.

A research team recently concluded from a survey of the California Correctional system that "there is no evidence to support any program's claim of superior rehabilitation efficacy." The single answer, then, to the question originally posed—"Will the clients act differently if we lock them up, or keep them locked up longer, or do something with them on the inside, or watch them more closely afterwards, or cut them loose officially?"—is "Probably not."[14]

A recent study of the California penal system revealed the real evil of the indeterminate sentence. "In good prisons, like those in California, physical degradation is replaced by psychological degradation." "To prison administrators, the indeterminate sentence is a potent instrument for inmate control. The corrections people never lose sight of its punitive advantages. . . ." "Overlaid on these are the modern therapy and treatment goals. The offender must not only pay his debt to society but in addition he must prove that the modern treatment method has worked, that he is cured, rehabilitated, and ready for parole." "In the opinion of many sociologists the combination of diagnosis, evaluation, treatment and classification so highly rated by Dr. Karl Menninger is in fact the Catch-22 of modern prison life, a grand hypocrisy in which custodial careers, administrative exigensies, and punishment are disguised as treatment." "The Adult Authority operates without a clear and nationally justified policy and is legally and scientifically unequipped for its responsibilities. As a result California general parole policy, reflecting emotion, not facts, has become increasingly conservative, punitive, and expensive."[15]

We still persist in reforming offenders and in reforming the criminal justice system rather than reforming the environment, and providing services rather than research, on the assumption that the causes of crime reside in the individual, not in the environment, and on the assumption that we do not need research because we already know how to rehabilitate offenders.

## NOTES

[1.] "I have Nothing to do With Justice" *Life,* March 12, 1971.

[2.] St. Petersburg Times, October 11, 1970.

[3.] *Time* Magazine, January 18, 1971.

[4.] St. Petersburg Times, March 20, 1971.

[5.] St. Petersburg Times, March 12, 1971.

[6.] *The Criminal Offender–What Should be Done,* The Report of the President's Task Force on Prisoner Rehabilitation, Washington, D.C., April, 1970, p. 1.

[7.] Ibid., pp. 1-20.

[8.] Ramsey Clark, *Crime in America,* New York: Simon and Schuster, 1970 p. 117.

[9.] Ibid., pp. 220-231.

[10.] *Congressional Record,* April 1, 1971, H 2391-2393.

[11.] *National Strategy for Youth Development and Delinquency Prevention,* Youth Development and Delinquency Prevention Administration, Department of Health, Education, and Welfare, Washington, D.C., January 21, 1971.

[12.] Corrections Digest, Washington, D.C., Vol. 2, No. 8 (April 21, 1971), p. 7.

[13.] Ibid., p. 10.

[14.] James Robison and Gerald Smith, "The Effectiveness of Correctional Programs," *Crime and Delinquency*, Vol. 17, No. 1 (January, 1971), p. 80.

[15.] Jessica Metford, "Kind and Usual Punishment in California" *Atlantic Monthly,* March, 1971, pp. 45-52.

# INDEX